P9-DMQ-874

Paris
day BY day®

5th Edition

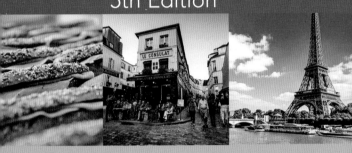

by Anna E. Brooke

FrommerMedia LLC

Contents

Published by:

Frommer Media LLC

Copyright © 2016 Frommer Media LLC. All rights reserved. No part of
this publication may be reproduced, stored in a retrieval system or
transmitted in any form or by any means, electronic, mechanical, pho-
tocopying, recording, scanning or otherwise, except as permitted
under Sections 107 or 108 of the 1976 United States Copyright Act,
without the prior written permission of the Publisher. Requests to the
Publisher for permission should be addressed to Support@Frommer-
Media.com.

Frommer's is a trademark or registered trademark of Arthur Frommer.

ISBN: 978-1-628-87240-8 (paper); ISBN 978-1-628-87241-5 (ebk)

Editorial Director: Pauline Frommer
Editor: Christine Ryan
Production Editor: Erin Geile
Photo Editor: Meghan Lamb
Cartographer: Roberta Stockwell
Compositor: Heather Pope
Indexer: Maro RioFrancos

Front cover photos, left to right: Sandwiches from Chambelland Bakery
©Aldo Sperber. Le Consulat in Montmartre ©anshar/Shutterstock.com.
The Eiffel Tower from the Seine River ©Viacheslav Lopatin.

Back cover photo: Enjoying an afternoon in the Jardin du Luxembourg.
©nito/Shutterstock.com.

For information on our other products and services, please go to
Frommers.com.

Frommer's also publishes its books in a variety of electronic formats.
Some content that appears in print may not be available in electronic
formats.

Manufactured in China

5   4   3   2   1

About This Guide

Organizing your time. That's what this guide is all about.

Other guides give you long lists of things to see and do and then expect you to fit the pieces together. The Day by Day guides are different. These guides tell you the best of everything, and then they show you how to see it in the smartest, most time-efficient way. Our authors have designed detailed itineraries organized by time, neighborhood, or special interest. And each tour comes with a bulleted map that takes you from stop to stop.

Hoping to follow Hemingway's footsteps, or to tour the highlights of the Louvre? Planning a walk through Montmartre, or a whirlwind tour of the very best that Paris has to offer? Whatever your interest or schedule, the Day by Days give you the smartest routes to follow. Not only do we take you to the top attractions, hotels, and restaurants, but we also help you access those special moments that locals get to experience—those "finds" that turn tourists into travelers.

The Day by Days are also your top choice if you're looking for one complete guide for all your travel needs. The best hotels and restaurants for every budget, the greatest shopping values, the wildest nightlife—it's all here.

Why should you trust our judgment? Because our authors personally visit each place they write about. They're an independent lot who say what they think and would never include places they wouldn't recommend to their best friends. They're also open to suggestions from readers. If you'd like to contact them, please send your comments our way at Support@FrommerMedia.com, and we'll pass them on.

Enjoy your Day by Day guide—the most helpful travel companion you can buy. And have the trip of a lifetime.

About the Author

Anna E. Brooke has authored six guidebooks on Paris and France for Frommer's, and her work has appeared in international publications such as *The Sunday Times Travel Magazine, Time Out,* and the *Financial Times.* She also writes children's fiction and composes lyrics and music for film and stage. She can be contacted on annaebrooke@gmail.com.

Advisory & Disclaimer

Travel information can change quickly and unexpectedly, and we strongly advise you to confirm important details locally before traveling, including information on visas, health and safety, traffic and transport, accommodations, shopping, and eating out. We also encourage you to stay alert while traveling and to remain aware of your surroundings. Avoid civil disturbances, and keep a close eye on cameras, purses, wallets, and other valuables.

While we have endeavored to ensure that the information contained within this guide is accurate and up-to-date at the time of publication, we make no representations or warranties with respect to the accuracy or completeness of the contents of this work and specifically disclaim all warranties, including without limitation warranties of fitness for a particular purpose. We accept no responsibility or liability for any inaccuracy or errors or omissions, or for any inconvenience, loss, damage, costs, or expenses of any nature whatsoever incurred or suffered by anyone as a result of any advice or information contained in this guide.

The inclusion of a company, organization, or website in this guide as a service provider and/or potential source of further information does not mean that we endorse them or the information they provide. Be aware that information provided through some websites may be unreliable and can change without notice. Neither the publisher nor author shall be liable for any damages arising herefrom.

Star Ratings, Icons & Abbreviations

Every hotel, restaurant, and attraction listing in this guide has been ranked for quality, value, service, amenities, and special features using a **star-rating system.** Hotels, restaurants, attractions, shopping, and nightlife are rated on a scale of zero stars (recommended) to three stars (exceptional). In addition to the star-rating system, we also use a **kids icon** to point out the best bets for families. Within each tour, we recommend cafes, bars, or restaurants where you can take a break. Each of these stops appears in a shaded box marked with a coffee-cup-shaped bullet 🍵.

The following **abbreviations** are used for credit cards:

AE	American Express	DISC	Discover	V	Visa
DC	Diners Club	MC	MasterCard		

Frommers.com

Now that you have this guidebook to help you plan a great trip, visit our website at **www.frommers.com** for additional travel information on more than 4,000 destinations. We update features regularly to give you instant access to the most current trip-planning information available. At Frommers.com, you'll find scoops on the best airfares, lodging rates, and car rental bargains. You can even book your travel online through our reliable travel booking partners. Other popular features include:

- Online updates of our most popular guidebooks

- Vacation sweepstakes and contest giveaways

- Newsletters highlighting the hottest travel trends

- Podcasts, interactive maps, and up-to-the-minute event listings

- Opinionated blog entries by Arthur Frommer himself

- Online travel message boards with featured travel discussions

A Note on Prices

In the "Take a Break" (🍴) and "Best Bets" sections of this book, we have used a system of dollar signs to show a range of costs for 1 night in a hotel (the price of a double-occupancy room) or the cost of an entree at a restaurant. Use the following table to decipher the dollar signs:

Cost	Hotels	Restaurants
$	under $130	under $15
$$	$130–$200	$15–$30
$$$	$200–$300	$30–$40
$$$$	$300–$395	$40–$50
$$$$$	over $395	over $50

How to Contact Us

In researching this book, we discovered many wonderful places—hotels, restaurants, shops, and more. We're sure you'll find others. Please tell us about them, so we can share the information with your fellow travelers in upcoming editions. If you were disappointed with a recommendation, we'd love to know that, too. Please write to: Support@FrommerMedia.com

Favorite Moments

2

13 Favorite Moments

13 Favorite Moments

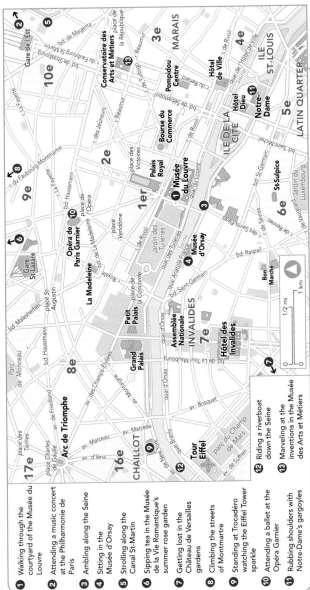

1. Walking through the courtyard of the Musée du Louvre
2. Attending a music concert at the Philharmonie de Paris
3. Ambling along the Seine
4. Sitting in the Musée d'Orsay
5. Strolling along the Canal St-Martin
6. Sipping tea in the Musée de la Vie Romantique's summer rose garden
7. Getting lost in the Château de Versailles gardens
8. Climbing the streets of Montmartre
9. Standing at Trocadéro watching the Eiffel Tower sparkle
10. Attending a ballet at the Opéra Garnier
11. Rubbing shoulders with Notre-Dame's gargoyles
12. Riding a riverboat down the Seine
13. Marveling at the inventions in the Musée des Arts et Métiers

Previous page: I.M. Pei's iconic glass pyramid dominates the courtyard of the Musée du Louvre.

Waiting for the Eiffel Tower to light up after dark, strolling along the Seine on a warm summer night—these could become your favorite moments in the world, not just in Paris. This is an electric city—a "moveable feast" (as Ernest Hemingway so aptly called it). The list of wonderful experiences to be had here is endless. Here are 13 of my favorites.

❶ Walking through the courtyard of the Musée du Louvre early in the morning, hurrying to be one of the first in line, and catching the sun glinting off the glass pyramids in the courtyard—it only heightens the excitement of seeing the masterpieces inside. *See p 30.*

❷ Taking in a music concert at the new Philharmonie de Paris. The main auditorium is wholly futuristic, like the inside of a wooden space ship—all sinuous lines and floating "clouds" (sound-reflecting surfaces designed to perfectly disperse the sound waves). The eclectic program is fab too, covering everything from classic symphonic works to fusion jazz. *See p 133.*

❸ Ambling along the Seine toward the islands, watching the tour boats cruise slowly by, the lights from their windows reflecting on the river. On summer nights, the riverside is packed, even after 10pm; sometimes it seems as if

You'll see everything from art stalls to street performers during a stroll along the Seine.

The light-filled sculpture hall in the Musée d'Orsay.

everybody in Paris is here. Bands play, lovers kiss, children frolic, everybody smiles—this is how life should be all the time.

❹ Sitting in the Musée d'Orsay in the center sculpture court, down below the entrance, looking up at the huge, ornate clock on the wall far above. Through the frosted glass around it, you can see the shadows of people passing by on invisible walkways. The sheer scale is astounding; the look is pure drama. And all around you, the works of history's most talented sculptors lounge, leap, and laugh silently. *See p 7.*

❺ Strolling along the Canal St-Martin, passing delicate iron bridges, locks, and the occasional fisherman. You could spend the better part of a day losing yourself in the bohemian boutiques, stopping at a cafe, and then continuing along to the Parc de la Villette for a

picnic in the park or a trip around the *Cité des Sciences*. *See p 68.*

⑥ Sipping tea in the Musée de la Vie Romantique's summer rose garden. The pink, ivy-clad house once frequented by George Sand and Frédéric Chopin feels like Paris's best-kept secret. Wind down in the garden over a Darjeeling tea and a *tarte du jour*, with just the buzzing of bees and the clinking of tea cups for company. *See p 38.*

⑦ Getting lost in the Château de Versailles gardens. This opulent château of the Sun King, Louis XIV, is the glittering highlight of any visit to the Île-de-France. Nothing can beat a day spent ambling through the terraced gardens, admiring the fountains and Marie Antoinette's hamlet. *See p 153,* ②.

⑧ Climbing the streets of Montmartre. This hilly, hopelessly romantic neighborhood is my favorite in all of Paris. A sweeping view of the city spreads out before you from every cross street. Every corner reveals another evocative stone staircase too steep to see all the way down, but at the bottom you know you'll find sweet old buildings painted pale colors and streets of old paving stones. *See p 17.*

⑨ Standing at Trocadéro, watching the Eiffel Tower sparkle at nightfall. It's the best place in town to take in the tower's elegant, filigree proportions, and that moment when somebody, somewhere, flicks the button to light it up is matchless. *See p 24.*

⑩ Attending a ballet at the Opéra Garnier. Whether you're seeing a traditional rendition of Tchaikovsky's *The Nutcracker* or a contemporary version of Prokofiev's *Romeo et Juliette*, the Charles Garnier–designed grande dame of performance spaces provides a breathtaking backdrop for ballet.

Climb the majestic central staircase, order champagne for the *entr'acte* (intermission), and then sink into your red velvet chair and admire Chagall's famous ceiling fresco before the lights go down. *See p 133.*

⑪ Rubbing shoulders with Notre-Dame's gargoyles. Climb the uneven stone steps to the top of Notre-Dame's towers, and you're in the precipitous realm of Quasimodo, where hideous stone sculptures stick out their tongues at the city below. The views from here are mesmerizing, especially on a cloudy day, when the sky looks moody. *See p 9,* ⑦.

⑫ Riding a riverboat down the Seine, where all the buildings are artfully lighted so they seem to glow from within. On warm nights, take an open-top boat and feel as if you can reach up and touch the damp, stone bridges as you pass beneath them. *See p 11.*

⑬ Marveling at the inventions in the Musée des Arts et Métiers. This museum is easy to miss, yet it contains some of the world's greatest inventions: Blaise Pascal's 17th-century calculator, the *Blériot 11* (the first plane to cross the English Channel), steam-powered carriages, and Henry Ford's Model T car and automated toys. It's a must-see for science fans big and small. *See p 39,* ⑥. ●

The extravagance of the gardens at Versailles rivals that of the palace itself.

The Best **in One Day**

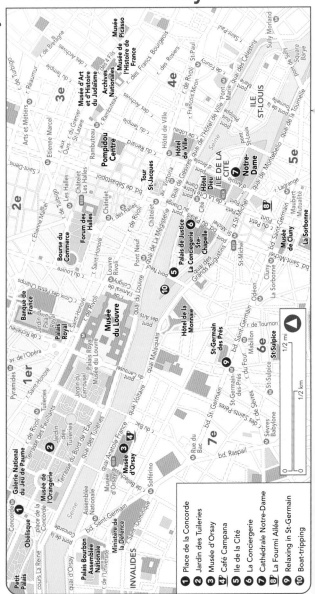

1 Place de la Concorde
2 Jardin des Tuileries
3 Musée d'Orsay
4 Café Campana
5 Ile de la Cité
6 La Conciergerie
7 Cathédrale Notre-Dame
8 La Fourmi Ailée
9 Relaxing in St-Germain
10 Boat-tripping

Previous page: Notre-Dame Cathedral's western facade.

This whirlwind 1-day tour covers everything I would want to see if I had only 24 hours in the City of Light. Start at the stately Place de la Concorde, then spend some time with the Musée d'Orsay's 19th-century masterpieces. Enjoy strolling the narrow cobblestone streets of Paris's islands before touring the iconic Cathédrale de Notre-Dame. Relax at a cafe in Saint-Germain for pre-dinner drinks, and end the day with a moonlit Seine cruise. It's an ambitious itinerary, so start early and wear comfortable shoes.
START: **Métro to Concorde.**

1 ★★ Place de la Concorde. From the city's largest square, you get immediate Paris gratification. First, admire the view of the Eiffel Tower, and then position yourself to see down the Champs Elysées to the Arc de Triomphe, a monument to Napoleon's conquests. Behind you are the Tuileries gardens and the Louvre museum. In the center of the square stands the 3,300-year-old Luxor Obelisk (a gift from Egypt in 1829), placed near the spot where Queen Marie-Antoinette was guillotined in 1793 during the Revolution. To your left, you'll see the Madeleine Church (see p 15)—a mirror image of the Assemblée Nationale across the Seine (home to the lower house of the French Parliament). This lovely viewpoint is your own instant postcard. Welcome to Paris. ⏱ 10 min. Go early in the morning to avoid crowds or just after sunset to see the edifices aglow. Free admission. Métro: Concorde.

2 Jardin des Tuileries. Place de la Concorde ends where the Louvre's stately sculpture-strewn gardens begin. On a space about the size of two football fields, chestnut trees shade winding paths. It's a beautiful place to walk, read, or admire works by such greats as Rodin and Maillol. See also the "Jardin des Tuileries" tour on p 90. ⏱ 20 min. End Mar–May & Sept daily 7am–9pm, June–Aug daily 7am–11pm, Oct to early Mar 7:30am–7:30pm. Métro: Tuileries or Concorde.

3 ★★★ Musée d'Orsay. Across the Seine on the Left Bank is the Gare d'Orsay. Built for the 1900 Universal Exhibition, this Belle

A fountain in Place de la Concorde, with the ancient Luxor Obelisk in the background.

The Tuileries gardens, between Place de la Concorde and the Louvre.

Epoque train station now houses a museum devoted to works created from 1848 to 1914. Fans of Impressionism will swoon at masterpieces by Manet, Renoir, Degas, Cézanne, and Monet. The Post-Impressionist collection includes pieces by van Gogh, Rousseau, and Gauguin. A huge, ornate clock and a 3m (9½ ft.) model of the Statue of Liberty by the French sculptor Auguste Bartholdi (1834–1904) dominate the light-filled central hall. Statues of robust maidens and eager men stand where the train tracks once lay, including the original of Carpeaux's *La Danse* (once controversial for its frolicking nude women), taken from the facade of Paris's Opéra Garnier (see p 15). ⏱ *2–3 hr. 1 rue de la Légion d'Honneur, 7th.* ☎ *01-40-49-48-14. www.*

musee-orsay.fr. *Admission 11€ ages 26 & over, 8.50€ ages 19–25, free for children 18 & under and visitors 25 & under from E.U. countries. Tues–Wed & Fri–Sun 9:30am–6pm, Thurs 9:30am–9:45pm. Métro: Solférino & Assemblée Nationale. RER C: Musée d'Orsay.*

4 **Café Campana.** Near the Impressionist galleries, the Musée d'Orsay's Art Nouveau–inspired restaurant serves tasty brasserie-style meals throughout the day. At tea time, indulge in coffee and delicious chocolate éclairs. *$$.*

5 ★★★ **Île de la Cité.** One of the most quintessentially Parisian experiences you can have is a stroll along the Seine to the Île de la Cité, the birthplace of Paris. Take a right as you leave the Musée d'Orsay. It's about a 15-minute walk to this island, home to **Notre-Dame Cathedral.** Cross onto the island at the **pont Neuf** (New Bridge), which despite its name is the oldest bridge in the city; note the statue of Henri IV, who commissioned the *pont* in 1578. To your right will be the pretty pink Place Dauphine, which opens onto the west wing of the **Palais de Justice,** Paris's law courts (Rue de Harlay). This is an active court building, so

Marie Antoinette awaited her execution in the foreboding Conciergerie.

Notre-Dame sits on an island in the Seine River.

unfortunately tourists are not welcome. But you can admire the majestic east facade (the main entrance) behind gilded gates, between the Conciergerie and Sainte-Chapelle (see the next stop of this tour). ⏱ *30 min. Métro: Pont Neuf.*

❻ ★★ La Conciergerie. The fairy-tale towers that soar above the north end of the island near the pont Neuf mark the fortress where Marie Antoinette was imprisoned before her execution. Its intimidating look is largely courtesy of an 1850s makeover, but most of the building is much older—several parts date to the 12th and 13th centuries, when it was a royal palace (the monarchs moved to the Louvre at the end of the 14th century). During the French Revolution, torture and execution were commonplace here, and it became a symbol of terror. You can visit a reconstruction of Marie Antoinette's cell as well as the former banquet halls and guardrooms, which date back to the Middle Ages. Next door is the 13th-century **Sainte-Chapelle** (buy a dual ticket upon arrival), a Flamboyant Gothic masterpiece built by Saint Louis (King Louis IX) It's famous for the

breathtaking "light show" cast on the interior when the sun shines through its jewel-like stained-glass windows, which recount the stories of the Bible and King Louis. ⏱ *1 hr. 2 bd. du Palais, 1st.* ☎ *01-53-40-60-80. www.conciergerie.monuments-nationaux.fr. Admission 8.50€ (14€ dual ticket) ages 26 & over, 6.50€ ages 19–25 (11€ dual ticket), free for children 18 & under and visitors 25 & under from E.U. countries. Daily 9.30am–6pm. Métro: Cité.*

❼ ★★★ Cathédrale de Notre-Dame. As you approach the eastern tip of the island, you'll see the familiar silhouette of one of the world's best-known cathedrals. Founded in 1160, Notre-Dame stood through wars of religion and centuries of kings (Napoleon also crowned himself emperor here in 1804) before losing its riches to plunderers during the Revolution. By the 19th century, it had fallen into disrepair and was scheduled for demolition until author Victor Hugo, who wrote *The Hunchback of Notre-Dame*, led a successful campaign for its restoration. Before you enter, look for **Point Zero** on the *parvis* (esplanade) outside. It's the center of Paris and the official spot from which all distances are measured in France.

Notre-Dame de Paris

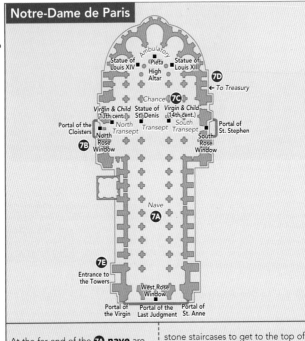

At the far end of the **7A** **nave** are three elaborately sculpted 13th-century portals: on the left, the Portal of the Virgin; in the center, the Portal of the Last Judgment; and on the right, the Portal of St. Anne. Above them all glow the ruby hues of the West Rose Window, its beauty surpassed only by the **7B** **North Rose Window.** The colors are especially vivid in the late afternoon. Near the altar is the 14th-century **7C** **Virgin and Child.** In the **7D** **treasury,** you'll find a collection of crosses and ancient reliquaries, including the Crown of Thorns (brought from the Sainte-Chapelle). To get an up-close look at the cathedral's famous gargoyles, you must climb 422 steps on old

stone staircases to get to the top of the 67m (220 ft.) **7E** **tower.** The non-acrophobic will love the views of the fanciful and detailed hobgoblins and chimeras. ⏲ *1 hr. 6 Parvis Notre-Dame/Place Jean Paul II, 4th.* ☎ *01-42-34-56-10. www.cathedraledeparis.com. Free admission to cathedral, 8.50€ to towers (free to under 18s and visitors 25 & under from E.U. countries), 4€ to treasury. Cathedral daily 8am–6:45pm (guided visits in English Wed–Thurs 2pm, Sat 2:30pm). Towers Apr–June, Sept daily 10am–6:30pm; July–Aug Mon–Thurs, Sun 10am–6:30pm, Fri–Sat 10am–11pm; Oct–Mar daily 10am–5:30pm. Treasury Mon–Fri 9:30am–6pm, Sat 9:30am–6:30pm, Sun 1:30–6:30pm. Métro: Cité.*

8 ★ La Fourmi Ailée. Escape the crowds around Notre-Dame by crossing the pont au Double to the Left Bank. A 5-minute walk past Square René Viviani brings you to the "Flying Ant" tearoom, where sticky cakes and excellent hot dishes, such as veal blanquette (17€), are served in a library-like dining room. *8 rue du Fouarre, 5th.* ☎ *01-43-29-40-99. $$.*

9 ★★ Relaxing in Saint-Germain. Head right as you leave the cafe and go up Rue Dante to join Boulevard Saint-Germain (turning right) and, after 5 minutes, the bustle of Saint-Germain-des-Prés. This area was the incubator for artistic creativity in the 1920s, for Nazi resistance in the 1940s, and for student revolution in the 1960s. These days, you can get a great cup of coffee, drop a wad of money on high-fashion clothes, or spend a night on the town. The best way to experience the neighborhood is to weave your way through glittering, tree-lined Boulevard Saint-Germain and its narrow side-streets, soaking up the atmosphere and stopping at shops and bars that spark your fancy. The district is also the realm

of Paris's historic literary cafes: the stylish **Café de Flore,** 172 bd. St-Germain (☎ 01-45-48-55-26), a favorite of the philosopher Jean-Paul Sartre; and the more touristy **Les Deux Magots,** 6 place St-Germain-des-Prés (☎ 01-45-48-55-26), a regular haunt of both Sartre and Hemingway. At either spot, you can linger over a *café* or enjoy a complete meal. Prices are high, but you can stay at your table and people-watch as long as you like.

10 ★★ Boat Tripping. After dinner, walk down to the riverside at the pont Neuf and catch one of Vedettes du Pont Neuf's long, low boats. As the boats navigate the river by night, the city's lights reflect in the Seine's inky waters like diamonds. Magical. *Tip:* Show your entry ticket from the Conciergerie or Notre-Dame's towers for a 2€ reduction. Internet tickets are also discounted. ⏱ *1 hr. Square du Vert Galant, 4th.* ☎ *01-46-33-98-38. www.vedettesdupontneuf.com. Tickets 14€ adults, 7€ children 4–12, free for children 3 & under. Mid Mar–Oct daily 10:30am–10:30pm, about every 30 min.; Nov–Early Mar daily 10:30am–9.30pm (10pm on weekends), about every 45 min.*

Outside Les Deux Magots cafe on Boulevard Saint-Germain.

12

The Best **in Two Days**

The Best Full-Day Tours

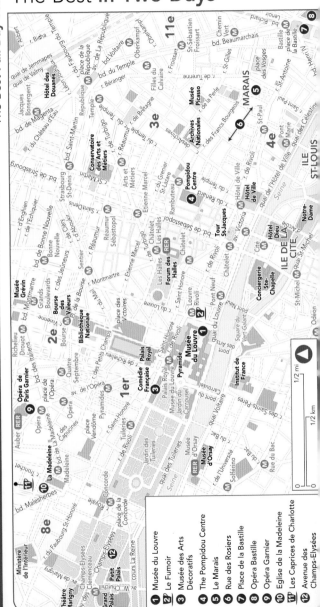

1 Musée du Louvre
2 Le Fumoir
3 Musée des Arts Décoratifs
4 The Pompidou Centre
5 Le Marais
6 Rue des Rosiers
7 Place de la Bastille
8 Opéra Bastille
9 Opéra Garnier
10 Eglise de la Madeleine
11 Les Caprices de Charlotte
12 Avenue des Champs-Elysées

If you followed the 1-day tour of Paris, you've already had a good introduction to the city, but there's so much more to see. Start early with coffee and fresh croissants. Le Nemours (2 Galerie de Nemours, 1st), nestled behind graceful columns opposite the Louvre and the historic Comédie Française theater (p 134), is an atmospheric spot that's perfect for people-watching. START: **Métro to Palais Royal–Musée du Louvre.**

❶ ★★★ Musée du Louvre.
Arrive early, or after 6pm on Wednesday or Friday (when the museum is open until 9:45pm), to catch the shortest lines at what is arguably the world's greatest art museum. The Louvre is so humongous you could easily spend a day in each wing and still not see everything. Overdosing on culture is best avoided by deciding what you want to see in advance. For help navigating the museum, opening times, and ticket prices, see the **Louvre tour** on p 30. ⏱ *2 hr.*

The vast wings of the Louvre contain some of the world's greatest works of art.

❷ ★★ Le Fumoir. This chic cafe with a convenient location near the Louvre and Arts Décoratifs museums has a faithful following among Paris's literary and media crowds. Sink into a Chesterfield armchair and order a refreshing fruit cocktail, or fill up on French classics with a Scandinavian twist. *6 rue de l'Amiral de Coligny, 1st.* ☎ *01-42-92-00-24. www.lefumoir.com. Métro: Louvre-Rivoli. $$$.*

❸ ★ Musée des Arts Décoratifs. This excellent museum (set inside the Louvre palace but separate from the Louvre museum) contains one of the world's most important collections of design and decorative art. It covers a breathtaking range of pieces, from medieval liturgical items, Art Nouveau and Art Deco furniture, and Gothic paneling to Renaissance porcelain and 1970s psychedelic carpets. Ten period rooms show how the

museum's collections would have looked in a real house. The most memorable are couturière Jeanne Lanvin's purple early–Art Deco boudoir and a grandiose Louis-Philippe bedchamber. If you have time, check out the rotating exhibitions at both the Fashion and Textile and Advertising and Graphic Design departments. The former comprises some 152,800 items of clothing and accessories (many by world-famous designers such as Yves Saint Laurent and Christian Dior), while the latter covers the evolution of advertising from the 18th century to today. ⏱ *1–1½ hrs. 107 rue de Rivoli, 1st.* ☎ *01-44-55-57-50. www.lesartsdecoratifs.fr. Admission 11€ ages 27 & over, 8.50€ ages 19–26, free for children 18 & under & visitors 26 & under from E.U. countries. Tues–Wed & Fri–Sun 11am–6pm, Thurs 11am–9pm. Métro: Palais-Royal Musée du Louvre.*

❹ ★★ The Pompidou Centre. If the Louvre's classic artworks leave you craving modernity, walk eastward to Paris's most avant-garde building, the Pompidou Centre—one of the world's leading modern and contemporary art museums. See p 13, ❶.

❺ ★★ Le Marais. I find nothing more relaxing than strolling the winding medieval streets of the Marais district—traditionally the city's old Jewish quarter and home to magnificent 17th- and 18th-century mansions (called *hôtels*). You can spend hours perusing its charming boutiques and tiny Jewish bakeries if you take the Marais tour (p 60). One of its most picturesque squares is the Place des Vosges—Paris's oldest square, remarkable for its perfect symmetry, formed by 36 red-brick–and–stone arcades with sharply pitched roofs. In 1615, a 3-day party was held here celebrating Louis XIII's marriage to Anne of Austria. ◷ *2 hr. Most Jewish shops and restaurants close Fri evening through Sat, the Jewish Sabbath. Many boutiques open Sun. Métro: St-Paul.*

🄶 ★ Rue des Rosiers, 4th. Two places on this street serve the best falafel sandwiches in town (from 5€): L'As du Falafel (no. 34, ☎ 01-48-87-63-60) and Chez Hanna (no.54, ☎ 01-42-74-74-99). Choose the one with the shortest queue; both serve soft pitas bursting with tahini sauce, pickled cabbages, and, of course, tasty chickpea balls. Unless it's raining, eat it on a bench in nearby Place des Vosges. (See previous stop.) *$.*

❼ ★ Place de la Bastille. Here stood the Bastille prison, a massive building that loomed ominously over the city as a symbol of royal authority. On July 14, 1789, a mob

The exoskeletal architecture of the Pompidou Centre.

attacked it, and its fall marked the beginning of the people's uprising that eventually led to the founding of the first French republic, in 1792. Today, the site is home to the modern Bastille Opera House and a busy traffic circle. The central column, the Colonne de Juillet, honors the casualties of the 1830 revolution. ◷ *15 min. Métro: Bastille.*

❽ ★ Opéra Bastille. This impossible-to-miss behemoth, which opened in 1989 as part of President Mitterrand's "Grand Travaux" (large-scale monument program), is the home of the Opéra National de Paris (together with the Opéra Garnier; see the next stop). Designed by Canadian-Uruguayan architect Carlos Ott, the building infamously ran over budget and had structural issues that took years to resolve. Today, however, the 80m-tall (262-ft.) monument has found its place in the landscape, and the operas performed in its 2,745-seat auditorium are of the highest standard. Tickets are sold online, or try your luck 40 minutes before the performance, when remaining tickets are sold off at a discount. ◷ *15 min. 2 place de la Bastille, 4th. ☎ 08-92-89-90-90*

(0.34€/min.) or 33-1-71-25-24-23 from abroad. www.operadeparis.fr. Tickets 5€–215€. Métro: Bastille.

⑨ ★★ Opéra Garnier. Charles Garnier's 1875 opera house goes beyond baroque and well into the splendors of rococo, and is hailed as one of most spectacular Italian-style theaters in the world. An elaborate ceiling painted by Marc Chagall in 1964 and an 8-ton chandelier dominate the main theater, while the facade is a riot of marble and flowing sculpture, with gilded busts and multihued pillars. This is where the Phantom did his haunting (a man-made lake below the opera house inspired novelist Gaston Leroux to create his tragic antihero). Even if you don't see a show, buy a visitor's ticket (11€, 7€ ages 13–25) to admire the flamboyant gilded interior, including the grand staircase where a salamander sculpture serves the double function of hiding electric cables and protecting the opera from fire: Paris's previous opera houses burned down, so Garnier included the salamander as a good-luck charm (according to legend, the creatures are fire-resistant). ◷ 20 min. Place de l'Opéra, 9th. ☎ 08-92-89-90-90 (0.34€/min.) or 33-1-71-25-24-23 from abroad. www.operadeparis.fr. Tickets 5€–215€. Visiting hours daily 10am–5pm; until 1pm on matinee performance days. Métro: Opéra, RER A: Auber.

⑩ ★★ Eglise de la Madeleine. Tear yourself away from the Art Nouveau–style department stores behind the opera house on Boulevard Haussmann (**Galeries Lafayette** and **Au Printemps,** p 84), and head west down Boulevard des Capucines to this neoclassical church, designed by Barthélémy Vignon in 1806 as a "temple of glory" for Napoleon Bonaparte. The exterior, which mirrors the Assemblée Nationale on the other side of Place de la Concorde, is marked by fluted Corinthian columns, while interior highlights include a wonderful frieze of the Last Judgment and a painting of the history of Christianity by Jules-Claude Ziegler. The square around the church, **Place de la Madeleine,** is a foodie paradise, with top-end restaurants and such luxury food shops as **Fauchon** (p 86). ◷ 30 min. Place de la Madeleine, 8th. ☎ 01-44-51-69-00. www.eglise-lamadeleine.com. Free admission. Daily 9:30am–7pm. Métro: Madeleine.

⑪ ★★ Les Caprices de Charlotte. Behind the Madeleine, gateaux fill this modern boulangerie's counter like exquisite gourmet jewels. Sidle up to a table and try the Paris-Brest (choux pastry filled with praline cream) washed down with piping hot tea or an espresso. The raspberry tartelettes are also superlative. 14 rue Castellane, 8th. ☎ 01-42-65-40-69. www.lescapricesdecharlotte.net. Mon–Sat 7am–8pm. Métro: Madeleine or Havre-Caumartin. $.

⑫ ★★ Avenue des Champs-Elysées. This bustling 2km (1¼-mile) avenue—the symbolic gathering place for national parades and sports victory celebrations, largely centered around Napoleon's early-19th-century **Arc de Triomphe** (p 24)—is inseparable from Paris in the minds of most people. It is also part of the city's **Golden Triangle** (along with av. Georges V and av. Montaigne), where Chanel, Louis Vuitton, and other designer boutiques stand alongside lavish hotels. You'll find plenty for tighter budgets, too: Such mass-market shops as H&M, Marks & Spencer, and Zara line the sidewalk along with cinemas, bars, the **Lido** cabaret (p 129), and the famous **Queen** nightclub (p 120).

The Best **in Three Days**

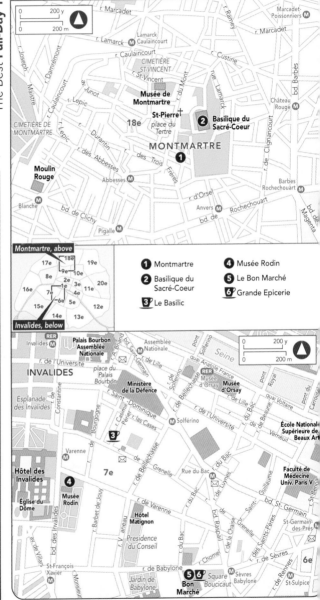

Montmartre, above

Invalides, below

1 Montmartre

2 Basilique du Sacré-Coeur

3 Le Basilic

4 Musée Rodin

5 Le Bon Marché

6 Grande Epicerie

After 2 jam-packed days, you may want to slow down a bit. A good way of getting a leisurely feel for two very different parts of the city is to spend the morning amid the cobblestones and windmills of Montmartre on the Right Bank before heading to the throng of boutiques in the Saint-Germain district, south of the Seine, in the afternoon. If you fancy slackening the pace even more, choose one of these two areas and follow the full-day tours on p 52 or p 64. START: **Métro to Abesses or Blanche.**

❶ ★★★ **Montmartre.** With its steep hills, staircase streets, quaint windmills, and sweeping views, this is the most romantic neighborhood in Paris, and many would say the most beautiful. Unfortunately, it's not exactly a secret—prepare yourself for some tacky souvenir shops and the ever-present tourist onslaught around the Sacré Coeur. Still, spending a morning wandering around the streets of Montmartre is enough to make the heart flutter (and not just from the exertion of climbing all those stairs). Take the Métro to Abesses or Blanche and head upward. Fall in love with such streets as Rue des Abbesses, Rue des Trois Frères, or Rue des Martyrs. Find the windmills on Rue Lepic or the famous one atop the titillating Moulin Rouge on the boulevard below. For more guidance, try the Montmartre walking tour on p 64. ⏱ *2 hr. Métro: Abesses or Blanche.*

❷ ★★★ **Sacré Coeur.** You can either take a funicular from the end of Rue Berthe or, better still, wander up to Sacré Coeur via the bustling Place du Tertre; however you get here, this white wedding-cake basilica will draw a gasp from you when it first hovers into view. Construction began in 1876 and didn't end until 1919—the whole thing was paid for by donations from the faithful to thank God for freeing Paris from the invaders of the 1870–71 Franco-Prussian War. The mosaics inside—on the ceiling, walls, and floors—are dizzying, and the panoramic view from the steps out front is almost as splendid as the one from its dome (300 steps higher), where a panorama unfolds 50km (30 miles) into the distance. The Sacré Coeur's bell, called La Savoyarde, is 3m (10 ft.) wide and weighs 18,835 kg (19 tons), making it the biggest bell in France. An audio-guide tour in English is

The Basilica Sacré Coeur crowns the highest hill in Paris.

The Thinker in the courtyard of the Musée Rodin.

available for your smartphone via a flash code at the entrance. ⏱ 1 hr. Place Saint-Pierre, 18th. ☎ 01-53-41-89-00. www.sacre-coeur-montmar tre.com. Free admission to basilica, 8€ to dome & crypt. Daily 6am–10:45pm (dome 9am–5pm Oct–Apr, 8:30am–8pm May–Sept). Métro: Abbesses or Anvers.

3 ★★ **Le Basilic.** On Rue Lepic, north of the Café des Deux Mou-lins (no. 15), where Amélie worked in the film of the same name, an honest two-course lunch of hearty French staples costs just 12€. Dishes—think Rossini-style beef with creamy potato gratin and a velveteen mousse au chocolat—are fresh and hearty, and the atmo-sphere is wholly Montmartrois. 33 rue Lepic, 18th. ☎ 01-46-06-78-43. www.lebasilic.fr. Daily 11:45am–mid-night. $.

4 ★★ **Musée Rodin.** A short Métro ride will bring you to this peaceful museum, where the sculp-tor Auguste Rodin once had his studio. Today his works

are scattered inside and outside a somber 18th-century mansion of gray stone. The Thinker perches pensively in the courtyard, while the lovers in The Kiss embrace in per-petuity inside. There's also a room devoted to the oft-overlooked works of Rodin's talented mistress, Camille Claudel. It's rarely crowded, so it's a good option when things are overwhelming at the Louvre. ⏱ 1 hr. Hôtel Biron, 79 rue de Varenne, 7th. ☎ 01-44-18-61-10. www.musee-rodin.fr. Admission 9€ ages 26 & over, 5€ ages 19–25, free for children 18 & under & visitors 25 & under from E.U. countries. Garden only 2€. Tues & Thurs–Sun 10am–5:45pm; Wed 1am–8:45pm. Métro: Varenne or Invalides. RER C: Invalides.

5 ★ **Shopping at Le Bon Marché.** If you haven't found everything you hoped to yet, come to this swank department store. The place is all very designer-label oriented, which may put some strains on the holiday budget. But this is Paris's oldest department store, and even the central escala-tors are worth photographing, so you should at least take a look. ⏱ 2 hr. 24 rue de Sèvres, 7th. ☎ 01-44-39-80-00. www.lebon marche.com. Mon–Sat 10am–8pm (Thurs–Fri until 9pm). Métro: Sèvres-Babylone.

6 ★ **Grande Epicerie.** In the building next to the Bon Marché, this grand food hall contains all the pâtés and cheeses your heart could desire. You can build yourself a gor-geous picnic, or take a seat in the excellent brasserie and let some-one else do all the work. There's even a happy hour (5–8pm, glass of wine 5€). 38 rue de Sèvres, 7th. ☎ 01-44-39-81-00. www.lagran deepicerie.com. Mon–Sat 8:30am–9pm. $$. ●

2 The Best Special-Interest Tours

Monumental Paris

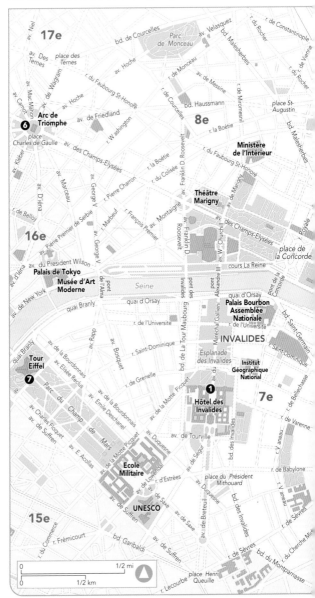

Previous page: Lines for admission to the Louvre can be long. Save time by buying tickets online in advance.

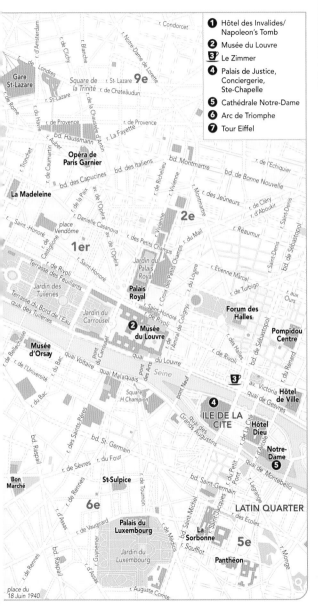

1 Hôtel des Invalides/
   Napoleon's Tomb
2 Musée du Louvre
3 Le Zimmer
4 Palais de Justice,
   Conciergerie,
   Ste-Chapelle
5 Cathédrale Notre-Dame
6 Arc de Triomphe
7 Tour Eiffel

This tour covers a lot of ground, so be prepared for lots of walking and, when your feet ache, metro-hopping. For your efforts, you'll see the city's most glorious edifices in one giant sweep. If you get an early start and keep moving, you should be able to make it to the Eiffel Tower (the last stop) by sunset. START: **Métro to Invalides.**

❶ ★★★ Hôtel des Invalides/ Napoleon's Tomb. The imposing Les Invalides complex, with its symmetrical corridors and beautiful Dôme church (Libéral Bruand and Jules Hardouin-Mansart's golden-domed masterpiece), was built in 1670 by Louis XIV as a military hospital and a showpiece of the Sun King's military power. Approach it from the cherub-clad pont Alexandre III to see it as intended, from the end of its perfectly balanced gardens, lined with canons. Inside, along with accouterments of Napoleon's life and death, is the Musée de l'Armée, with enough historic weaponry (vicious battle-axes, clumsy blunderbusses) to mount another revolution. Among the collection's gems are a German Enigma machine, used by Hitler's

Napoleon's tomb at Hôtel des Invalides.

army to encrypt messages, and suits of armor worn by the kings and dignitaries of France, including one worn by Louis XIV and François I's exquisite "armor suit of the lion," inspired by Classical war heroes. The complex also contains the Charles de Gaulle Monument, a high-tech audiovisual attraction covering the whole of de Gaulle's life, particularly his role in World War II; the Musée des Plans Reliefs, the collection of scale-model cities Vauban, Louis XIV's military engineer, used for planning military attacks; and of course, Napoleon's beautiful, over-the-top tomb, set inside the Dôme church, featuring giant statues that represent his victories. You can also see his death mask and an oil painting by Paul Delaroche, painted at the time of Napoleon's first banishment in 1814. ◷ *1 hr. 129 rue de Grenelle, 7th.* ☎ *01-42-44-38-77. www. invalides.org. Admission 9.50€ ages 26 & over, 7.50€ ages 18–25, free for children 17 & under & visitors 25 & under from E.U. countries. Nov–Mar daily 10am–5pm; Apr–Oct daily 10am–6pm. Oct–June closed 1st Mon of the month. Charles de Gaulle Monument closed Mon. Métro: Invalides, Varenne or La Tour Maubourg; RER C: Invalides.*

❷ ★★★ Musée du Louvre. The home of da Vinci's *Mona Lisa* is one of the world's largest and best museums, set in Paris's former royal palace. It's worth spending a day here (see "Exploring the Louvre," p 30), but for this tour, admire it from the outside. ◷ *20 min.*

A subterranean passage undercuts traffic, leading pedestrians safely to the Arc de Triomphe.

3 ★ **Le Zimmer.** Jules Verne, Marcel Proust, and Igor Stravinski once frequented this storied, 19th-century brasserie. During WWII, the "Honneur de la Police" (underground police Résistance) secretly occupied its cellars. Today, it's an atmospheric spot–all mirrors and red velvet–for lunch with terrace views onto your next stop, the Conciergerie. The 20€ menu is good value. *1 place du Châtelet, 1st.* ☎ *01-42-36-74-03, www.lezimmer. com. Métro: Châtelet. $$.*

4 ★★★ **Palais de Justice, Conciergerie & Sainte-Chapelle.** Take the Pont au Change to the Île de la Cité and walk down Boulevard du Palais. Immediately on your right is the complex made up of the Conciergerie (formerly a prison, now a museum), the Palais de Justice (law courts, not open to visitors), and the exquisite Sainte-Chapelle church. Once a palace, the Conciergerie was converted to a prison during the Revolution and became a symbol of terror—Paris's answer to the Tower of London. Carts once frequently pulled up to the Conciergerie to haul off fresh victims for the guillotine. Among the few imprisoned here who lived to tell the tale was American political theorist and writer Thomas Paine. Inside, you can learn about the bloody history of the Conciergerie and visit some of the old prison cells, including a re-creation of Marie Antoinette's. The Palais de Justice is still the center of the French judicial system and thus doesn't accept tourists, but you can peek through its grand, gated entrance as you make your way to the Sainte-Chapelle—stunning in afternoon light. It was built in the 13th century to hold a crown of thorns that King Louis IX believed Christ wore during his crucifixion (the crown is now in Notre-Dame). The chapel's stained-glass windows comprise more than 1,000 scenes depicting the Christian story from the Garden of Eden through to the Apocalypse, shown on the great Rose Window. (Read them from bottom to top and from left to right.) The stained glass of Sainte-Chapelle is magnificent in daylight, glowing with reds that have inspired the saying "wine the color of Sainte-Chapelle's windows." ⏱ *1 hr. 2–6 bd. du Palais, 1st.* ☎ *01-53-40-60-80. www.con ciergerie.monuments-nationaux.fr. Conciergerie 8.50€ ages 26 & over,*

A view of the Eiffel Tower from the carousel in the Luxembourg Gardens.

6.50€ ages 18–25, free for ages 17 & under & visitors 26 & under from E.U. countries; Sainte-Chapelle 8.50€ ages 26 & over, 5.50€ ages 18–25, free for children 17 & under & visitors 26 & under from E.U. countries. Combined ticket Conciergerie & Sainte-Chapelle 14€; concessions 11€ or free entry, as above. Daily 9:30am–6pm (Sainte-Chapelle until 9pm on Wed mid-May to mid-Sept). Métro: Cité or Châtelet (exit place du Cnâtelet).

❺ ★★★ Cathédrale Notre-Dame.
For a good view of the buttresses, take the short bridge—pont de l'Archevêché—just behind the cathedral to Île Saint-Louis. ⏱ *1 hr. See p 9,* ❼.

❻ ★★★ Arc de Triomphe.
The world's largest triumphal arch was commissioned by Napoleon in 1806 to commemorate the victories of his Grande Armée. The monument is engraved with the names of hundreds of generals (those underlined died in battle) who commanded French troops in Napoleonic victories. The arch was finished in 1836, after Napoleon's death. His remains, brought from St. Helena in 1840, passed under it on the journey to his final resting place at the Hôtel des Invalides. These days, the arch is the focal point of state funerals and the site of the Tomb of the Unknown Soldier, in whose honor an eternal flame burns. It's also a huge traffic circle, representing certain death to pedestrians, so you reach the arch via an underground passage (well-signposted). The constant roar of traffic can ruin the mood, but the view from the top (accessible via elevator or stairs) makes enduring the din worthwhile. The last leg of your tour is a 20-minute walk away. You can also hop back on the Métro to Trocadéro or flag down a taxi on the Champs Elysées. ⏱ *45 min. The Arc de Triomphe is open late at night, so if you prefer a nighttime view, you can put this off until after dinner. Place Charles de Gaulle–Etoile, 8th.* ☎ *01-55-37-73-77. www. arc-de-triomphe.monuments-nation-aux.fr. Admission 9.50€ ages 26 & over, 7.50€ ages 18–25, free for children 17 & under & visitors 25 & under from E.U. countries. Apr–Sept daily 10am–11pm; Oct–Mar daily 10am–10:30pm. Métro/RER: Charles de Gaulle–Etoile.*

❼ ★★★ Tour Eiffel.
At last. It's the Eiffel Tower to English speakers and the *Tour Eiffel* to the French-speaking world, but whatever you call it, it is synonymous with Paris.

The tower was meant to be temporary, built by Gustave-Alexandre Eiffel (who also created the framework for the Statue of Liberty) in 1889 for the Universal Exhibition. It weighs 7,000 tons but exerts about the same pressure on the ground as an average-size person sitting in a chair. Praised by some and denounced by others, the tower created as much controversy in the 1880s as I.M. Pei's glass pyramid at the Louvre did in the 1980s. The tower, including its antenna, is 324m (1,062 ft.) high, and from the top you can see for 65km (40 miles). But the view *of* the tower is just as important as the view *from* it. If you go to Trocadéro on the Métro and then walk from the Palais de Chaillot gardens across the Seine, you'll get the best view (not to mention photo opportunities). I always come right at sunset or just after dark when the tower's 20,000 bulbs sparkle for 5 minutes every hour on the hour from nightfall to 1am. Inside the tower's lacy ironwork are restaurants, bars, and historic memorabilia. Take your time, take selfies over the new transparent floor on the 1st level, or even book a table at Alain Ducasse's pricey restaurant **Le Jules Verne** (reserve 3 months in advance for an evening meal;

☎ 01-45-55-61-44, www.lejules-verne-paris.com), and enjoy sweeping views from the second level as you dine. If your pockets aren't that deep, the brasserie 58 Tour Eiffel, on the first floor, is a panoramic compromise. Or opt for a glass of bubbly from the tiny top floor champagne bar—no more than a barman behind a hatch. *Tip:* To save time in line, buy your tickets online in advance or book a guided tour. The tower's smartphone app is also worth downloading. ⏲ *2 hr. Champ de Mars, 7th.* ☎ *01-44-11-23-23. www.tour-eiffel.fr. Admission via lift to 1st or 2nd floor 11€ adults, 8.50€ ages 12–24, 4€ ages 4–11; lift to top floor 17€ adults, 15€ ages 12–24, 10€ ages 4–11; stairs to 1st and 2nd floors 7€ adults, 5€ ages 12–24, 3€ ages 4–11, free for children 3 & under. Open by lift mid-Sept to early June daily 9:30am–11:45pm (last lift to top 10:30pm); mid-June to early Sept daily 9am–12:45am (last lift to top 11pm). By stairs mid-Sept to early-June daily 9:30am–6:30pm (last entry 6pm); mid-June to early-Sept daily 9am–12:45am (last entry midnight). Métro: Trocadéro, Ecole Militaire, or Bir-Hakeim. RER: Champs-de-Mars-Tour-Eiffel.*

Paris with Kids

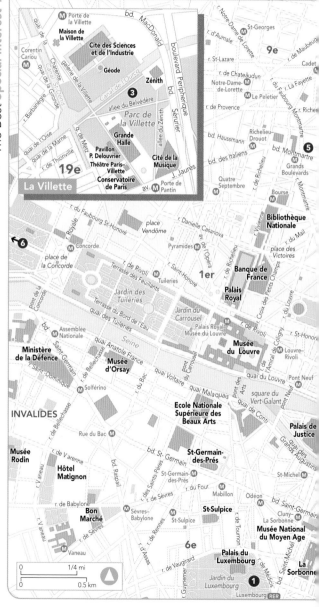

Porte de la Villette
Maison de la Villette
Cité des Sciences et de l'Industrie
Géode
Zénith
bd. MacDonald
Corentin Cariou
quai de la Charente
galerie de la Villette
quai de la Gironde
Canal de l'Ourcq
boulevard Périphérique
Sérurier
allée du Belvédère
Parc de la Villette
❸
Grande Halle
Pavillon P. Delouvrier
Théâtre Paris–Villette
Conservatoire de Paris
Cité de la Musique
J. Jaurès
Porte de Pantin
av.
quai de l'Oise
quai de la Marne
r. de Metz
r. de Thionville
r. de Flandre
19e
La Villette
allée du Zénith

Notre-Dame de Lorette
St-Georges
r. d'Aumale
9e
r. St-Lazare
Cadet
r. de Chateâudun
Notre-Dame-de-Lorette
Le Peletier
r. de Provence
r. du Faubourg Montmartre
r. La Fayette
r. de Maubeuge
r. Riche...
Richelieu-Drouot
bd. Haussmann
bd. des Italiens
bd. Montmartre
❺
Grands Boulevards
r. de Richelieu
Montmartre
Quatre Septembre
Bourse
r. Royale
r. du Faubourg St-Honoré
place Vendôme
r. Danielle Casanova
av. de l'Opéra
place des Victoires
Bibliothèque Nationale
r. Vivienne
r. du Mail
❻
Concorde
Pyramides
Saint-Honoré
1er
r. de Richelieu
place des Victoires
place de la Concorde
r. de Rivoli
Terrasse des Feuillants
Tuileries
Banque de France
Croix des Petits Champs
Palais Royal
pont de la Concorde
Jardin des Tuileries
Terrasse du Bord de l'Eau
quai des Tuileries
Jardin du Carrousel
Palais Royal–Musée du Louvre
r. de Rivoli
Musée du Louvre
r. de l'Amiral Coligny
r. St-Honoré
Louvre–Rivoli
Assemblée Nationale
Seine
quai Anatole France
Musée d'Orsay
pont du Carrousel
quai Voltaire
quai Malaquais
quai du Louvre
pont des Arts
square du Vert-Galant
quai de Conti
Pont Neuf
Ministère de la Défence
r. Saint-Germain
r. de Bellechasse
r. du Bac
bd.
Solférino
r. Saint-Dominique
Ecole Nationale Supérieure des Beaux Arts
Palais de Justice
quai des Grands Augustins
INVALIDES
r. de Bellechasse
Rue du Bac
bd. St-Germain
St-Germain-des-Prés
St-Germain-des-Prés
St-Michel
Musée Rodin
r. de Varenne
bd. Raspail
r. des Saints-Pères
r. du Four
Mabillon
Odéon
bd. Saint-Germain
Hôtel Matignon
r. de Babylone
Sèvres-Babylone
St-Sulpice
Cluny–La Sorbonne
Musée National du Moyen Age
r. V. Vaneau
Bon Marché
r. des Rennes
r. de Tournon
St-Sulpice
r. de Sèvres
6e
r. Guynemer
r. d'Assas
Vaneau
Palais du Luxembourg
r. de Vaugirard
Jardin du Luxembourg
❶
r. de Médicis
La Sorbonne
bd. Saint-Michel
Luxembourg RER

0   1/4 mi
0   0.5 km

1 Jardins du Luxembourg
2 Muséum National
d'Histoire Naturelle
& Ménagerie du Jardin
des Plantes
3 Parc de la Villette
4 Parc Zoologique de Paris
5 Grévin
6 Jardin d'Acclimation

Let's face it: Most kid-approved attractions are outdoors, which means you're dangerously reliant on good weather. But this tour has been designed for you to dip into at will, to keep the brood smiling come rain or shine. Look for the "kids" icon in chapter 6 to find family-friendly dining options around the city. And if the best-laid plans fail, you can always rush them off for a day at Disneyland Paris (p 156). START: **Métro to Odéon or RER to Luxembourg.**

❶ Jardins du Luxembourg.

Kids can run amok in these elegant gardens, which are done in classic French style, with urns and statuary and trees planted in patterns. Statues peek out everywhere as children sail toy boats on the ponds, ride the ponies, or catch a puppet show, if you get lucky with timing. Kids can also watch the locals play *boules* (lawn bowling), but are unlikely to be invited to join in. Don't miss the swings in the play area, the old-fashioned merry-go-round, and (if you're with toddlers) the sandpits. ⏱ *1 hr. Métro: Odéon. RER: Luxembourg.*

❷ Muséum National d'Histoire Naturelle & Ménagerie du Jardin des Plantes.

The giant whale skeleton that greets you at this natural history museum lets you know right off the bat that the kids are going to be fine here. Beyond those bones in the Galerie de l'Evolution are more skeletons of dinosaurs and stuffed animals, lined-up like a queue for Noah's Ark, plus adjacent galleries filled with sparkling minerals, and hothouses of rare plants. In the surrounding gardens (the Jardin des Plantes), there's also a wonderful little zoo with small animals, birds, crocodiles and wild cats. ⏱ *90 min. 56 rue Cuvier, 5th.* ☎ *01-40-79-54-79. www.mnhn.fr. Admission 13€ adults, 9€ ages 3–16, free for children 2 & under (1 full-price ticket gives reduced price access to the Menagerie). Wed–Fri & Mon 9am–5pm, Sat–Sun 9am–6pm. Métro: Jussieu or Gare d'Austerlitz.*

❸ ★★★ Parc de la Villette.

In the rejuvenated northeast part of town, this retro-futurist, canal-side succession of gardens is a fab place for kids to run around. There's the **Géode IMAX cinema** (26 av. Corentin-Cariou, ☎ 01-40-05-79-99; admission 12€ adults, 9€ 25 and under; www.lageode.fr), a wonderful

Toy boats in the Jardins du Luxembourg.

The Paris Zoo dates back to 1931.

children's science museum, **La Cité des Sciences** (30 av. Corentin-Cariou; ☎ 01-40-05-70-00; www.cite-sciences.fr; admission 12€ adults, 10€ ages 7–25, 3€ for children under 6), and the new **Philharmonie de Paris** (see p 133), a post-modernist philharmonic hall with a music museum displaying over 1,000 instruments, including Chopin's piano (222 av. Jean Jaurès, 19th; ☎ 01-44-84-44-84, www.philharmoniedeparis.fr; admission 7€ adults, free for visitors 26 and under). ⏱ *3 hr. 19th. Métro: Porte de la Villette or Porte de Pantin.*

❹ **Parc Zoologique de Paris.** Created as a temporary exhibition for the 1931 Colonial Fair, the Paris Zoo was so successful it became permanent in 1934. Today's park is a zoo of the future, dedicated to endangered species, and split into five conservation areas, called "biozones," corresponding to habitats in Patagonia (South America), the Sahel (Africa), Europe, Madagascar, and tropical French Guiana. For something special, treat the kids to breakfast with the giraffes (the largest herd in Europe); it's a splurge, but it's magical. (Wed, Sat–Sun before the park opens, ☎ 01-70-94-50-25/resa.pzp@mnhn.fr; 60€ adults, 50€ ages12–25, and 45€ ages 3–11). ⏱ *2 hr. Intersection of ave Daumesnil and the route du Lac, 12th. www.parczoologiquedeparis.fr.* ☎ *08-11-22-41-22. Admission 22€ adults, 17€ children 12–25, 14€ children 3-11, free 2 and under. Mid-Oct to June daily 9:30am–7:30pm (until nightfall Thurs), July to early-Oct daily 10am–5pm. Métro: Porte-Dorée.*

❺ **Grévin.** At this waxworks museum, kids will enjoy wandering among stars—both French (Edith Piaf) and international (soccer star Zlatan Ibrahimovic). Among the 300 wax figures, you'll find heads of state, artists, writers, and historical figures—at times, the museum even verges on educational. ⏱ *1 hr. 10 bd. Montmartre, 9th.* ☎ *01-47-70-85-05. www.grevin.com. Admission 25€ adults 18 & up, 22€ children 15–17, 18€ children 6–14, free for children 5 & under. Mon–Fri 10am–6:30pm, Sat–Sun 10am–7pm. Times may vary seasonally. Closed 1st week in Oct. Métro: Grands-Boulevards.*

❻ ★★ **Jardin d'Acclimatation.** Let the kids while away a sunny afternoon here. You can start with a ride on a narrow-gauge train from porte Maillot to the entrance (daily, roughly every 30 min. from 10am–7pm; until 8pm Fri & Sun). Inside, there's a house of mirrors, an archery range, miniature golf, a small (and vaguely worrying) zoo, a bowling alley, a puppet theater, playgrounds, kid-size rides, shooting galleries, and food stalls. Kids can ride ponies and paddle about in boats—they can even drive little cars. Bear in mind that it's only for little ones; teenagers will hate it. ⏱ *2–3 hr. Bois de Boulogne, 16th.* ☎ *01-40-67-90-82. www.jardindacclimatation.fr. Admission 3€ to enter, then 2.90€ for each attraction, or 35€ for 15 rides; free for children 3 and under. June–Sept daily 10am–7pm (until 8pm Sun & bank holidays); Oct–May daily 10am–6pm. Métro: Sablons or Porte Maillot.*

Exploring the Louvre

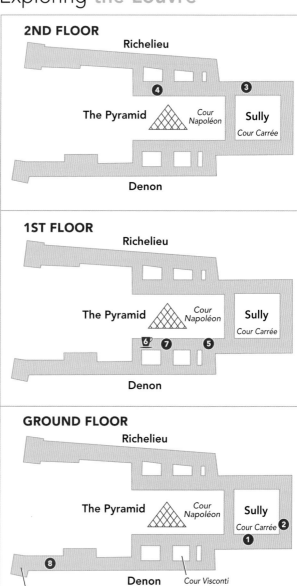

2ND FLOOR

Richelieu

The Pyramid · *Cour Napoléon* · **Sully** · *Cour Carrée*

Denon

1ST FLOOR

Richelieu

The Pyramid · *Cour Napoléon* · **Sully** · *Cour Carrée*

Denon

GROUND FLOOR

Richelieu

The Pyramid · *Cour Napoléon* · **Sully** · *Cour Carrée*

Cour Visconti

Denon

Port des Lions

1. Venus de Milo
2. Colossal Statue of Ramesses II
3. The Card Sharper
4. The Lacemaker
5. Winged Victory of Samothrace
6. Café Mollien
7. Mona Lisa
8. Italian Sculpture
9. Cour Visconti

THE PYRAMID

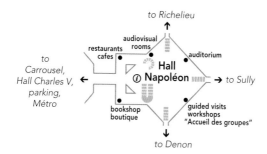

to Richelieu

audiovisual rooms

restaurants cafes

auditorium

to Carrousel, Hall Charles V, parking, Métro

Hall Napoléon

to Sully

bookshop boutique

guided visits workshops "Accueil des groupes"

to Denon

LOWER GROUND FLOOR

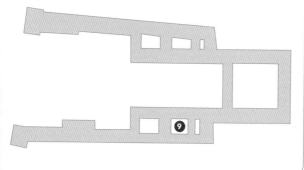

Before becoming a museum, the Musée du Louvre was France's main royal palace. In 1527, François I demolished most of the old castle to build a new one, which makes up part of the building you see today. (François also inadvertently founded part of the museum's collection—the *Mona Lisa* and *Virgin of the Rocks* once hung in his bathroom.) The rest of the building was completed over the centuries, particularly by Henri II and Napoleon whose apartments may be visited on the 1st floor (if you're from the U.S., remember that the French first floor is your second floor). More recent additions include the glass pyramids designed by I. M. Pei (in 1989) and the Cour Visconti extension, which houses a wonderful Islamic art collection. START: **Métro to Palais Royal–Musée du Louvre.**

Travel Tip

Laid out end to end, the Louvre would be the size of several football fields, so put aside at least 3 to 4 hours to get a general feel for the place and browse a bit between stops. Pick up a map when you arrive at the museum and use it to find my suggested selection of works—the floor and rooms are marked for each entry.

❶ ★★★ Venus de Milo. Begin your tour in Greek Antiquities, where *Venus* stands alluringly, her drapery about to fall to the floor. The statue dates to 100 B.C. Myths about her abound—one story maintains that her arms were knocked off when she was hustled onto a French ship. Another claims she was rescued from a pottery kiln. Both are untrue—she was found buried as you see her now, along with part of an arm, a hand holding an apple, and a pair of small columns, one of which fit neatly into her base and bore the inscription ALEXANDROS, SON OF MENIDES, CITIZEN OF ANTIOCH, MADE THIS STATUE. Sadly, those parts were all lost over time. *Ground floor, Room 16.*

❷ ★ Colossal Statue of Ramesses II. On the same level, enter the Ancient Egypt

department, where you'll see this intriguing statue of King Ramesses II sitting in pharaonic splendor (albeit with a damaged nose). Ramesses was the third pharaoh of the 19th dynasty. He reigned for 67 years (1279–1213 A.D.; the second longest reign in Egyptian history), died aged 96, and had over 200 wives and concubines. His names and titles can be seen on his belt buckle, and on the back and sides of his throne. *Ground floor, Room 12.*

❸ ★★ The Card Sharper. In Room 24, on the second floor, you'll find Georges de la Tour's sensational *Tricheur (The Card*

After all these millennia, Venus de Milo still manages to work the crowd.

The Louvre: Practical Matters

The main entrances to the Musée du Louvre, 1st (☎ 01-40-20-53-17; www.louvre.fr) are at 99 rue de Rivoli, inside the Carousel du Louvre underground shopping mall, and the glass pyramid in the main courtyard. However, the lesser-known Porte des Lions entrance (in the Denon wing; cross place du Carousel and walk toward the Tuileries gardens; it's on your left) is often quiet (call the day before to check it's open: ☎ 01-40-20-53-17). Tickets can be bought inside the museum, but expect a long line. To jump the queues, use the automatic ticket machines inside the Carousel du Louvre (just after the entrance at 99 rue de Rivoli) or buy them in advance at a FNAC (p 132) or online (www.ticketweb.com if you're from the United States or Canada, or www.fnactickets.com or www.ticket master.fr if you're not), then go to the Passage Richelieu entrance, 93 rue de Rivoli.

To beat the crowds, arrive shortly after opening or after 6pm Wednesday or Friday. Admission is 16€, free for children 18 and under and visitors 25 and under from E.U. countries, and free for everyone the first Sunday of the month (Oct–Mar). Hours are Wednesday to Monday 9am to 6pm (until 9:45pm Wed and Fri), Closed Tuesday. Métro: Palais Royal–Musée du Louvre and Louvre Rivoli.

Sharper), painted around 1630. In this gorgeous work, complex relationships play out in shimmering colors. In the center, a courtesan holds her hand out for a glass of wine poured by a servant. Her cheating friend holds cards behind his back as she casts a colluding glance at him. The chubby-cheeked youth in the embroidered shirt is the victim of a plot. A cruel tale, playfully told. *2nd floor, Room 24.*

❹ ★★★ *The Lacemaker.* The *Lacemaker* (around 1664) is one of Johannes Vermeer's most famous paintings. It shows a young woman bent over her work, her shape forming a subtle pyramid, and her face, hair, and rich yellow blouse aglow. The book in the foreground is probably the Bible and sets the moral and religious tone of the painting. Vermeer's unique use of

color and light are exemplified in this work, which is usually surrounded by a crowd of admirers. *2nd floor, Room 38.*

❺ ★ *Winged Victory of Samothrace.* Head toward the Denon Wing, where at the top of the Daru stairs stands Nike, the goddess of victory, her wings flung back in takeoff, and the fabric of her skirts swirling around her, as fine as silk. The statue's origins are uncertain. Most scholars date it to somewhere between 220 and 190 B.C. The statue was discovered on the Greek island of Samothrace in 1863, and its base was discovered in 1879. In 1950, one of the statue's hands was found; it's on display in a glass case near the statue. An inscription on the statue's base includes the word RHODHIOS (Rhodes) and this, along with the fact that the statue stands

The Mona Lisa once hung over François I's bathtub.

on the prow of a ship, has led some scholars to theorize that the piece was commissioned in celebration of a naval victory by Rhodes. Others believe it was an offering made by a Macedonian general after a victory in Cyprus. Regardless of its origins, this glorious work is considered one of the best surviving Greek sculptures from that period. *Top of the Daru staircase.*

⑥ ★ Café Mollien. Ready for a break? Café Mollien, by the French painting department, is particularly enjoyable in the summertime, when the outdoor rooftop terrace is open. Choose between sandwiches, salads, and hot dishes such as pasta. The iced coffee with whipped cream is good on a hot day. *$.*

⑦ ★★★ *Mona Lisa.* This lady's enigmatic smile and challenging eyes draw scores of admirers daily. Though the identity of the subject has long been under debate (Was she the wife of an Italian city official? Is she meant to be in mourning? Is "she" a man—perhaps even a self-portrait of da Vinci himself?), many specialists say she is Lisa Gherardini, wife of 16th-century

Florentine cloth merchant Francesco del Giocondo (hence the work's alternative title, La Gioconda).The painting has been through a lot over the years. It was stolen in 1911 (by a Louvre employee who simply put the painting under his coat and walked out with it) and wasn't recovered until 1913. During World War II, it was housed in various parts of France for safekeeping. In 1956, the painting was severely damaged after someone threw acid on it. In 1962 and 1963, it toured the United States, and was shown in New York City and Washington, D.C. In 1974, it was shown in Tokyo and Moscow. All the hype and history aside, some find actually seeing Leonardo da Vinci's *Mona Lisa* (painted between 1503 and 1507) a disappointment. It's a very small painting (just 77cm tall, 53cm wide) and has been kept behind glass since it was attacked by a vandal in the 1990s. That, along with the crowds surrounding it, makes it difficult to connect with. Despite these shortcomings, few come to the Louvre without stopping by. *1st floor, Room 6.*

⑧ ★★★ Italian Sculpture. Make your way down to the ground floor of the Denon Wing and head to Room 4, which is filled with exquisite Italian sculptures. Michelangelo's two statues are among the most dramatic in the room—the muscular arms of his *Rebellious Slave* are tensed furiously against his bindings, while the *Dying Slave* seems resigned to his fate. Both were commissioned in 1505 by Pope Julius II as funerary art. Look across the room for the delicate wings of Cupid, who clutches the breast of Psyche in a pas de deux in pure white marble in Antonio Canova's *Cupid Awakening Psyche* (1793). It is love carved in stone. *Ground floor, Room 4; the collection continues on the lower-ground floor immediately below.*

⑨ ★★★ Cour Visconti.

Opened in 2012, the newly refurbished Cour Visconti section provides the Louvre's more than 2,000 pieces of Islamic art with an appropriately prominent setting. The fascinating collections (including many lavish pieces made for heads of state) highlight the development of Islamic art from its beginnings in the 7th century up until the early 19th, showing the differences in artistic styles according to culture, geography, and era. *Lower-ground floor, Rooms 1 to 9.*

Paris for Museum Lovers

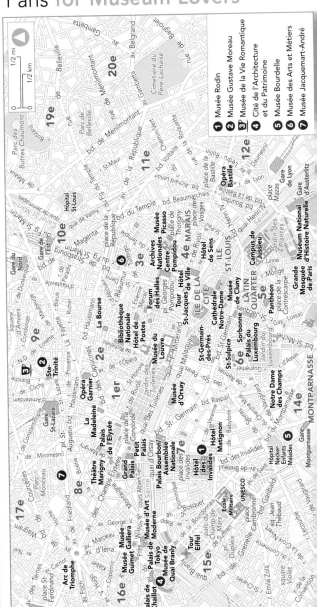

1 Musée Rodin
2 Musée Gustave Moreau
3 Musée de la Vie Romantique
3' Cité de l'Architecture et du Patrimoine
5 Musée Bourdelle
6 Musée des Arts et Métiers
7 Musée Jacquemart-André

You'd need a lifetime to fully explore the hundreds of museums in Paris. Once you've visited the behemoths (the Louvre, Musée d'Orsay, and Centre Pompidou), there are dozens of beautiful, more intimate addresses dedicated to sculpture, inventions, and architecture. This section is not a tour per se, but a list to be dipped into as you please. START: Métro to Varennes.

Save on Admission Fees

The permanent collections of all of Paris's 14 municipal museums are free (see www.parismusees.paris.fr for a full list). If you plan to visit several nonmunicipal museums over 2, 4, or 6 days, you'll save money with the Paris Museum Pass (www.paris museumpass.com; 2 days 42€, 4 days 56€, 6 days 69€), available for purchase at more than 60 participating museums and online.

❶ ★★ Musée Rodin. This peaceful museum, housed in the building that was once sculptor Auguste Rodin's studio, can't help but inspire thoughts of romance. *The Thinker* ponders in the sublime gardens, while the lovers in *The Kiss* are locked in a permanent embrace inside. ① *1 hr. Hôtel Biron, 79 rue de Varenne, 7th.* ☎ *01-44-18-61-10. www.musee-rodin.fr. Admission museum 9€ ages 26 & over, 7€ ages 18–25, free for children 18 & under, & visitors 25 & under from E.U. countries; gardens 2€. Tues–Sun 10am–5:45pm. Métro: Varenne or Invalides. RER C: Invalides.*

❷ ★★ Musée Gustave Moreau. Painter Gustave Moreau was around at the same time as the Impressionists, but he worked against the prevailing mood, drawing inspiration from the Bible, Greek mythology, Leonardo da Vinci, and Indian miniatures. This atmospheric museum, where he lived and worked, reveals Moreau's obsession with knick knacks and furniture, which are displayed alongside his fabulous mythical beasts and fantasy worlds. ① *1 hr. 14 rue de la Rochefoucauld, 9th.* ☎ *01-48-74-38-50. www.musee-moreau.fr. Admission 6€ adults, 4€ ages 19–25, free for ages 18 & under, free for everyone 1st Sun of the month. Wed–Mon 10am–12:45pm & 2–5:15pm. Métro: Trinité.*

The Thinker strikes a contemplative pose outside the Musée Rodin.

3 ★★★ **Musée de la Vie Romantique.** Hidden from the rest of the world is this charming, green-shuttered 18th-century mansion that once housed composers Gioachino Rossini and Frédéric Chopin, novelist George Sand, and painter Eugène Delacroix. But what really takes the gâteau (cake), quite literally, is the rose garden, which doubles as an outside tearoom. Decadence is yours for the price of your café and tarte au citron (lemon tart). *16 rue Chaptal, 9th.* ☎ *01-55-31-95-67. www.parismusees.paris.fr. Tues–Sun 10am–6pm. Free admission. Métro: Pigalle, St-Georges, or Blanche.*

4 kids ★★ **Cité de l'Architecture et du Patrimoine.** Comprising 8 sq. km (3 sq. miles) of space in the east wing of the Palais de Chaillot, the City of Architecture and Heritage contains more than 850 breathtaking full-size copies of French architectural treasures, including molded portions of churches, châteaux, and great French cathedrals, such as Chartres. There are also reconstructions of modern architecture, the centerpiece of which is an apartment by Le Corbusier. ⏱ *2 hr. Palais de Chaillot, 1 place du Trocadéro, 16th.* ☎ *01-58-51-52-00. www.citechaillot. fr. Admission 8€ adults, 6€ ages 19–25, free for ages 18 & under & visitors 25 & under from E.U. countries, free for everyone 1st Sun of the month. Wed & Fri–Mon 11am–7pm, Thurs 11am–9pm. Métro: Trocadéro.*

5 ★★ **Musée Bourdelle.** Hidden away from the hustle and bustle of Montparnasse is the workshop where Rodin's star pupil, sculptor Antoine Bourdelle (1861–1929), lived and worked. The sumptuous array of statues, many inspired by Greek mythology, includes Centaure Mourant (The Dying Centaur) writhing in agony; Penelope, Ulysses's wife, who waited 20 years for her husband to return; and, in the gorgeous walled garden, the colossal General Alvear horse statue (part of an allegorical monument that was never finished). ⏱ *90 min. 18 rue Antoine-Bourdelle, 15th.* ☎ *01-49-54-73-73. www.bour delle.paris.fr. Free admission. Tues–Sun 10am–6pm. Closed public holidays. Métro: Montparnasse-Bienvenue.*

The Cité de l'Architecture et du Patrimoine is a must-see for architecture buffs.

Greek mythology inspired many of the sculptures at the Musée Bourdelle.

6 kids ★★★ **Musée des Arts et Métiers.** This museum, founded in the 18th century by Abbot Grégoire as "a store for useful new inventions," is an absolute gem. Housed in the former Benedictine church and priory of Saint-Martin-des-Champs, it exhibits some of the world's greatest inventions, from Pascal's calculating devices and celestial spheres to the first computers, steam-powered vehicles, and even airplanes (including the monoplane Louis Blériot flew across the English Channel in 1909). ⏲ *2 hr. 60 rue Réamur, 3rd.* ☎ *01-53-01-82-00. www.arts-et-metiers.net. Admission 8€ adults, 5.50€ ages 19–25, free for ages 18 & under & visitors 25 & under from E.U. countries. Free for everyone 1st Sun of the month, and Thurs after 6pm. Tues–Wed & Fri–Sun 10am–6pm, Thurs 10am–9:30pm. Métro: Arts et Métiers.*

7 kids ★★ **Musée Jacquemart-André.** This decorative-arts museum, set in the stately former home of the collectors it's named for—Nélie Jacquemart and Edouard André—houses an array of rare 18th-century French paintings and furnishings, 17th-century Dutch and Flemish paintings, and Italian Renaissance works fit for a king. The salons drip with gilt and the ultimate in fin-de-siècle style. Works by Bellini, Carpaccio, Uccello, van Dyck, Rembrandt, Tiepolo, Rubens, Watteau, Boucher, Fragonard, and Mantegna hang on almost every wall. If you fancy a decadent snack, Mme. Jacquemart's high-ceilinged tearoom complies, with delicious sticky cakes and piping-hot tea (served 11:45am–5:30pm). ⏲ *1 hr. 158 bd. Haussmann, 8th.* ☎ *01-45-62-11-59. www.musee-jacquemart-andre.com. Admission 12€ adults, 10€ ages 7–17, free for children 6 & under. Daily 10am–6pm (until 8:30pm on Mon during temporary exhibitions). Métro: Miromesnil or St-Philippe du Roule.*

A sumptuous salon in the Musée Jacquemart-André.

Paris's Best Modern Art

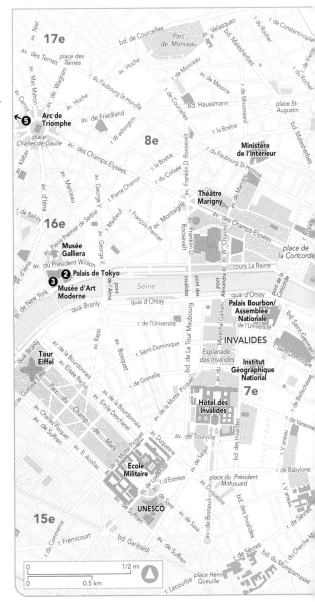

17e

av. Niel
av. des Ternes   place des
Ternes
r. du Faubourg St-Honoré
bd. de Courcelles
Parc
de Monceau
r. de Constantinople
av. Velasquez
bd. Malesherbes
r. du Rocher
r. de Vienne
r. du Rocher

av. Carnot
av. Mac Mahon
av. de Wagram
av. Hoche
av. Hoche
r. de Monceau
av. de Messine
bd. Haussmann
r. de Courcelles
r. de Miromesnil
place St-
Augustin
bd. Malesherbes

5 Arc de
Triomphe
place
Charles de Gaulle
av. de Friedland
r. Washington
av. des Champs-Elysées
8e
r. la Boétie
r. du Faubourg St-Honoré
**Ministère
de l'Intérieur**

av. Kléber
av. d'Iéna
av. Marceau
r. Pierre Charron
r. la Boétie
r. du Colisée
Franklin D. Roosevelt
av. de Matignon

16e
av. George V
r. Marbeuf
r. François Pav. Montaigne
**Théâtre
Marigny**
av. des Champs-Elysées

r. de Belloy
av. Pierre Premier de Serbie
av. George V
Franklin D.
Roosevelt
av. W. Churchill
place de
la Concorde

**Musée
Galliera**
av. du President Wilson
2 **Palais de Tokyo**
3 **Musée d'Art
Moderne**
pont de
l'Alma
Seine
quai d'Orsay
cours La Reine
pont des
Invalides
pont
Alexandre III
pont de la
Concorde

av. de New York
quai Branly
r. de l'Université
Maréchal Galliéni
quai d'Orsay
**Palais Bourbon/
Assemblée
Nationale**
r. de l'Université
bd. Saint-Germain

Quai Branly
**Tour
Eiffel**
av. Rapp
av. de la Bourdonnais
av. Bosquet
r. Saint-Dominique
r. de La Tour Maubourg
INVALIDES
Esplanade
des Invalides
**Institut
Géographique
National**
r. Saint-Dominique

av. Gustave Eiffel
av. Elisée Reclus
Parc
du
Champ
de
Mars
av. de la Bourdonnais
av. Emile Deschanel
r. de Grenelle
av. de la Motte Picquet
av. de
**Hôtel des
Invalides**
7e
r. de Bellechasse
r. de Varenne

av. Charles Floquet
av. de Suffren
av. E. Acollas
av. de la Motte Picquet
av. Duquesne
bd. des Invalides
r. V aneau

**Ecole
Militaire**
av. de Lowendal
r. d'Estrées
place du Président
Mithouard
av. Duquesne
r. de Babylone
r. V aneau

15e
r. du Commerce
r. Frémicourt
av. de Suffren
bd. Garibaldi
av. de Saxe
av. de Saxe
UNESCO
av. de Breteuil
bd. des Invalides
bd. de Sèvres
r. de Sèvres

0		1/2 mi
0	0.5 km	

place Henri
Queuille
r. Lecourbe
r. des
bd. du Montparnasse
du Cherche M

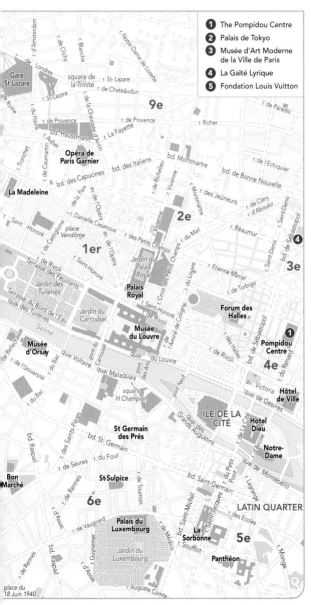

1 The Pompidou Centre
2 Palais de Tokyo
3 Musée d'Art Moderne de la Ville de Paris
4 La Gaîté Lyrique
5 Fondation Louis Vuitton

You only have to look at the Louvre's glass pyramid or the Pompidou Centre's madcap exterior to realize that Parisians can be unconventional when they put their minds to it—something that's also reflected in the city's art scene, which includes everything from edgy art squats to sleek museums and galleries. Here's where to find Paris's most exciting modern and contemporary art venues, both big and small. START: **Métro to Rambuteau.**

❶ kids ★★★ The Pompidou Centre. This benchmark art venue, designed by Richard Rogers and Renzo Piano, holds the largest collection of modern art in Europe. The permanent collections cover 20th- and 21st-century art, with some 40,000 rotating works. The fifth floor is dedicated to modern art from 1905 to 1960 (Fauvism, Cubism, interwar art, Surrealism, abstraction, and neorealism). Floor four covers 1960 to the modern day, providing themed rooms that focus on such movements as antiform art (*arte povera*) and video installations. Go it alone, or opt for the English audio-guided visit. Don't miss the stunning view of Paris from the top floor. ⏱ *2 hr. Place Georges Pompidou, 4th.* ☎ *01-44-78-12-33. www.centre-pompidou.fr. Admission 14€ ages 26 & over, 11€ students & ages 19–26, free for children 18 & under & visitors 26 & under from E.U. countries. Wed–Mon 11am–9pm (until midnight for some exhibitions & 11pm Thurs). Métro: Rambuteau or Hôtel de Ville. RER A & B: Châtelet-les-Halles.*

The Palais de Tokyo is the place in Paris for contemporary art installations.

❷ ★ Palais de Tokyo. This "Site de Création Contemporaine" is a showcase for experimental art on a big scale. Inside its stripped-back interior, international artists fill the space with temporary exhibitions. It also wows with two good eateries: Tokyo Eat, a manga-chic canteen (12pm–1am) and Monsieur Bleu, a

The Pompidou Centre houses Europe's biggest collection of modern art.

The Gehry-designed Fondation Louis Vuitton houses exhibition space, an auditorium, and Le Frank restaurant.

posh neo–Art Deco brasserie with a cocktail bar and an Eiffel Tower–view terrace (12pm–2am). ⏱ *2 hr. 13 av. du President Wilson, 16th.* ☎ *01-81-97-35-88. www.palaisdetokyo.com. Admission 10€ ages 27 & over, 8€ ages 19–26, free for children 18 & under. Wed–Mon noon–midnight. Métro: Alma-Marceau or Iéna. RER C: Pont d'Alma.*

❸ ★★ **Musée d'Art Moderne de la Ville de Paris.** Take yourself on a journey through 20th-century "isms": Fauvism, Cubism, Surrealism, realism, expressionism, and neorealism to be exact, with works by such artists as Braque, Dufy, Picasso, Léger, and Matisse. In addition to the permanent collection, expect fascinating retrospectives on major 20th-century artistic movements, plus thematic exhibitions on the best of today's artistic pickings. *11 av. du Présdent Wilson, 16th.* ☎ *01-53-67-40-00. www.mam. paris.fr. Free admission for permanent collections. Tues–Sun 10am–6pm (until 10pm Thurs for temporary exhibitions). Métro: Alma-Marceau or Iéna. RER C: Pont d'Alma.*

❹ **La Gaîté Lyrique.** Set inside a former Belle Epoque theater, this multidisciplinary arts center specializes in digital art by both recognized and up-and-coming names. Displays are consistently cutting-edge, featuring disciplines like music, graphic design, fashion, and even video games. *3 bis rue Papin, 3rd.* ☎ *01-53-01-52-00. www. gaite-lyrique.net. Admission 7.50€ ages 26 & over, 5.50€ ages 25 & under. Tues–Sat 2–8pm, Sun 2–6pm. Closed mid-Aug to mid-Sept. Métro: Réaumur-Sébastopol/Arts et Métiers.*

❺ ★ **Fondation Louis Vuitton.** Sydney's opera house meets a space-age galleon in this vast, whimsical art space (built by American architect Frank Gehry). Amid its glass sails, sunken water-features and clever lighting are big, stark spaces spattered with paintings, a state-of-the-art auditorium and an excellent bookshop. Chic Le Frank restaurant serves contemporary French cuisine. *8 ave du Mahatma Gandhi, 16th.* ☎ *01-40-69-96-00. www.fondationlouisvuit ton.fr. Admission 14€ ages 27 & over, 10€ ages 25 & under, & students with a valid card, 5€ ages 4–18, free ages 3 & under. Mon, Wed–Thurs 12–7pm, Fri 12–11pm, Sat–Sun 11am–8pm. Métro: Les Sablons or by electric shuttle from Place Charles de Gaulle (corner of Ave Friedland).*

Hemingway's Paris

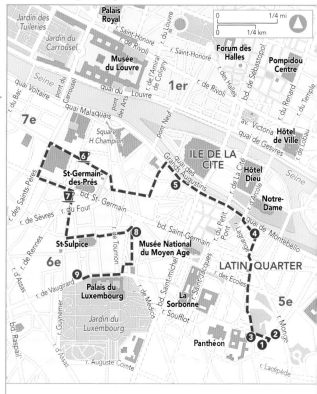

1. Marché Mouffetard
2. Ernest & Hadley's apartment
3. Hemingway's first apartment
4. Shakespeare & Company
5. Booksellers along the quai des Grands Augustins
6. Café Pré aux Clercs
7. Les Deux Magots
8. Shakespeare & Company's original site
9. Hemingway's last apartment

For fans of Papa Hemingway, a trip to Paris is a pilgrimage. This is where Hemingway honed his craft, bullied F. Scott Fitzgerald, and charmed Gertrude Stein. Here he married more than once and had countless mistresses, not the least of which was Paris herself. Oh sure, he cheated on her with Cuba and Spain, but we all know Paris is the one he *really* loved. This tour follows his spectacular rise and charts the beginning of his fall. START: **Métro to Censier Daubenton.**

1 ★ Marché Mouffetard. At the beginning of his memoir, *A Moveable Feast,* Hemingway describes spending time on Rue Mouffetard's "wonderful narrow crowded market street." That description still fits—it's narrow, crowded, and wonderfully Parisian.

2 Ernest & Hadley's Apartment. Several blocks up Rue Mouffetard, Rue du Cardinal-Lemoine branches off to the right. A few houses down, on the fourth floor of no. 74, a 22-year-old Hemingway and his wife Hadley rented their first Parisian apartment together in 1921. *74 rue du Cardinal-Lemoine, 5th.*

3 Hemingway's Writing Apartment. When he first moved to Paris as a writer for the *Toronto Star* newspaper, Hemingway took a grimy, cheap room on the top floor of a hotel on Rue Descartes to write in peace. The building—as a small wall plaque says—was also where

One of the secondhand booksellers along the Quai des Grands Augustins.

Rue Mouffetard.

French poet Paul Verlaine died in 1896. *39 rue Descartes, 5th.*

4 ★ Shakespeare & Company. Walk toward the river for about 15 minutes, first on Rue Descartes (which joins Rue Montagne St-Geneviève) through Place Maubert, then down Rue F. Sauton, and then take a sharp left onto Rue de la Bucherie to reach Paris's best expat bookstore. In the 1920s, it was at 12 rue de l'Odéon (see stop **8** on this tour) and belonged to American publisher Sylvia Beach. It was at that location that Hemingway broke a vase when he read a bad review, that Henry Miller used to "borrow" books and never bring them back, and that James Joyce's *Ulysses* was first published. The current location is still a favorite of writers for its eccentric attitude and wonderful selection of books. ⏱ *30 min–1 hr. 37 rue de la Bucherie, 5th.* ☎ *01-43-25-40-93. www.shakespeare andcompany.com. Daily 10am–11pm. Métro: St-Michel.*

Un serveur at Les Deux Magots in Saint-Germain-des-Prés.

❺ Booksellers along Quai des Grands Augustins. Hemingway frequently shopped here among the secondhand book peddlers (called *bouquinistes*) along the edge of the Seine. Now, as then, their collections are bewilderingly eclectic and somewhat hit-and-miss—like a flea market for books. I once saw the complete Harry Potter collection, in English, next to a book of French erotica. 🕑 *30 min–1 hr. Quai des Grands Augustins, 6th.*

❻ Café Pré aux Clercs. Next you'll come to a series of cafes where you can take a well-deserved rest, as Hem surely would, over a whiskey or a glass of the house red. The first cafe is this charming one reached by walking down Rue des Grands Augustins. (No. 7 was once Pablo Picasso's studio.) Turn onto Rue St-André des Arts, and then right along Rue de Seine and left onto the antiques-shop-lined Rue Jacob, which brings you to Rue Bonaparte and this cafe. It was one of Hem's early haunts, a short walk from the Hotel d'Angleterre, where he slept (in room no.14) on his first night in Paris. Continue down rue Bonaparte and you'll get to

more-famous (and more-touristy) Les Deux Magots. *30 rue Bonaparte, 6th.* ☎ *01-83-76-16-53. www.restaurant-preauxclercs.com. $$–$$$.*

❼ ★★ Les Deux Magots. Loop down noisy Rue des Saints-Pères to the more sophisticated hustle of Boulevard Saint-Germain, and soon you'll see the glass front of this cafe, which has gotten more mileage out of the gay '20s than any flapper ever could have. This was the preeminent hangout of the arty expat crowd, where Hemingway charmed the girls, picked fights with the critics, and hassled tourists. The feel today is admittedly touristy, and the food pricey, but it's still a good place to have a coffee and wonder what he'd think of it all now. *6 place St-Germain-des-Prés, 6th.* ☎ *01-45-48-55-25. www.lesdeuxmagots.fr. $$–$$$.*

❽ Shakespeare & Company's Original Site. You can get in a bit of shopping at the posh boutiques on Rue Saint-Sulpice before turning right onto Rue de l'Odéon and passing a plaque marking the site of the original Shakespeare & Company bookstore. *12 rue de l'Odéon, 6th.*

❾ Hemingway's Last Apartment. After turning down Rue de Vaugirard and walking past the French Senate, look for this narrow lane near the Jardins du Luxembourg. The impressive building at no. 6 was Hemingway's last Paris apartment. From the look of its ornate stonework, and heavy gates, you might get the idea that he'd written a successful novel (*The Sun Also Rises*) and left poor Hadley for somebody richer (Pauline Pfeiffer). And so he had. Here, he wrote *A Farewell to Arms*, and began his descent into alcoholism. *6 rue Férou, 6th.* ●

3 The Best
Neighborhood Walks

The **Latin** Quarter

1. Place St-Michel
2. Rue du Chat-qui-Pêche
3. Eglise St-Séverin
4. Eglise St-Julien-le-Pauvre
5. Musée National du Moyen Age (Thermes de Cluny)
6. La Sorbonne
7. Eglise de la Sorbonne
8. Le Panthéon
9. Les Papilles

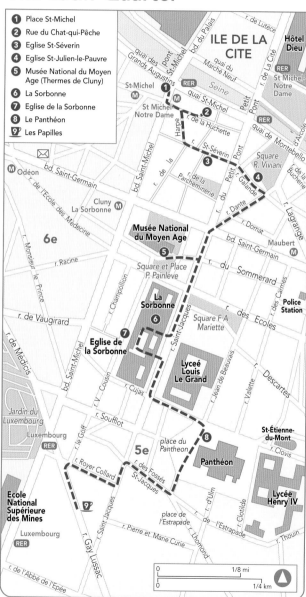

Previous page: Luxembourg Palace and Gardens, in Saint-Germain-des-Prés.

In the 1920s, this Left Bank neighborhood was the heart of Parisian cafe society. You'll still find plenty of cafes, plus universities and shops, all constantly buzzing with activity. Traditionally arty, intellectual, and bohemian, the area also has a history of political unrest. Today, it is still one of Paris's most interesting, not to mention picturesque, quarters to explore. START: **Métro to St-Michel.**

1 Place Saint-Michel. An elaborate 1860 fountain of Saint Michael presides over this bustling cafe- and shop-lined square, where skirmishes between occupying Germans and French Resistance fighters once took place. This is the beginning of busy Boulevard Saint-Michel, which was trendy long ago but is now a disappointing line of fast-food chains and down-market stores. It is, however, the main student quarters, and a young, lively atmosphere pervades.

2 Rue du Chat-qui-Pêche. Turn left down Rue de la Huchette, bypassing its endless kabob and pizza joints to reach this street, which is one of the narrowest in Paris, at just 1.8m (6 ft.) wide. Plenty of local tales exist about the history of the name ("Street of the Cat Who Fishes"), but nobody knows for sure.

The Fontaine Saint-Michel, at the center of Place Saint-Michel.

Gargoyles at Eglise Saint-Séverin.

3 Eglise Saint-Séverin. This charming medieval church was built in the early 13th century and reconstructed in the 15th. Don't miss the gargoyles projecting from the roof. Inside, linger over the rare Georges Rouault etchings from the early 20th century, and the abstract 1970s stained-glass windows in the apse chapels. ⏱ *30 min. 1 rue des Pretres St-Séverin, 5th.* ☎ *01-42-34-93-50. www.saint-severin.com. Mon–Sat 11am–7:30pm, Sun 9am–8:30pm.*

4 Eglise Saint-Julien-le-Pauvre. Take Rue Saint-Séverin to Rue Galande and, after snapping photos of its quaint old houses, find this Melkite Greek church, which dates, at least in part, to 1170. Note the unusual capitals covered in carved vines and leaves. The garden contains one of the oldest trees in Paris and has one of my favorite views of Notre-Dame. ⏱ *20 min. Rue St-Julien-le-Pauvre, 5th.* ☎ *01-43-54-52-16.*

The Musée National du Moyen Age is home to the famous Lady and the Unicorn tapestries.

www.sjlpmelkites.fr. Mon–Sat 9:30am–noon & 3–6:30pm. Métro: Cluny–La Sorbonne.

⑤ ★★ Musée National du Moyen Age–Thermes de Cluny. With one of the world's strongest collections of medieval art, this small, manageable museum is a gem. Most visitors come to see the *Lady and the Unicorn* tapestries, but there's much more here than long-haired maidens and mythical creatures: This 15th-century Gothic building sits atop 2nd-century baths. The Gallo-Roman pools are in excellent shape—the

Cafes along Place de la Sorbonne.

frigidarium (cold bath) and tepidarium (warm bath) can still be clearly seen (although you can no longer take a dip). 🕐 1 hr. 6 place Paul-Painlevé, 5th. ☎ 01-53-73-78-00. www.musee-moyenage.fr. Admission 8€ ages 26 & over, 6€ ages 18–26 from outside E.U., free for ages 25 & under from E.U. countries & 17 & under from outside E.U.; free for everyone 1st Sun of the month. Wed–Mon 9:15am–5:45pm. Métro: Cluny–La Sorbonne.

⑥ ★ La Sorbonne. France's most famous university, dating back some 700 years, has all the venerable buildings and confident, scraggly-haired students you might imagine. Teachers here have included Thomas Aquinas, and the alumni association counts Dante, Calvin, and Longfellow among its past members. This is a sprawling place, and only the courtyard and galleries are open to the public (9am–5pm) when school is in session—follow the crowds and the scarce signs to get a peek. Or book a guided tour (in French only; Mon–Fri and one Sat per month). 🕐 30 min. 12 rue de la Sorbonne, 5th. ☎ 01-40-46-23-48. www.sorbonne.fr. Admission for guided tour adults 9€, students 4€. Métro: Cluny–La Sorbonne.

7 ★ Eglise de la Sorbonne.
On the grounds of the Sorbonne, this 17th-century church holds the elaborate tomb of Cardinal Richelieu (1585–1642). Richelieu was a staunch defender of the monarchy's power and did much to unify the French state. The extraordinary statue at its feet is poignantly named *Learning in Tears*. The figure mourning at the cardinal's feet represents science, and the one supporting him represents religion. ⏱ *30 min. Rue de la Sorbonne, 5th.*

8 ★★ Le Panthéon. This magnificent building was built (1764–1790) by Louis XV as a tribute to Saint Geneviève. Since the Revolution, however, it's been used to honor more earthly heroes. France's great dead are entombed here, including Voltaire, Rousseau, Zola, and Hugo. Recent additions include Alexandre Dumas (2002) and Marie Curie (in 1995), who was one of only two women here until 2015, when WWII *résistantes* Geneviève de Gaulle-Anthonioz (de Gaulle's niece) and Germaine Tillion were accepted. Appropriately, Foucault's

pendulum is here—the famous device, which proved that the Earth rotates on an axis, was said to hang from "the eye of God." Although the pendulum appears to swing, it's not moving—the Earth is. ⏱ *1 hr. Place du Panthéon, 5th.* ☎ *01-44-32-18-00; www.pantheon.monuments-nationaux.fr. Admission 7.50€ ages 26 & over, 6€ ages 18–26 from outside E.U., free for ages 25 & under from E.U. countries & 17 & under from outside E.U. Daily 10am–6pm (Apr–Sept until 6:30pm). Métro: Cardinal Lemoine. RER B: Luxembourg.*

9 Les Papilles. Dying for a break? This is just the place. The owners of this sweet Provençal-style bistro are dedicated to Southern French food and adventurous wine. The small menu changes with the seasons, and the wines change with the owners' moods. If it's available, try the excellent stewed chicken or the hearty cassoulet. *30 rue Gay-Lussac, 5th.* ☎ *01-43-25-20-79. www.lespapillesparis.fr. RER B: Luxembourg. $$.*

Le Panthéon, an 18th-century memorial hall honoring France's greatest intellectuals.

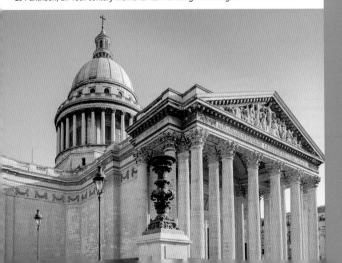

Saint-Germain-des-Prés

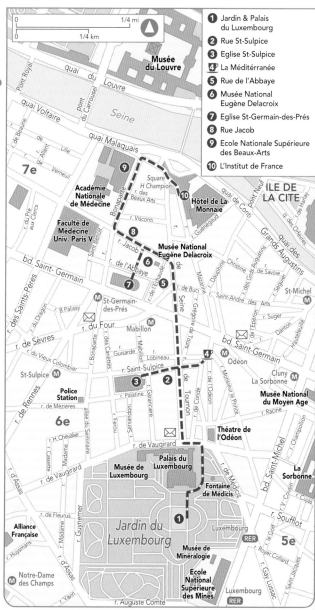

1 Jardin & Palais du Luxembourg
2 Rue St-Sulpice
3 Eglise St-Sulpice
4 La Méditérranée
5 Rue de l'Abbaye
6 Musée National Eugène Delacroix
7 Eglise St-Germain-des-Prés
8 Rue Jacob
9 Ecole Nationale Supérieure des Beaux-Arts
10 L'Institut de France

This neighborhood was the place to be in the 1920s. Here the literati met the glitterati and *tout* Paris marveled at the ensuing explosion of creativity and alcoholism. On these streets, Sartre fumed while Hemingway and Fitzgerald drank and quarreled. Today the bookshops have been replaced by designer boutiques, but it's still the place to go for a night on the town. START: **Métro to Luxembourg.**

1 ★★★ kids Jardins & Palais du Luxembourg. There's a certain justice in the fact that this former palace, built between 1615 and 1627 for the widow of Henry IV, is now home to the democratically elected French Senate. The lovely Italianate building also houses the Musée du Luxembourg, famed for its world-class temporary art exhibitions (19 rue de Vaugirard, 6th; ☎ 01-40-13-62-00; www.museedu luxembourg.fr). Most people, however, come for the gardens. Hemingway claimed to have survived a winter by catching pigeons here for his supper, and Gertrude Stein used to cross the gardens on her way to sit for Picasso. The classic formal gardens are well groomed and symmetrically designed. And there are statues everywhere—more than 80 of them vie for your attention—a long-haired French queen, a nymph playing a flute, a stern effigy of poet Charles Baudelaire. It's fanciful

and delightful; you could spend hours here and not discover all its secrets. Particularly popular with families are the pond in which children float wooden boats, the games area, and pétanque (French boules) pitches. ① *1 hr. Métro: Odéon. RER: Luxembourg.*

2 Place & Rue Saint-Sulpice. Turn down any street on the river side of the gardens and walk a few blocks to Place Saint-Sulpice and its surrounding streets. Welcome to shopping heaven (or window-shopping purgatory). This is where you'll find all the usual designer suspects for your inspection—agnès b., YSL, perfumer Annick Goutal, and more. If you want to stock up for a picnic, pop down to 8 rue du Cherche-Midi to Poilâne bakery for some of the city's best breads and sandwiches to go. Or turn onto Rue Bonaparte, where Pierre Hermé (at no. 72) makes the city's most delicious macaroons.

Palais du Luxembourg, home to the French Senate.

The elegant interior of the Ecole Nationale Supérieure des Beaux-Arts.

❸ ★★ Eglise Saint-Sulpice.

Filled with paintings by Delacroix, including *Jacob's Fight with the Angel*, this is a wonderful church in which to meditate and take in some gorgeous frescoes. The church has one of the world's largest organs, comprising 6,700 pipes—a national treasure, especially when it's played (see www.stsulpice.com for a schedule). ⓞ *30 min. Rue St-Sulpice, 6th.* ☎ *01-42-34-59-98. www.pss75.fr/saint-sulpice-paris. Daily 7:30am–7:30pm.*

❹ La Méditérranée.

A short walk away lies this restaurant, filled with murals by 20th-century stage designers Christian Bérard and Marcel Vertés and paintings by Picasso and Chagall. It was once a haunt of Jacqueline Kennedy, Picasso, and Jean Cocteau (whose work enlivens the plates and menus). The chef delivers creative interpretations of traditional dishes,

The mighty pipe organ at Eglise Saint-Sulpice.

including an incredible bouillabaisse, thick with seafood. *2 place de l'Odéon, 6th.* ☎ *01-43-26-02-30. www.la-mediterranee.com. Métro: Odéon. $$$.*

❺ Rue de l'Abbaye.

Saint-Germain was built around an old abbey that once towered over this street, although there's virtually nothing left of it today. With houses and churches built from brick, the street is charming, particularly Rue de Furstenberg—once the abbot's stables, it's now filled with upscale design shops and galleries.

❻ ★ Musée National Eugène Delacroix.

The Romantic painter Eugène Delacroix lived and worked in this lovely house on Rue de Furstenberg from 1857 until his death in 1863. The museum sits on a charming square and has a romantic garden. Most of his major works are in the Louvre (you may buy a joint ticket for the Louvre, 15€), but the collection here is unusually personal, including an early self-portrait and letters and notes to such friends as Baudelaire and George Sand. You can also see his work in the Chapelle des Anges in Eglise Saint-Sulpice (see stop ❸ on this tour). ⓞ *1 hr. 6 rue de Furstenberg, 6th.* ☎ *01-44-41-86-50. www.musee-delacroix.fr. Admission 7€ adults, free for children 17 & under & visitors 25 & under from E.U. countries. Wed–Mon 9:30am–5:30pm. Métro: St-Germain-des-Prés.*

❼ ★ Eglise Saint-Germain-des-Prés. This exquisite little church is the oldest in Paris. It dates to the 6th century, when a Benedictine abbey was founded here by Merovingian king Childebert, although little remains from that time. Its aged columns still bear their medieval paint in breathtaking detail. You can visit the tomb of the French philosopher René Descartes (1596–1650) in the second chapel. On the right as you enter, look into the Chapelle de Saint-Symphorien. It was here, during the revolution, that many clergymen were imprisoned before being executed just outside on the square. ⏱ 30 min. 3 place St-Germain-des-Prés, 6th. ☎ 01-55-42-81-10. www.eglise-sgp.org. Mon–Sat 8am–7:45pm, Sun 9am–8pm. Métro: St-Germain-des-Prés.

❽ Rue Jacob. This elegant street, with clean lines and classic 19th-century architecture, was once home to such illustrious residents as the author Colette and the composer Richard Wagner. Today, it holds charming bookstores and antiques shops and is all very posh-bohemian.

❾ Ecole Nationale Supérieure des Beaux-Arts. Turn onto Rue Bonaparte and walk toward the river to reach this fine-arts school, where the main attraction is the architecture. The school occupies a 17th-century convent and the 18th-century Hôtel de Chimay. Attending an exhibition (held frequently) will grant you a peek inside, but if none is on, just wander down Rue Bonaparte, which is lined with lovely small art galleries. ⏱ 30 min. 14 rue Bonaparte, 6th. ☎ 01-47-03-50-00. www.ensba.fr. Courtyard Mon–Fri 9am–5pm; during exhibitions Tues–Sun 1–7pm. Métro: St-Germain-des-Prés.

❿ L'Institut de France. Turn right along the river and you'll see an elegant domed baroque building, home to five subgovernmental agencies all lumped together as the rather ominously named L'Institut. Here the Académie Française zealously guards the purity of the French language from "Franglais" encroachment, while other, lesser-known agencies (Sciences, Inscriptions et Belles Lettres, Beaux Arts, and Sciences Morales et Politiques) do . . . whatever it is they do. It's all a bit intimidating (academy members are known as "the Immortals"), and all buildings are closed to the public, but it's possible to arrange in advance for a guided tour (available in English). ⏱ 15 min. 23 quai de Conti, 6th. ☎ 01-44-41-44-41. www.institut-de-france.fr. Guided tours 2nd Sun of the month (request via website only). Métro: St-Germain-des-Prés or Louvre Rivoli.

The imposing Institut de France houses several government agencies.

The Islands

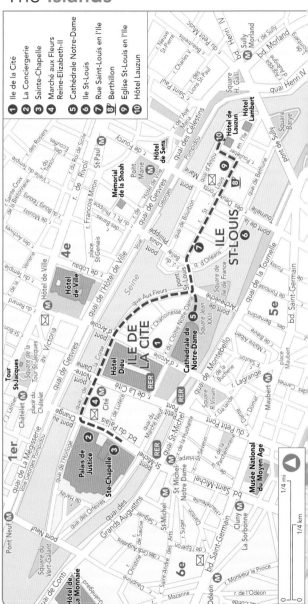

The Île de la Cité is where it all began. By the time the Romans came in 52 B.C., the Celtic Parisii tribe had been living on the Île de la Cité for about 200 years. Over the next 2 millennia, Paris was expanded by the Romans, Franks, Merovingians, and Capetian kings, but the city's soul remains here, around Notre-Dame cathedral. Across the pont Saint-Louis, Île Saint-Louis (former marshlands) is a coveted residential area filled with glorious 17th-century mansions. This tour takes you through both islands and along some of the loveliest stretches of the Seine. START: **Métro to Cité.**

❶ Île de la Cité. By medieval times, this was a thriving island town with huddles of houses and narrow streets. But it was all swept away in the 19th century by Baron Haussmann when he evicted some 25,000 people to make way for the large administrative buildings we see today, such as the law courts. Few have written more movingly about its heyday than Victor Hugo, who invites the reader "to observe the fantastic display of lights against the darkness of that gloomy labyrinth of buildings; cast upon it a ray of moonlight, showing the city in glimmering vagueness, with its towers lifting their great heads from that foggy sea." You have only to climb Notre-Dame's towers to see what he's talking about: On a cloudy day, dramatic skies cast eerie light over the island. Linking the Île de la Cité to the city at large

is the pont Neuf, embellished by a statue of Henri IV. The name means "new bridge"—ironic considering that it's Paris's oldest bridge, dating back to the 16th century. A staircase below leads to the Square du Vert-Galant, my favorite riverside picnic spot.

❷ ★ La Conciergerie. This intimidating building, originally a medieval royal palace, was converted into a prison during the Revolution and became an object of terror at a time when idle accusations could result in spontaneous executions. Marie Antoinette, Danton, and Robespierre all were held here before being guillotined. Today, you can see the cells where they were held and the rooms where they were tried and condemned. A strange and interesting place. *See p 9,* ❸.

Pont Neuf, at the western end of Île de la Cité.

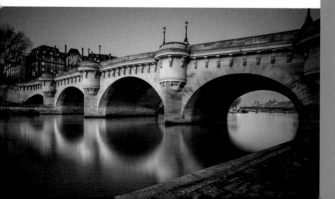

Tiny Sainte-Chapelle is known for its dazzling stained-glass windows.

③ ★ Sainte-Chapelle. Tucked away among the huge Conciergerie and the vast law courts of the Palais de Justice is this tiny church—a precious place seemingly made almost entirely of dazzling stained-glass windows. One of the loveliest things you can do is visit at night for a classical music concert. You'll find a list of concerts on the website. *See p 23,* **③**.

④ Marché aux Fleurs Reine-Elizabeth-II. Recently renamed after Queen Elizabeth II, to commemorate the 70th anniversary of the Normandy landings in WWII, this vivid flower market must be one of the most photographed places in the city—and for good reason. On Sunday, it's transformed into a bird market, but the standard of living for the animals presented is questionable. ⏲ *30 min. Place Louis Lépine, Quai de la Corse, Quai des Fleurs, 4th. Mon–Sat 8am–7:30pm, Sun 8am–7pm. Métro: Cité.*

⑤ ★★★ Cathédrale Notre-Dame. This world-famous cathedral is more beautiful in person than on film. Climb its towers to see snarling gargoyles and sweeping panoramas of the city. *See p 9,* **⑦**.

⑥ Île Saint-Louis. Despite its central location, the Île Saint-Louis still feels like a tranquil backwater, removed, somehow, from the rest of the buzzing city. The 17th-century buildings lining the narrow streets are some of the city's most expensive properties, and many of them have hosted, at one point or another, French literary stars, such as Racine and Molière. A bourgeois arty crowd still frequents the many art galleries around. It's a lovely place to wander, and so tiny that it's almost impossible to get lost.

⑦ Rue Saint-Louis-en-l'Île. The Île Saint-Louis's central artery is

Climb Notre-Dame's tower and you'll be rewarded with close-ups of gargoyles and sweeping city views.

Peaceful Île Saint-Louis.

gorgeous, narrow, and lined with restaurants and boutiques selling art, clothes, precious stones and minerals, food, hats, and jewelry. Hôtel Chenizot, at no. 51, has fantastic carved dragons and bearded fauns on its facade. Go through the door and admire the sculpted facade in the courtyard beyond. A second courtyard also contains craft shops and galleries. The end of the street closest to the Île de la Cité is a great place to get a photo of Notre-Dame.

8 **Berthillon.** On Île Saint-Louis, even the ice-cream stores are sophisticated. This place proves it, with polite crowds queuing outside for cones to go, and others perched at the tables inside to try the lemon, hazelnut, and mango flavors favored by the locals—the chocolate is especially divine. *31 rue St-Louis-en-l'Île, 4th, www. berthillon.fr. Métro: Pont Marie. $.*

9 **Eglise Saint-Louis-en-l'Île.** This 17th-century church, vastly overshadowed by Notre-Dame, has wonderful rococo-baroque architecture, including a lovely sunburst above the altar. Not as dramatic as its famous neighbor, but it's more intimate and enchanting. ○ *20 min. 19 rue St-Louis-en-l'Île, 4th. ☎ 01-46-34-11-60. www.saintlouis enlile.catholique.fr. Tues–Sun 10am–1pm & 3–7:30pm. Métro: Pont Marie.*

10 **★★ Hôtel Lauzun.** This astonishing place, with fantastic drains in the shapes of sea serpents, was where poets Baudelaire and Théophile Gautierthe hosted famously long, hazy hashish parties. Baudelaire wrote *Les Fleurs du Mal* while living here, although it's hard to see how he could have been so depressed living somewhere so pretty. The building takes its name from a former occupant, the duc de Lauzun. He was a favorite of Louis XIV until he asked for the hand of the king's cousin, the Duchesse de Montpensier. Louis refused and had Lauzun tossed into the Bastille. Eventually the duchesse convinced Louis to release him, and they married secretly and moved here in 1682. *17 quai d'Anjou. Generally closed to the public, although guided tours are becoming more frequent. Check with the tourist office or try www.guideapolis.fr (French-only tours). Métro: Pont Marie.*

The Marais

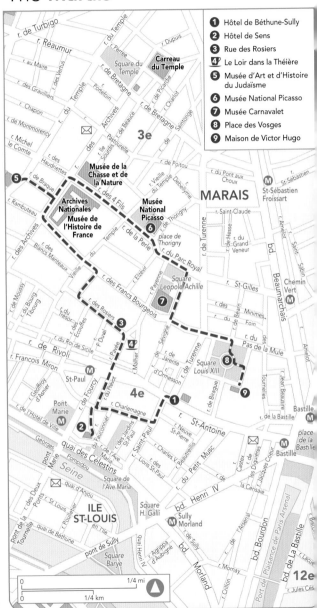

1 Hôtel de Béthune-Sully
2 Hôtel de Sens
3 Rue des Rosiers
4 Le Loir dans la Théière
5 Musée d'Art et d'Histoire du Judaïsme
6 Musée National Picasso
7 Musée Carnavalet
8 Place des Vosges
9 Maison de Victor Hugo

When the Île de la Cité became overcrowded in the 17th century, it was here, to what had been swampland, that the wealthy Parisians moved, filling the streets with fashionable mansions called *hôtels*. Over the years, it became the center of the city's Jewish community, although today the gay and lesbian community has also adopted the area. Its many boutiques and diverse buildings make for excellent shopping and exploring. START: **Métro to St-Paul.**

❶ Hôtel de Béthune-Sully. Out of the Métro, turn right on Rue Saint-Antoine and walk through the wooden doorway at no. 62. The relief-studded facade of this gracious mansion dazzles just as much as when it was first designed as the residence of the family of Maximilien de Béthune, duke of Sully, Henri IV's famous minister, in 1625. It stands as one of the finest Louis XIII structures in Paris and, although the building is closed to the public, the charming walled garden is open during office hours (and on weekends from around 9am–6pm). A "secret" door leads to the Place des Vosges (see ❽, below). ◷ *30 min. 62 rue St-Antoine, 4th. www.sully.monuments-nationaux.fr. Métro: St-Paul.*

❷ Hôtel de Sens. Given the leaded windows and fairy-tale turrets, you might not be surprised to find that this 15th-century mansion has a gloriously ornate courtyard in

The Hôtel de Béthune-Sully is one of the finest 17th-century buildings in Paris.

which you can wander at will most afternoons. Once a private home for archbishops and, later, queens, it now holds a fine-arts library, the Bibliothèque Forney. ◷ *20 min. 1 rue du Figurier.* ☎ *01-42-78-14-60. Courtyard Mon–Fri 8am–8:30pm, Sat–Sun 9am–8:30pm (until 7:30pm Sept–Apr). Métro: St-Paul.*

The Hôtel de Sens once housed the archbishops of Sens.

The meticulously manicured topiary of the Musée Carnavalet.

3 Rue des Rosiers. Perhaps the most colorful and typical street remaining from the time when this was the city's Jewish quarter, Rue des Rosiers (Street of the Rosebushes) meanders among the old buildings with nary a rose to be seen. It is jam-packed with falafel cafes and shops, though, and makes a plum spot for a cheap lunch.

4 ★ Le Loir dans la Théière. This bustling cafe serves some of the best salads and homemade cakes in the Marais. There's usually a queue to get a table, but it's worth the wait—especially for the humongous lemon meringue pies (7.50€ a slice). *3 rue des Rosiers, 4th.* ☎ *01-42-72-90-61.* **$.**

Strolling along colorful Rue des Rosiers.

5 ★ Musée d'Art et d'Histoire du Judaïsme. This museum was created in 1948 to protect the city's Jewish history after the Holocaust. It's a moving place, with excellent Jewish decorative arts from around Europe—German Hanukkah lamps, a wooden sukkah cabin from Austria—and documents related to the continent's Jewish history. There's also a memorial to the Jews who lived in the building in 1939, 13 of whom died in concentration camps. ⏱ *45 min. Hôtel de St-Aignan, 71 rue du Temple, 3rd.* ☎ *01-53-01-86-60. www.mahj.org. Mon–Fri 11am–6pm, Sun 10am–6pm. Admission 8€ ages 26 & up, 4.50€ ages 18 to 25, free for ages 18 & under. Métro: Rambuteau.*

6 ★★ Musée National Picasso. This fabulous museum's permanent collection boasts some 5,000 works by Pablo Picasso (though not all are on show at once). Pieces from his Blue period, Surrealist paintings and Cubist sculptures sit alongside startling assemblages of Picasso's own art collection, with works by Modigliani and Renoir. A showpiece in its own right is the building—the Hôtel Salé—one of the most extravagant 17th-century mansions in Paris, built by salt-tax farmer and advisor to Louis XIV Pierre Aubert (hence the building's name: "salé" means "salty"). The magnificent central staircase was based on Michelangelo's stair plan for the Laurentian Library in Florence. ⏱ *1 hr. Hôtel Salé, 5 rue du Thorigny, 3rd.* ☎ *01-85-56-00-36. www.museepicassoparis.fr. Tues–Sun 9:30am–6pm. Admission 13€ ages 27 & up, free for ages 18 and under & visitors 25 & under from E.U. countries. Métro: Saint-Paul.*

❼ Musée Carnavalet. The Renaissance palace that houses this free museum was acquired by Mme de Carnavalet (hence its name), but is most associated with the letter-writing Mme de Sévigné, who moved here in 1677 to be with her daughter and poured out nearly every detail of her life in her letters. Several salons cover the Revolution, and others display furniture from the Louis XIV period to the early 20th century, including a replica of Marcel Proust's cork-lined bedroom. Also on view are the chessmen Louis XVI used to distract himself while waiting to go to the guillotine. ⏱ *1 hr. 16 rue des Francs-Bourgeois, 3rd.* ☎ *01-44-59-58-58. www.carnavalet.paris.fr. Tues–Sun 10am–6pm. Free admission. Métro: St-Paul or Chemin Vert.*

❽ Place des Vosges. This is Paris's oldest square and was once its most fashionable; today it's arguably its most adorable, with perfect brick-and-stone pavilions rising above covered arcades. Its perfect symmetry might be why so many

Striking Chinese-inspired decor in the Maison de Victor Hugo.

writers and artists (Descartes, Pascal, Gautier, and Hugo) chose to live here. See p 14, ❺.

❾ Maison de Victor Hugo. The writer of *Les Misérables* lived here from 1832 to 1848, and his home has been turned into a tiny shrine, with period rooms dedicated to his life and works. Room 3 is particularly impressive, with an Oriental-style medley of black, green, and red panels and porcelain. The decor is based on the Chinese room at Hauteville Fairy in Guernsey, where Hugo's mistress, Juliette Drouet, lived during the couple's exile from France (after Napoleon III's coup d'état). The views from the windows offer an interesting panorama over the pink-brick Place des Vosges. ⏱ *30 min. 6 place des Vosges, 4th.* ☎ *01-42-72-10-16, www.maisonsvictorhugo. paris.fr. Free admission. Tues–Sun 10am–6pm. Métro: St-Paul or Bastille.*

Lounging on the lawns of the Place des Vosges.

Montmartre & the Sacré Coeur

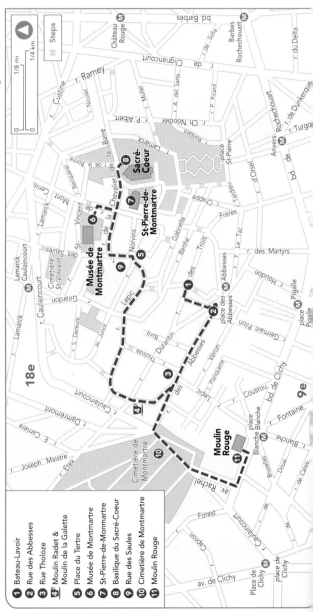

8 Sacré-Coeur

7 St-Pierre-de-Montmartre

6 Musée de Montmartre

11 Moulin Rouge

18e

9e

1 Bateau-Lavoir
2 Rue des Abbesses
3 Rue Tholoze
4 Moulin Radet & Moulin de la Galette
5 Place du Tertre
6 Musée de Montmartre
7 St-Pierre-de-Monmartre
8 Basilique du Sacré-Coeur
9 Rue des Saules
10 Cimetière de Montmartre
11 Moulin Rouge

Artsy, graceful, undulating Montmartre does something to your heart. From the moment you see its narrow, tilting houses, still windmills, and steep streets, you're in love. This part of town—known as the La Butte, or "the Hill" in the 18th arrondissement—was a rural village separate from Paris until 1860. Then, in the 1880s, Renoir and Toulouse-Lautrec helped make it a lair of artists—a legacy that lives on today. It all starts at the Abbesses Métro station—designed by French architect Hector Guimard, it's one of only two stations in Paris that still has its original Art Nouveau roof (the other is Porte Dauphine, in the 16th). START: **Métro to Abbesses.**

1 Bateau-Lavoir. This building is called the "cradle of Cubism." While living here from 1904 to 1912, Picasso painted *The Third Rose* (of Gertrude Stein) and *Les Demoiselles d'Avignon.* Today, it's filled with art studios, with some occasionally open to view. ⏱ *10 min. 13 place Emile Goudeau. Métro: Abbesses.*

2 Rue des Abbesses. On this street, the unusual rust-red church with the turquoise mosaics is the neo-Gothic Saint-Jean-de-Montmartre, built early in the 20th century. Peek inside to see its delicately weaving arches.

Winding streets lead up to the Sacré Coeur.

The Saint-Jean-de-Montmartre church.

Many excellent cafes and dress shops line this street.

3 Rue Tholoze. Rue des Abbesses soon brings you to this steep, narrow street, with an adorable windmill at the top. Halfway up is Studio 28, which was the city's first proper art-house cinema, named after the year it opened. It showed Buñuel's *L'Age d'Or* in 1930, and outraged locals ripped the screen from the wall. Today, it still shows arty flicks and has a tiny bar.

This moulin (windmill), atop Rue Tholoze, is the subject of a recently authenticated van Gogh painting.

4 **Moulin Radet & Moulin de la Galette.** The Moulin Radet windmill, confusingly enough, tops a restaurant called Le Moulin de la Galette, after the dance hall that once stood here, inspiring such artists as Renoir. The food here is traditionally French and moderately priced. *83 rue Lepic.* ☎ *01-46-06-84-77. www.lemoulin delagalette.fr. $$.*

5 **Place du Tertre.** This old square would be lovely were it not for the tourists—and the artists chasing you around, threatening to draw your caricature. You can buy some very good original paintings here, but you'll have to haggle to get a reasonable price. The perpetual hubbub can be entertaining—it's charming and awful all at once.

6 **Musée de Montmartre & Jardins Renoir.** This oasis of calm will give you a good look at Montmartre's artistic history. There are pictures of 19th-century Montmartre, rural and lined with windmills, along with a few Toulouse-Lautrec posters and the like. The

gardens—named after Auguste Renoir, who lived on-site from 1875 to 1877—offer heartwarming cityscapes and views over Montmartre's vineyard (see **9**). ⏱ *45 min. 12 rue Cortot, 8th.* ☎ *01-49-25-89-37. www.museedemontmartre.fr. Admission 9.50€ ages 26 & over, 7.50€ ages 18–25, 5.50€ ages 10–17, free for children 10 & under. Daily 10am–6pm. Métro: Abbesses or Lamarck-Caulincourt.*

7 **Saint-Pierre-de-Montmartre.** Follow the winding roads ever upward to this early-Gothic Benedictine abbey, now a small church. This is one of the city's oldest churches (from 1133), and its simplicity in the shadow of the Sacré Coeur is refreshing. ⏱ *15 min. Rue du Mont-Cenis.*

8 ★★ **Sacré Coeur.** The creamy white domes of this basilica soar high above Paris. Inside is an artistic and architectural explosion of color and form; out front are sweeping views of the gorgeous city in soft pastels. Unmissable. *See p 17,* **2**.

Iconic Sacré Coeur crowns the highest summit in Paris.

Montmartre Cemetery provides a peaceful respite from the neighborhood's bustling streets and squares.

⑨ Rue des Saules. Head down Rue des Saules, pausing to admire the oft-photographed cabaret Au Lapin Agile (www.au-lapin-agile.com), which was a favorite hangout of Picasso's back when it was called Cabaret des Assassins. It's still usually crowded with tourists, strange fans of old French music, and those seeking Picasso's muse. Opposite, notice the small patch of vines, a throwback from the days when Montmartre was a wine-growing village separate from Paris. The Clos Montmartre harvest (red wine) is celebrated annually in October over a very boozy weekend.

⑩ ★★ Cimetière de Montmartre. Retrace your steps and follow Rue Lepic back down past no. 54, where van Gogh lived with his brother Theo. Turn right onto Rue Joseph-de-Maistre and then left onto Rue Caulaincourt to this quiet resting place. Get a map from the gatehouse—it will help you find the graves of Truffaut, Stendhal,

Degas, and many others. But don't follow it too closely—it doesn't list most of the graceful statues of exquisitely tragic women draped across tombs, nor does it tell you where the most beautiful trees stand, or where the light dapples through just so. You'll have to discover those treasures on your own. ⏱ 1 hr. Access on Rue Rachel by stairs from Rue Caulaincourt, 18th. ☎ 01-53-42-36-30. Free admission. Mon–Sat 8am–6pm, Sun 9am–6pm (Mar 16–Nov 5 until 5:30pm). Métro: Blanche.

⑪ Moulin Rouge. Immortalized by Toulouse-Lautrec (and more recently, Nicole Kidman), this bright red windmill hasn't changed much with time. Just as the windmill remains outside, the cancan still goes on inside. It's all just as tawdry and tacky as it was when Toulouse-Lautrec downed one absinthe after another to endure it, but it's still the most traditional place to see real cancan in Paris. See p 129.

Canal Saint-Martin & Villette

1. Canal St-Martin
2. Hôpital St Louis
3. L'Hôtel du Nord
4. Quai de Valmy shops
5. Bassin de la Villette
6. Bar Ourcq
7. Canal de l'Ourcq
8. Parc de la Villette

This tour will take you past legacies of early-20th-century industrialized Paris—its tree-lined piers, iron footbridges, old factories, and warehouses—relics that evoke the days when Edith Piaf lifted the spirits of the nation with her soulful "La Vie en Rose" (1946). Today, this area, both scruffy and cosmopolitan, is one of the city's most happening districts. Its bohemian vibe and new canal-side galleries and cafes make it a fun place to stroll. In summer, the Parc de la Villette—with its science and music museums, IMAX cinema, and open-air film festival—is a hip place to hang out.
START: **Métro to République.**

❶ ★ Canal Saint-Martin. Walk across Place de la République to Rue Beaurepaire, lined with trendy shops and cafes. At the end of the street, you're on Quai de Valmy. The Canal Saint-Martin, built between 1805 and 1825, begins at Bastille but hides underground until it gets to Boulevard Richard Lenoir. This is the prettiest stretch, lined with chestnut trees and iron footbridges that beg to be photographed. If you saw the film *Amélie,* you might recognize the canal from the stone-skimming scene.

Opposite Rue Beaurepaire, cross the footbridge and go up Avenue Richerand.

❷ Hôpital Saint-Louis. The Saint-Louis hospital was founded by Henri IV to house plague victims away from the city center and was built in the same style as Place des Vosges (p 63). Enter and then leave via the left wing, past the chapel. *Av. Claude-Vellefaux.*

Turn left onto Rue de la Grange aux Belles and note the spot where the Montfauchon gibbet (or gallows) once stood. Erected in 1233 and used for nearly 400 years, the macabre structure served as a place to execute criminals and display their hanging corpses. Then, turn right onto Quai de Jemmapes.

❸ L'Hôtel du Nord. Director Marcel Carné's 1938 film Hôtel du Nord made this building (which still has its original facade) famous. Today, it's a bistro serving hearty French cuisine with a typical 1930s interior—a fine choice for lunch. *102 quai de Jemmapes, 10th.* ☎ *01-40-40-78-78. www.hoteldunord.org. $$.*

An iron footbridge on the Canal Saint-Martin.

Along the Quai de Valmy.

Cross back over the Canal onto Quai de Valmy.

④ ★ Quai de Valmy shops. New boutiques keep appearing along this stretch of the canal (and its adjacent streets). The best ones are **Artazart**, on Quai de Valmy (no. 83; ☎ 01-40-40-24-00), a cutting-edge bookshop stocking glossy art and design publications. Farther up, at no. 95, you'll find kitsch clothes and collectables by **Antoine & Lili** (☎ 01-40-37-41-55). On Rue de Lancry, don't miss **Chez Chiffons** (no. 47; ☎ 06-72-28-91-14), the latest hot spot for affordable ladies' vintage designer

apparel; and at no. 2 rue de Marseille, **Centre Commercial** (☎ 01-42-02-26-08) stocks funky clothes and accessories by up-and-coming French designers.

⑤ Bassin de la Villette. At the top of the Canal Saint-Martin, you reach the circular Barrière de la Villette, one of the few remaining 18th-century tollhouses designed by Nicolas Ledoux (now a lively cafe). The modernist fountains in front channel your view up the Canal de l'Ourcq past the twin MK2 cinema complex. If you're a film buff, spend a few moments in the MK2's specialized bookshop (Quai

Houseboats docked on Canal Saint Martin.

The Géode in the Parc de la Villette is a 3-D IMAX theater.

de la Loire, 19th). If you fancy a film in English, look out for VO *(version originale)* written next to the title (providing it's an English-language film, of course!).

6 **Bar Ourcq.** Cheap drinks make this a popular bar with residents, especially on a hot day, when boules can be hired at the bar for a game of pétanque on the sand in front of the door. Be daring and challenge a local to a game (opens 3pm). *68 quai de la Loire, 19th.* ☎ *01-42-40-12-26. $.*

Walk northward along the Canal de l'Ourcq.

7 **Canal de l'Ourcq.** Created in 1813 by Napoleon to provide drinking water and an additional route for transporting goods, this stretch is now characterized by 1960s and '70s tower blocks. It is separated from the Bassin de la Villette by an unusual 1885 hydraulic lifting bridge.

8 **kids** ★★★ **Parc de la Villette.** The city's former abattoir district is now a vast retro-futurist park with wide-open lawns and play areas for children. On site is also the excellent **Cité des Sciences** museum (☎ 01-40-05-70-00; www.cite-sciences.fr), with a section entirely dedicated to kids (Cité des Enfants); the **Philharmonie de Paris** music museum and concert hall (☎ 01-44-84-44-84; www.philharmoniedeparis.fr; p 133); the **Zenith** concert hall (www.le-zenith.com), where international bands play; and the **Geode** 3-D IMAX movie theater, whose silver dome sparkles in the sunlight. In August, the park becomes an outdoor cinema *(cinéma en plein-air)* with Europe's biggest inflatable screen. *Av. Corentin-Cariou, 19th.* ☎ *01-40-03-75-75. www.villette.com. Métro: Porte de la Villette or Porte de Pantin.*

Montparnasse

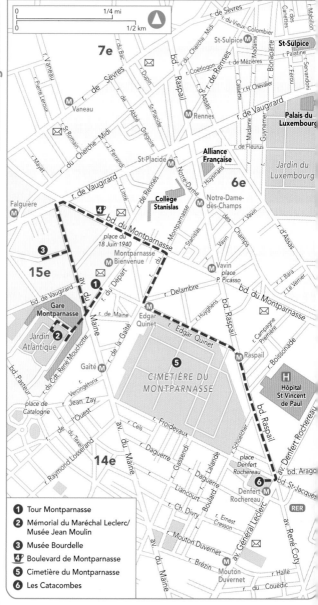

1 Tour Montparnasse

2 Mémorial du Maréchal Leclerc/
   Musée Jean Moulin

3 Musée Bourdelle

4 Boulevard de Montparnasse

5 Cimetière du Montparnasse

6 Les Catacombes

When Montmartre artists did their jobs so well that the neighborhood became popular and rents went up, they all moved to Montparnasse. Before long, Picasso, Léger, and Chagall had joined Man Ray, Henry Miller, and Gertrude Stein on its somewhat forbidding streets. In terms of beauty, the two areas don't compare—concrete is abundant in Montparnasse, but it offers plenty of sights to keep you busy. START: **Métro to Montparnasse-Bienvenue.**

① kids **★ Tour Montparnasse.** Completed in 1973 and rising 210m (689 ft.) above the skyline, Paris's most famous inner-city skyscraper was denounced by some as "bringing Manhattan to Paris." The city soon outlawed any further structures of this size in the heart of the city. Today, it is frequented for its panoramic viewing platform on the 56th floor. Take in the skyline before splurging on a cocktail or dinner in the touristy Ciel de Paris restaurant (☎ 01-40-64-77-64), famed for its views. *33 av. de Maine, 15th.* ☎ *01-45-38-52-56. www.tourmontparnasse56.com. Admission 15€ adults, 12€ ages 16–20, 9.20€ ages 7–15, free for children 6 & under. Apr–Sept daily 9:30am–11:30pm; Oct–Mar Sun–Thurs 9:30am–10:30pm, Fri–Sat & eve of public holidays 9:30am–11pm. Last lift 30 min. before closing. Métro: Montparnasse-Bienvenüe.*

② **Mémorial du Maréchal Leclerc/Musée Jean Moulin.** This rooftop museum fills you in on World War II France and the French Resistance. The absorbing film archives and the art—which includes posters exhorting residents of occupied France to work in Germany—show what the French endured. ⏲ *1 hr. 23 allée de la 2e DB Jardin Atlantique (above Grandes Lignes of Gare Montparnasse), 15th.* ☎ *01-40-64-39-44. www.ml-leclerc-moulin.paris.fr. Admission free for permanent collection. Exhibitions: 5€ adults, 2.50€ ages 14–26, free for children 13 & under. Tues–Sun 10am–6pm. Métro: Montparnasse-Bienvenüe.*

③ **Musée Bourdelle.** Surrounded by pretty gardens, this museum is where French sculptor Antoine Bourdelle (1861–1929) worked. It was here that he pioneered 20th-century monumental sculpture, and you can't help but feel dwarfed by the sheer size of his masterpieces, which—as you walk through his atmospheric old atelier and gardens—each tell their own mythical story. Bourdelle is buried in the Cimetière de Montparnasse, stop **⑤** of this tour.

The view from the 56th floor of the Tour Montparnasse.

The Tour Montparnasse inspired a law preventing additional skyscrapers in the center of Paris.

4 **Boulevard du Montparnasse.** Just a block from the train station, this well-traveled street gets busiest at night, when its brasseries and cinemas are aglow, but at any time of day the enticing aromas may lure you to one of its many creperies or brasseries. Succumb to a full meal at no.108, Le Dôme, now a seafood restaurant ($$); or at no.102, La Coupole, a fabulous Art Deco brasserie ($$). A bit farther along, at no. 171, La Closerie des Lilas, includes among its former fans an unlikely combination of Picasso, Trotsky, Lenin, and Hemingway ($$$).

5 ★ **Cimetière du Montparnasse.** A short walk down Boulevard Edgar-Quinet, past its many attractive cafes, takes you to this well-known burial ground. For literary and philosophical types, it's a must-see, with the graves of Samuel Beckett, Charles Baudelaire, and Man Ray, as well as the shared grave of Simone de Beauvoir and Jean-Paul Sartre, usually covered in tiny notes of intellectual affection from fans. *3 bd. Edgar-Quinet, 14th.*

☎ *01-44-10-86-50. There's a map posted to the left of the main gate. Free admission. Mon–Fri 8am–6pm, Sat 8:30am–6pm, Sun 9am–6pm. Métro: Edgar Quinet.*

6 ★★ **kids Les Catacombes.** Just before the Revolution, Paris's cemeteries were bursting at the seams, spreading disease. To solve the problem, millions of bones were transferred underground into the quarried tunnels that sprawl beneath the Denfert-Rochereau district. These catacombs, 18m (60 ft.) underground, can be visited today. It feels incredibly strange seeing miles of neatly stacked bones and skulls, and it's surprisingly rather moving. The sign at the appropriately eerie entrance reads "STOP! THIS IS THE EMPIRE OF DEATH!" Older kids will love it; younger ones will probably have nightmares. ⏱ *1 hr. 1 avenue du Colonel Henri Roi-Tanguy, 14th.* ☎ *01-43-22-47-63. www.catacombes.paris.fr. Admission 10€ ages 27 & older, 18€ ages 18–26, free for children 17 & under. Tues–Sun 10am–8pm (last ticket sold at 6.45pm). Métro/RER B: Denfert-Rochereau.* ●

Six million skeletons stretch 910m (2,986 ft.) through underground tunnels in Les Catacombes beneath Paris.

Shopping **Best Bets**

Best **Department Store**
★ Le Bon Marché, *22–24 rue de Sèvres, 7th (p 84)*

Best **Flea Market**
Marché aux Puces de St-Ouen, *Rue des Rosiers, 94300 Saint-Ouen (p 82)*

Best **Contemporary Art**
★ Art Generation, *67 rue de la Verrerie, 4th (p 82)*

Best Working **Art Atelier**
★ 59 Rivoli, *59 rue de Rivoli, 1st (p 82)*

Best **Children's Clothing**
★ Bonpoint, *6 rue de Tournon, 6th (p 83)*

Best **Toy Store**
Joué Club, *5 bd. des Italiens, 2nd (p 83)*

Best **Place to Buy a Picnic Lunch**
★★★ Maison Plisson, *93 bd Beaumarchais, 3rd (p 86)*

Best **Trendy Jewelry**
★★ Servane Gaxotte, *55 rue des Saints Pères, 6th (p 88)*

Best **Kitchenware**
E. Dehillerin, *18 rue Coquillière, 2nd (p 88)*

Best **Vintages Wines**
★★★ Ryst Dupeyron, *79 rue du Bac, 7th (p 87)*

Best **Place for English-Language Books & Magazines**
Galignani, *224 rue de Rivoli, 1st (p 83)*

Best **Place for Gifts**
★★★ Deyrolle, *45 rue du Bac, 7th (p 87)*

Best **Gourmet Food**
★ Fauchon, *26–30 place de la Madeleine, 8th (p 86)*

Best **Porcelain**
★★ Manufacture Nationale de Sèvres, *4 place André Malraux, 1st (p 84)*

Best **Place for a Hipster**
Kiliwatch, *64 rue Tiquetonne, 2nd (p 86)*

Best **Place for Perfume**
★★★ Serge Lutens, *142 Galerie de Valois, 1st (p 88)*

Below: High-end togs for tots at Bonpoint. Previous page: Passage Jouffroy, a 19th-century shopping arcade.

Right Bank (8th & 16th–17th)

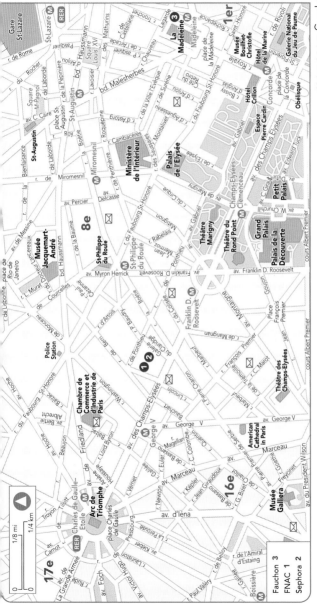

Fauchon	3
FNAC	1
Sephora	2

The Best Shopping

Right Bank (1st–4th & 9th–11th)

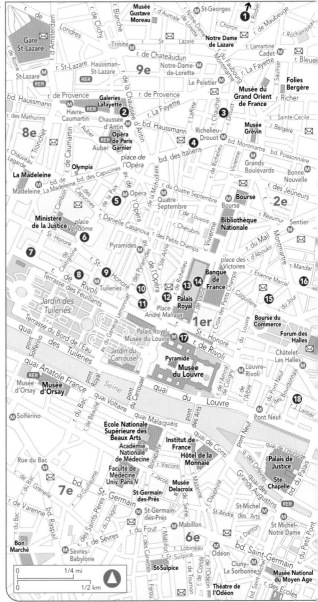

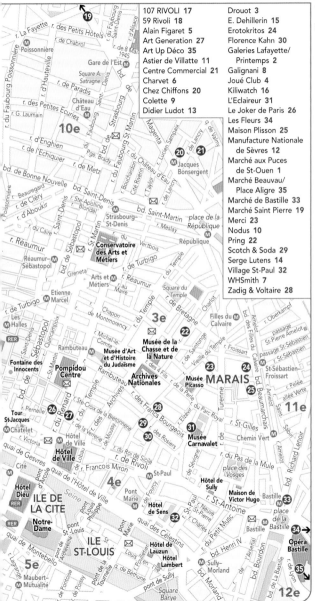

107 RIVOLI **17**
59 Rivoli **18**
Alain Figaret **5**
Art Generation **27**
Art Up Déco **35**
Astier de Villatte **11**
Centre Commercial **21**
Charvet **6**
Chez Chiffons **20**
Colette **9**
Didier Ludot **13**

Drouot **3**
E. Dehillerin **15**
Erotokritos **24**
Florence Kahn **30**
Galeries Lafayette/
    Printemps **2**
Galignani **8**
Joué Club **4**
Kiliwatch **16**
L'Eclaireur **31**
Le Joker de Paris **26**
Les Fleurs **34**
Maison Plisson **25**
Manufacture Nationale
    de Sèvres **12**
Marché aux Puces
    de St-Ouen **1**
Marché Beauvau/
    Place Aligre **35**
Marché de Bastille **33**
Marché Saint Pierre **19**
Merci **23**
Nodus **10**
Pring **22**
Scotch & Soda **29**
Serge Lutens **14**
Village St-Paul **32**
WHSmith **7**
Zadig & Voltaire **28**

The Best Shopping

Left Bank (5th–6th)

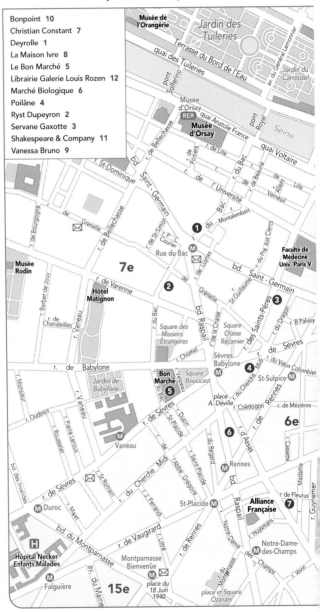

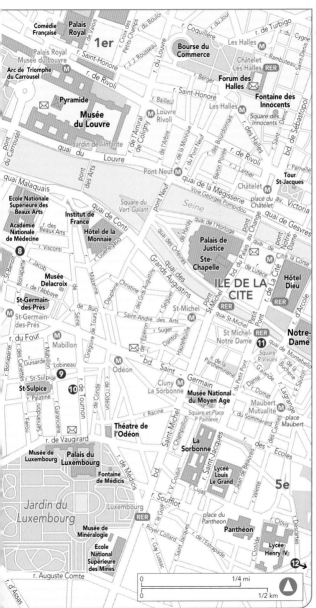

Comédie Française
Palais Royal
1er
Palais Royal Musée du Louvre
Arc de Triomphe du Carrousel
r. Saint-Honoré
r. de Rivoli
Louvre Rivoli
Bourse du Commerce
Les Halles
Châtelet Les Halles RER
Forum des Halles
Pyramide
Musée du Louvre
Jardin de l'Infante
quai du Louvre
Saint-Honoré
Les Halles
Fontaine des Innocents
Square des Innocents
r. de Rivoli
Pont Neuf
quai de la Mégisserie
Seine
Voie Georges Pompidou
Tour St-Jacques
quai Malaquais
Ecole Nationale Supérieure des Beaux Arts
Institut de France
Hôtel de la Monnaie
Square du Vert-Galant
quai de Conti
quai de l'Horloge
Châtelet
place de l'av. Victoria
Châtelet
quai de Gesvres
Académie Nationale de Médecine
r. des Beaux Arts
r. Visconti
8
Palais de Justice
Ste-Chapelle
ILE DE LA CITÉ
Cité la Corse
Hôtel Dieu
Musée Delacroix
r. de l'Abbaye
St-Germain-des-Prés
St-Germain-des-Prés
r. du Four
Mabillon
Lobineau
St-Sulpice
9
10
St-Sulpice
r. de Tournon
Odéon
St-Michel
St-Michel-Notre Dame RER
Notre-Dame
11
quai de Montebello
Cluny La Sorbonne
Musée National du Moyen Age
Maubert Mutualité
place Maubert
Théâtre de l'Odéon
Square et Place P Painlevé
La Sorbonne
des Ecoles
5e
Musée de Luxembourg
Palais du Luxembourg
Fontaine de Médicis
Lycée Louis Le Grand
Luxembourg RER
Jardin du Luxembourg
Musée de Minéralogie
Ecole National Supérieure des Mines
r. Soufflot
place du Panthéon
Panthéon
Lycée Henry IV
12
r. Auguste Comte
r. d'Assas

0 — 1/4 mi
0 — 1/2 km

Shopping A to Z

Antiques & Collectibles
Drouot GRANDS BOULEVARDS This venerable auction house is just the place to find fine art, collectibles, and a surprisingly large number of bargains. Come the day before the sale (11am–6pm) or between 11am and noon on auction day to peruse the items. During the sale, a simple hand gesture is enough to bid. But even if you don't buy, it's a fun show. *9 rue Drouot, 9th.* ☎ *01-48-00-20-20. www.drouot.com. MC, V. Métro: Richelieu-Drouot. Map p 78.*

Marché aux Puces de St-Ouen NORTH OF MONTMARTRE This massive, permanent site, one of the largest flea markets in Europe, contains many 18th- and 19th-century treasures, but you'll have to haggle for them. Beware of pickpockets. *All around Rue des Rosiers in St-Ouen 94300. From the Métro, walk north along av. de la Porte de Clignancourt (18th), then av. Michelet and turn right.* ☎ *01-40-11-77-36. www. marcheauxpuces-saintouen.com. MC, V (some stalls cash only). Métro: Porte de Clignancourt. Map p 78.*

Shopping for antiques at Marché aux Puces de St-Ouen.

Village St-Paul MARAIS This cluster of antiques and art dealers spreads across four interlocking courtyards and sells quality early-20th-century furniture, bric-a-brac, and art. *23–27 rue St-Paul, 4th. No phone. www.levillagesaintpaul. com. MC, V (some boutiques cash only). Métro: St-Paul. Map p 78.*

Art
★ **59 Rivoli** CHÂTELET This former art squat is now a fanciful, cutting-edge residence for artists who open their ateliers to show off works in progress as well as finished pieces. It's one of the few places that lets buyers deal directly with creators. *59 rue de Rivoli, 1st.* ☎ *01-44-61-08-31. www.59rivoli. org. Most artists accept cash only. Métro: Châtelet. Map p 78.*

★ **Art Generation** MARAIS Prices here range from 60€ to 2,800€ for original, cutting-edge photographs, paintings, sculpture, video, and drawings. Who knows— the pieces you buy might be worth much more one day. *67 rue de la Verrerie, 4th.* ☎ *01-53-01-83-88. www.artgeneration.fr. MC, V. Métro: Hôtel de Ville. Map p 78.*

★ **Art Up Déco** BASTILLE Part of the fabulous Viaduc des Arts (boutiques and craft shops nestled beneath the arches of a converted 19th-century viaduct), this is the place to pick up affordable contemporary paintings, photos, and sculptures by France's up-and-coming artists. Prices start at around 60€ and rarely go over 3,000€. *39-41 avenue Daumesnil, 12th.* ☎ *01-46-28-80-23. www.artup-deco.com. MC, V. Métro: Gare de Lyon or Ledru Rollin. Map p 78.*

Shakespeare & Company has long been a hub for English-speaking expats.

Books

Galignani TUILERIES This wood-paneled bookstore, opened in 1801, sells a vast selection of books in French and English. *224 rue de Rivoli, 1st. ☎ 01-42-60-76-07. www.galignani.com. MC, V. Métro: Tuileries. Map p 78.*

★★ **Librairie Galerie Louis Rozen** LATIN QUARTER This is the place to pick up literary curiosities, from 1930s editions of *Robin Hood* to '70s make-your-own paper airplane kits. There's a beautiful range of vintage photography books too. *8 rue Lacépède, 5th. ☎ 01-43-43-53-53. www.librairie galerielouisrozen.com. Métro: Place Monge. Map p 80.*

★★★ **Shakespeare & Company** LATIN QUARTER The most famous bookstore in Paris is still a joyous, higgledy-piggledy labyrinth of tomes. Expats gather here to swap books and catch readings in English. *37 rue de la Bucherie, 5th. ☎ 01-43-25-40-93. www.shakespeare andcompany.com. MC, V. Métro: Maubert-Mutualité. Map p 80.*

★★ **WHSmith** CONCORDE Come to this English-language bookshop for British and American bestsellers and classics. The upstairs kids' area is an Ali Baba's cavern of fairy stories, teen lit, and games. And you can load up on BBC TV series in the DVD section. *248 rue de Rivoli, 1st. ☎ 01-44-77-88-99. www.whsmith.fr. MC, V. Métro: Concorde. Map p 78.*

Children's Fashion & Toys
★ **Bonpoint** CONCORDE This place borders on haute couture for kids, so be warned. The diminutive outfits—presented in a stately 18th-century mansion—are tailored, traditional, and expensive. *6 rue de Tournon, 6th. ☎ 01-40-51-98-20. www.bonpoint.com. AE, MC, V. Métro: Odéon. Map p 80.*

Joué Club GRANDS BOULE-VARDS Set down an old-world covered passage, this place is like a toy village. You'll find teddies, dolls, pirate ships, Disney superheroes, and even Eiffel Tower Lego sets. *5 bd. des Italiens, 2nd. ☎ 01-53-45-41-41. http://villageparis.joueclub drive.fr. AE, MC, V. Métro: Richelieu-Drouot. Map p 78.*

Le Joker de Paris MARAIS Fun for adults as well as kids, this tiny boutique is packed to the gills with board games, toy soldiers, card tricks, puzzles, chess sets, and even dartboards. *77 rue de la Verrerie, 4th. ☎ 01-42-71-21-25. www. lejokerdeparis.fr. MC, V. Métro: Hôtel de Ville. Map p 78.*

An artist's gallery at 59 Rivoli.

China & Porcelain

★ Astier de Villatte PALAIS ROYAL This space once housed Napoleon's silversmith. Nowadays, it sells top-of-the-line handmade tableware and knickknacks inspired by 17th- and 18th-century designs. *173 rue St-Honoré, 1st.* ☎ *01-42-60-74-13. www.astierdevillatte.com. MC, V. Métro: Palais-Royal. Map p 78.*

La Maison Ivre ST-GERMAIN-DE-PRES Handmade country-style pottery fills this adorable kitchenware shop. There's an emphasis on Provençal and artisanal ceramics. *38 rue Jacob, 6th.* ☎ *01-42-60-01-85. www.maison-ivre.com. MC, V. Métro: St-Germain-des-Prés. Map p 80.*

★★ Manufacture Nationale de Sèvres PALAIS ROYAL This is where the porcelain giant Sèvres sells the plates off which kings and presidents dine. *4 place André Malraux, 1st.* ☎ *01-47-03-40-20. www.sevresciteceramique.fr. MC, V. Métro: Palais Royal. Map p 78.*

Concept & Department Stores

Colette LOUVRE This swank fashion citadel carries men's and women's apparel by some of the city's most promising young talent, in addition to music, housewares, and art. It's for sophisticated shoppers with high credit-card limits. For a reprieve, try the excellent restaurant downstairs. *213 rue St-Honoré, 1st.* ☎ *01-55-35-33-90. www.colette.fr. AE, MC, V. Métro: Tuileries or Pyramides. Map p 78.*

Galeries Lafayette/Printemps OPERA Although separate entities, these department stores with Art Nouveau cupolas stand like twin temples to shopping along the Boulevard Haussmann. Galeries Lafayette stocks more than 90 designers and has a sumptuous food gallery (Lafayette Gourmet). Printemps has a vast shoe department (more than 200 brands) and six floors of both mid-range and designer fashion. *Galeries Lafayette: 40 bd. Haussmann, 9th.* ☎ *09-69-39-75-75. www.galerieslafayette.com. AE, MC, V. Printemps: 64 bd. Haussmann, 9th.* ☎ *01-42-82-50-00. www.printemps.com. AE, MC. Métro for both: Opéra or Chausée d'Antin Lafayette. RER: Auber. Map p 78.*

★ Le Bon Marché INVALIDES Paris's oldest department store is jammed with luxury boutiques, such as Dior and Chanel, for both men and women. If you grow weary of the clothes, check out the dazzling Grande Épicerie food hall. *22–24 rue de Sèvres, 7th.* ☎ *01-44-39-80-00. www.lebonmarche.fr. AE, DC, MC, V. Métro: Sèvres-Babylone. Map p 80.*

★★★ Merci MARAIS/BASTILLE This is Paris's first ever charity concept store. Items aren't always secondhand (some clothes, furniture lines, and other items have been created especially for the shop), and prices aren't always low, but there are bargains to be had. The money raised goes to humanitarian organizations. There's also a funky cafe. *111 bd. Beaumarchais, 3rd.* ☎ *01-42-77-01-90. www.merci-merci.com. MC, V. Métro: St-Sébastien–Froissart. Map p 78.*

Fashion

Alain Figaret OPERA One of France's foremost designers of men's shirts offers a broad range of fabrics and elegant silk ties. *21 rue de la Paix, 2nd.* ☎ *01-42-65-04-99. www.alain-figaret.fr. AE, MC, V. Métro: Opéra. Map p 78.*

Sunday Shopping

Most shops close on Sundays, except in the Marais (Métro: St-Paul), at Bercy Village (Métro: Cour St-Emilion), and in the Carousel du Louvre underneath the Louvre museum (99 rue de Rivoli; Métro: Palais Royal–Musée du Louvre).

Charvet OPERA Charvet made shirts for fashionable Frenchmen for years before he was discovered by English royalty. (The company has made shirts for Prince Charles.) Shop here for crisp men's and women's designs in lush fabrics. *28 place Vendôme, 1st.* ☎ *01-42-60-30-70. www.charvet.com. MC, V. Métro: Opéra. Map p 78.*

★★★ Didier Ludot PALAIS ROYAL Recent and rare vintage haute couture and buyers with an eye for young talent (i.e., sussing out the vintage clothes of the future) make Didier Ludot exceptional. *20–24 Galerie de Montpensier, Palais Royal, 1st.* ☎ *01-42-96-06-56. www. didierludot.fr. MC, V. Métro: Palais Royal–Musée du Louvre. Map p 78.*

Erotokritos BASTILLE/MARAIS This small boutique offers trendy men's and women's fashions with a fun, eccentric edge: Think gingham skirts, schoolboy-style men's shorts, and customizable bags. *109 bd Beaumarchais, 3rd.* ☎ *01-42-78-14-04. www.erotokritos.com. MC, V. Métro: St-Sébastien Froissart. Map p 78.*

L'Eclaireur MARAIS This futuristic-looking boutique stocks the likes of Dries Van Noten, Comme des Garçons, and Carpe Diem, as well as exclusive one-offs by lesser-known designers. Its wild interior is worth seeing even if you don't buy. *40 rue de Sevigné, 3rd.* ☎ *01-48-87-10-22. www.leclaireur.com. MC, V. Métro: St-Paul. Map p 78.*

Pring sells pretty accessories in a rainbow of colors.

Galeries Lafayette's stained-glass cupola is classified as a historic monument.

Marché Saint Pierre MONT-MARTRE D.I.Y. fashionistas flock to this fabric market and its surrounding shops to hunt for everything from Toile de Jouy prints to sleek velvets and see-through cottons. There are fabulous buttons and ribbons too. *2 rue Charles Nodier, 18th.* ☎ *01-46-06-92-25. MC, V. Métro: Anvers. Map p 78.*

Nodus TUILERIES This men's shirt specialist has floor-to-ceiling displays of shirts in every color as well as a few accessories, including cuff links and ties. *274 rue St-Honoré, 1st.* ☎ *01-42-60-35-13. www. nodus.fr. AE, DC, MC, V. Métro: Tuileries. Map p 78.*

Fashion: Parisian-Style Dressing
Centre Commercial CANAL ST. MARTIN This hipster HQ is a fab place to pick up men's and women's clothes with an arty flair. Labels are hand-picked French, British, and Danish so there's little chance you'll find the same items elsewhere in Paris. *2 rue de Marseille, 10th.* ☎ *01-42-02-26-08. www. centrecommercial.cc. Métro: Jacques Bonsergent. Map p 78.*

At Fauchon you can shop for chocolates and pastries or provision an upscale picnic at the delicatessen.

Chez Chiffons CANAL ST-MARTIN This small boutique offers exceptional vintage pieces by luxury designers, plus one-off items by lesser-known brands. *47 rue de Lancry, 10th.* ☎ *06-72-28-91-14. www. chezchiffons.fr. MC, V. Métro: Jacques Bonsergent. Map p 78.*

Kiliwatch ETIENNE MARCEL You'll find a mix of one-off vintage finds alongside funky, modern street wear, hoodies, leather, and even sunglasses at this trendsetting boutique. Start at the back, work your way forward, and enjoy the treasure hunt. *64 rue Tiquetonne, 2nd.* ☎ *01-42-21-17-37. www.kiliwatch.fr. Métro: Etienne Marcel. Map p 78.*

★★★ Pring MARAIS Amid minimalist art galleries and progressive designer boutiques, this women's accessories shop carries a gorgeous, rainbow-hued array of sexy neo-Cinderella shoes and matching purses. A dream. *11 bis rue Elzevir, 3rd.* ☎ *09-80-33-10-10. www.pring paris.com. Métro: Saint-Sébastien-Froissart or St. Paul. Map p 78.*

Scotch & Soda MARAIS Hippie-chic ethnic-print jackets, pastel tie-dye T-shirts, and floaty floral-print dresses: This store sells women's daywear with just enough attitude to be carried into the evening. *42 rue Vieille du Temple, 4th.* ☎ *01-42-71-02-67. www.scotch-soda.com. MC, V. Métro: St-Paul. Map p 78.*

Vanessa Bruno SAINT-GERMAIN-DES-PRES Bruno's unique clothes are deeply feminine without being frilly. Her years in Japan gave her an appreciation for sleek lines and simple, clean fabrics. Great bags, too. *25 rue St-Sulpice, 6th.* ☎ *01-43-54-41-04. www.vanessa bruno.com. AE, DC, MC, V. Métro: Odéon. Map p 80.*

Zadig & Voltaire MARAIS This is one of several Z&V branches in Paris. Shelves are stocked with hip clothes in classic styles for men and women. Cotton tops, cashmere sweaters, and faded jeans are big sellers. *42 rue des Francs-Bourgeois, 3rd.* ☎ *01-44-54-00-60. www.zadig-et-voltaire.com. AE, MC, V. Métro: St-Paul or Hôtel-de-Ville. Map p 78.*

Food & Drink
Christian Constant LATIN QUARTER Chocoholics rejoice: The chocolates at this divine shop are made with exotic ingredients and sold by the kilo. *37 rue d'Assas, 6th.* ☎ *01-53-63-15-15. www.chris tianconstant.fr. MC, V. Métro: St-Placide. Map p 80.*

★ Fauchon MADELEINE This fabulous upscale mega-delicatessen will fill your stomach as fast as it empties your wallet. Must be seen to be believed. *24-26, 30 place de la Madeleine, 8th.* ☎ *01-70-39-38-00. www.fauchon.com. MC, V. Métro: Madeleine. Map p 77.*

★ Florence Kahn MARAIS This Jewish bakery, one of the best in the city, has all the heavy cakes, poppy seeds, apples, and cream cheese you could want. *24 rue des Ecouffes, 4th.* ☎ *01-48-87-92-85. www.florence-kahn.fr. No credit cards. Métro: St-Paul. Map p 78.*

★★★ Maison Plisson MARAIS This store is a picnicker's dream, selling farm-fresh vegetables, award-winning charcuterie, and rows of hand-picked wines in the basement. Their neo-canteen next door sports a fabulous bakery and serves top-notch, wholesome food at meal times. *93 bd. Beaumarchais, 3rd.* ☎ *01-71-18-19-09. www.lamai sonplisson.com. MC, V. Métro: Che-min Vert or Saint-Sébastien-Froissart. Map p 78.*

★★★ **Poilâne** ST-GERMAIN-DES-PRES One of the city's best-loved bakeries, with irresistible apple tarts, butter cookies, and crusty croissants. Get in line. *8 rue du Cherche-Midi, 6th.* ☎ *01-45-48-42-59. www.poilane.fr. MC, V. Métro: St-Sulpice. Map p 80.*

★★★ **Ryst Dupeyron** ST-GERMAIN-DES-PRES Fill up on vintage wines and specialty whis-kies in this family-run gem of a liquor store founded in 1905. Gour-met treats, such as foie gras and prunes in brandy, and friendly ser-vice complete the experience. *79 rue du Bac, 7th.* ☎ *01-45-48-80-93, www.maisonrystdupeyron.com. MC, V. Métro: Rue du Bac. Map p 80.*

Food & Drink: Markets
Marché Beauvau/Place Aligre
LEDRU ROLLIN The Marché d'Aligre is one of Paris's cheapest fruit, vegetable, and flower mar-kets—and one of the best (Tues–Sun 9am–1pm and 4–7:30pm). The more expensive, covered Marché Beauvau offers uncompromisingly

All the produce is organic at Marché Biologique in Saint-Germain.

Foodies will swoon over the vast selec-tion of cheeses in Paris's markets.

good meat, fish, and cheese. *Place d'Aligre, 12th. Cash only. Métro: Ledru-Rollin. Map p 78.*

Marché Biologique SAINT-GERMAIN Along Boulevard Ras-pail, this organic market (Sun 9am–3pm) sells top-notch produce, often locally sourced, plus hot soups, crêpes, and oysters to go. *Bd. Ras-pail (between rue du Cherche-Midi and Rue de Rennes), 6th. Cash only. Métro: Rennes. Map p 80.*

★★ **Marché de Bastille** BAS-TILLE This huge market (Thurs 7:30am–2:30pm; Sun 7am–3pm) is an excellent source for local cheese, meat, and fresh fish. Street perform-ers usually liven up the experience. *Bd. Richard Lenoir, 11th. Cash only. Métro: Bastille. Map p 78.*

Gifts & Jewelry
107 RIVOLI LOUVRE You don't need a ticket to enter the Arts Décoratifs' museum shop—the best place in central Paris to find cut-ting-edge, design-themed jewelry, tableware, fashion accessories, and beautiful coffee-table books. It's not cheap, but it's well worth a browse. *107 rue de Rivolit, 1st.* ☎ *01-42-60-64-94. www.lesartsdecoratifs.fr. MC, V. Métro: Palais Royal-Musée du Lou-vre. Map p 78.*

★★★ **Deyrolle** SAINT-GERMAIN This taxidermy/curiosity shop is filled with stuffed wildlife. The chances of

A taxidermy display at Deyrolle.

you leaving with a tiger in your bag are slim, but there are oodles of nature books, garden gadgets, and jewelry. The butterfly cabinets upstairs are particularly dazzling. *45 rue du Bac, 7th.* ☎ *01-42-22-32-31. www.deyrolle.com. MC, V. Métro: Rue du Bac. Map p 80.*

★★ **Les Fleurs** BASTILLE Hidden down a tiny passageway, this understatedly trendy boutique's jewelry and bags became so popular that they had to open a second store (a 5-minute walk away). Both boutiques are worth checking out; the first for its trinkets, the second for its hand-picked range of household items. *6 passage Josset & 5 rue Trousseau, 11th.* ☎ *01-43-55-12-94, www.boutiquelesfleurs.com. AE, MC, V. Métro: Ledru Rollin. Map p 78.*

★★ **Servane Gaxotte** SAINT-GERMAIN In this tiny jewelry shop, exquisite necklaces and trinkets take on the forms of delicate little dolls and whimsical animals, such as deer and rabbits. It's a girly heaven and utterly Parisian. *55 rue des Saint-Pères, 6th.* ☎ *01-42-84-39-93. www.servanegaxotte.com. MC, V. Métro: Saint Germain des Près. Map p 80.*

Kitchen
E. Dehillerin LES HALLES This shop has outfitted great chefs for nearly 2 centuries. Nothing here comes cheap, but a Dehillerin sauté pan is forever. *18 rue Coquilliére, 1st.* ☎ *01-42-36-53-13. www.e-dehillerin.fr. MC, V. Métro: Les Halles. Map p 78.*

Music & Tickets
FNAC CHAMPS-ELYSEES This supermarket of culture (with various branches) is where you can pick up CDs and vinyl of French and international artists, DVDs, video games, and electronics. It's also a convenient place to buy tickets for concerts, plays, sports events, and museums, both inside the stores and online at www.fnac.com. The branch on the Champs-Elysées stays open until midnight. *74 av. des Champs Elysées, 8th.* ☎ *08-25-02-00-02. AE, DC, MC, V. Métro: George V. Map p 77.*

Perfume & Makeup
Sephora CHAMPS ELYSEES Yes it's a chain, but this branch of Sephora is the biggest—a mini cosmetic department store offering a nail bar, makeup lessons and even a perfume bottle engraving service. *70-72 avenue des Champs Elysées, 8th.* ☎ *01-53-93-22-50. www.sephora.fr. MC, V. Métro: Georges V or Franklin D. Roosevelt. Map p 77.*

★★★ **Serge Lutens** PALAIS ROYAL This purple Belle Epoque boutique is so beautiful it's worth seeing even if you don't buy any fragrances or makeup. This is one of a handful of boutiques to sell Lutens's "exclusives" perfume range. *142 galerie de Valois, 1st.* ☎ *01-49-27-09-09. www.serge-lutens.com. AE, MC, V. Métro: Palais Royal. Map p 78.* ●

5 The Best of the **Outdoors**

Jardin des Tuileries

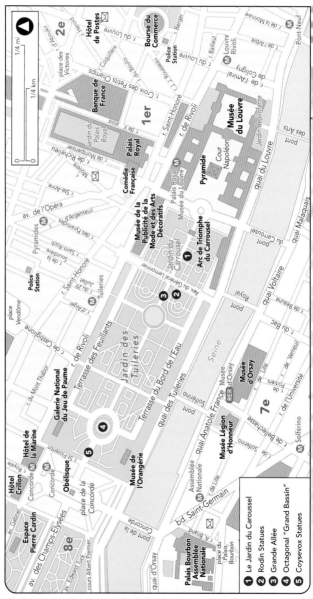

1. Le Jardin du Carousel
2. Rodin Statues
3. Grande Allée
4. Octagonal "Grand Bassin"
5. Coysevox Statues

The Roue de Paris is a transportable Ferris Wheel that has traveled around the world.

More a statue garden than, as its name implies, a "garden of tiles" (the clay earth here was once used to make roof tiles), the Tuileries stretches from the Louvre all the way down to the Place de la Concorde. Under lacy chestnut trees, paths branch and curl off the dusty main allée, and each seems to hold something to charm you—statues, ice-cream stands, and ponds surrounded by chairs in which you can read or simply relax and contemplate the beauty around you. It's open daily from 7am to 9pm in summer and from 7am to 5:45pm in winter. START: **Métro to Tuileries or Concorde.**

① Le Jardin du Carrousel.
Start by the glass pyramid and walk past the Arc de Triomphe du Carrousel—an elaborate arch ordered by Napoleon in 1806 and copied from the Septimus Severus Arch in Rome—into the eastern edge of the Tuileries, the Jardin du Carrousel. (Just so you know, the last word refers to equestrian exhibitions—there's no merry-go-round here.) The gold-tipped obelisk you see gleaming at the end (the Luxor Obelisk, a gift from Egypt) marks the Place de la Concorde. Look around and you'll find beautiful boxwood hedges, among which 20 graceful statues by Aristide Maillol seemingly play hide and seek.

② Rodin Statues. Keep walking until you cross Avenue du Général-Lemonnier. Four typically graceful statues by Auguste Rodin (*The Kiss, Eve, Meditation,* and *The Shadow*) flank the paths. The glimmering golden statue in the distance at Place des Pyramides is *Joan of Arc*; she assembled her army against the British from a spot not far from here, on Avenue de l'Opéra.

③ Grande Allée. Off to the sides of the Grande Allée, a number of modern statues peek at you from the greenery—Henry Moore's *Figure Couchée* lounges leisurely, and Alberto Giacometti's *Grande Femme II* sits near Jean Dubuffet's dazzling *Le Bel Costume*. Particularly beguiling is *The Welcoming Hands*—a collage of intertwined hands, by Louise Bourgeois.

④ Octagonal "Grand Bassin." The statues surrounding this pond date from the days when this was a royal park fronting the ill-fated Palais Tuileries, which burned to the ground during a battle in 1871. The statues are all allegories—of the seasons, French rivers, the Nile, and the Tiber.

⑤ Coysevox Statues. At the end of the garden, at the gates facing the Place de la Concorde, are copies of a set of elaborate statues originally created by Charles-Antoine Coysevox (1640–1720), one of Louis XIV's sculptors. They depict the gods Mercury and Fame riding winged horses.

The Grand Bassin in the Jardin des Tuileries is surrounded by statues.

Cimetière du Père-Lachaise

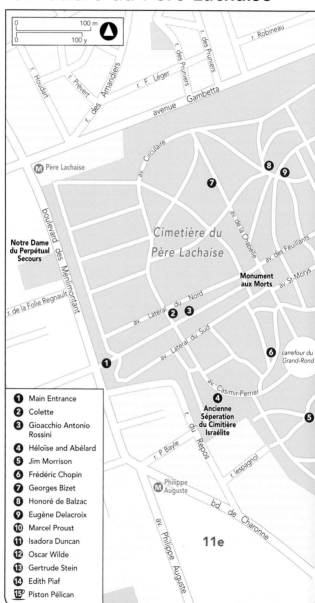

1. Main Entrance
2. Colette
3. Gioacchio Antonio Rossini
4. Héloïse and Abélard
5. Jim Morrison
6. Frédéric Chopin
7. Georges Bizet
8. Honoré de Balzac
9. Eugène Delacroix
10. Marcel Proust
11. Isadora Duncan
12. Oscar Wilde
13. Gertrude Stein
14. Edith Piaf
15. Piston Pélican

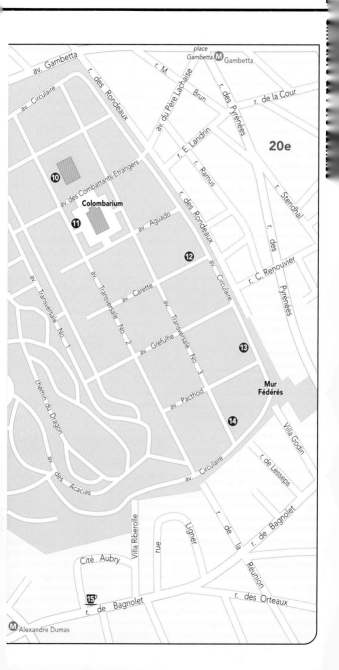

Père-Lachaise became one of the world's most famous cemeteries when Jim Morrison died (or didn't die, as some fans believe), in 1971. Almost immediately, Morrison's grave became a site of pilgrimage and the place filled with tourists, most of whom you can avoid if you stay away from Morrison's grave. Aside from its VIP RIPs, Père Lachaise is a peaceful place to get away from the hubbub of city life. It's also a magnet for lovers of sculpture, who can admire some of Europe's most intricate and beautiful 19th-century tombstones. START: **Métro to Philippe-Auguste or Père Lachaise.**

① Main Entrance. Start by picking up a free map at the gate. *8 bd. de Ménilmontant.* 📞 *01-55-25-82-10. Free admission. Daily 8am (8:30am Sat, 9am Sun & public holidays) to 6pm (until 5:30pm in winter). Métro: Philippe-Auguste or Père-Lachaise.*

② Colette. French writer Sidonie-Gabrielle Colette published 50 novels. Her most famous story, *Gigi,* became a successful Broadway play and film. When she died in 1954, she was given a state funeral but was refused Roman Catholic rites because of her naughty lifestyle. *Section 4.*

③ Gioacchio Antonio Rossini. The Italian composer is best known for the operas *The Barber of Seville* and *William Tell,* the overture of which is one of the most famous in the world. His dramatic style led to his nickname among other composers—"Monsieur Crescendo." *Section 4.*

④ Héloïse & Abelard. If you turn right down Avenue du Puits, near Colette's grave, you'll soon come to the oldest inhabitants of the cemetery. These star-crossed medieval lovers were kept apart their entire lives by Héloïse's family. Their passionate love letters to one another were published and have survived the ages. Abelard died first. Local lore maintains that when Héloïse died, a romantic abbess opened Abelard's grave to put Héloïse's body inside, and his corpse opened its arms to embrace his long-lost love. *Section 7.*

⑤ Jim Morrison. If you must visit Morrison's grave, follow the crowds. The bust that once stood at the head of the tomb was stolen years ago by one of his "fans." The cigarette butts stubbed out on the grave are also courtesy of his "fans." As are the graffiti and the stench of old beer. What a mess. *Section 6.*

⑥ Frédéric Chopin. Retrace your steps across Avenue Casimir-Périer to section 11, where you'll find the elaborate grave of the piano maestro marked with a statue of Erato, the muse of music. *Section 11.*

Famed pianist Frédéric Chopin's tomb.

The tombstone of Honoré de Balzac.

series of books, *A la Recherche du Temps Perdu (In Search of Lost Time)*, yet he's considered one of the world's great writers. *Section 85.*

⓫ Isadora Duncan. The tragic death of this marvelous modern dancer is legendary—she favored long, dramatic scarves and convertibles, and one day one of those wrapped around the other and that was the end of Isadora. *Section 87.*

⓬ Oscar Wilde. The bluntly named Avenue des Etrangers Morts pour la France (Avenue of Dead Foreigners, basically) leads to the fantastical tomb of this gay 19th-century wit and writer. The size of the member with which the statue atop the grave was equipped was quite the buzz in Paris until a vengeful woman knocked it off. *Section 89.*

⓭ Gertrude Stein. The early-20th-century writer, art collector, and unlikely muse shares a simple double-sided tomb with her longtime companion, Alice B. Toklas. *Section 94.*

⓮ Edith Piaf. Just one more stop before you collapse—the resting place of famed French songbird Edith Piaf, beloved by brokenhearted lovers and gay men everywhere. *Section 97.*

⓯ Exit. If possible, leave the cemetery at Rue de la Réunion (this exit sometimes closes early), and from there head right down Rue de Bagnolet to the Alexandre Dumas Métro station. On the way, shabby-chic bar Piston et Pélican is perfect for a glass of wine alongside arty crowds. Stay after 9pm for live music. *15 rue de Bagnolet, 20th.* ☎ *01-43-71-15-76. www.piston pelican.com. Open from 5pm.*

❼ Georges Bizet. The 19th-century composer of the impossibly infectious opera *Carmen* died 3 months after the premiere of his most famous work, convinced it was a failure. *Section 68.*

❽ Honoré de Balzac. The passionate French novelist wrote for up to 15 hours a day, drinking prodigious quantities of coffee to keep him going. His writing was often sloppy and uninspired, but it makes an excellent record of 19th-century Parisian life. *Section 48.*

❾ Eugène Delacroix. This dramatic and intensely romantic painter's *Liberty Leading the People* is a lesson in topless inspiration. In stark contrast, his tomb is sobriety incarnate: just a dark stone sculpture shaped like a coffin and decorated with a single row of white-centered flowers. *Section 49.*

❿ Marcel Proust. The wistful 19th-century novelist died before he could finish editing his famous

Exploring the **Bois de Boulogne**

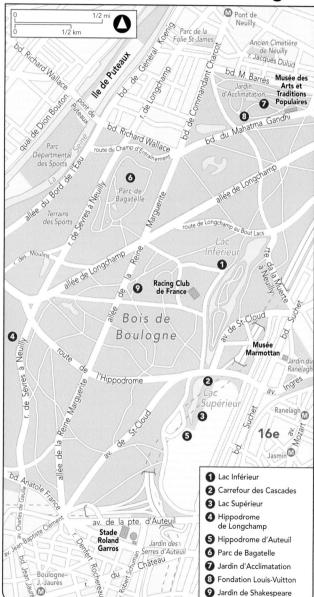

1 Lac Inférieur
2 Carrefour des Cascades
3 Lac Supérieur
4 Hippodrome de Longchamp
5 Hippodrome d'Auteuil
6 Parc de Bagatelle
7 Jardin d'Acclimatation
8 Fondation Louis-Vuitton
9 Jardin de Shakespeare

This former forest, once used for royal hunts, has two personalities. By day, it's a family park where children gambol and ride ponies, while walkers and cyclists take in the beauty of its lakes and waterfalls. By night, it's one of the city's busiest prostitution districts and a hub for other nefarious activities, so make sure you get out before sundown. While you're there, however, you're in for a bucolic day amid birds, woodlands, and 19th-century tropical greenhouses. Between May and September, you can even take in classical theater (in English and French) among the sweet-scented roses of the Jardin de Shakespeare. START: **RER to Avenue Foch.**

❶ Lac Inférieur. Most easily accessed by way of Avenue Foch, this unfairly named lake (it's the larger of the two) has two picturesque islands connected by fanciful footbridges. You can rent a boat and paddle across to the islands' cafes and restaurants. On a hot summer day, it's also a perfect spot for a picnic.

❷ Carrefour des Cascades. The scenic walkway between the upper and lower lakes is an attraction in itself, with willows dipping their branches languorously in the water, and a handsome, manmade waterfall creating a gorgeous backdrop. You can even walk under the waterfall.

❸ Lac Supérieur. The smaller of the two lakes has more of everything you find on the larger lake, with lots of boats to paddle and several restaurants and cafes dotted about.

❹ Hippodrome de Longchamp. If your euros are burning a hole in your pocket, head to the southern end of the park, where two horse-racing courses—the excellent Hippodrome de Longchamp and the smaller Hippodrome d'Auteuil (see next stop)—offer galloping action. The Grand Prix held at Longchamp each June is a major derby and gets the ladies out to the track in their finest hats. *Route des Tribunes, 16th.* ☎ *01-44-30-75-00. www. france-galop.com. Métro: Porte Maillot then bus 244 and get off at Carrefour de Longchamp.*

❺ Hippodrome d'Auteuil. This racetrack, the smaller of the two in Bois de Boulogne, is known for its heart-pounding steeplechases and obstacle courses. *Route d'Auteuil aux Lacs, 16th.* ☎ *01-40-71-47-47. www.france-galop.com. Métro: Porte d'Auteuil-Hippodrome.*

Bois de Boulogne is known as the green lung of the French capital.

Bois de Boulogne: Practical Matters

Bois de Boulogne is open daily from dawn to dusk. Because it's such a large park, there are several entrances and several public transportation options. Nearby Métro stops include Les Sablons (north, on av. Charles de Gaulle), Porte Maillot (northeast, on av. de la Grande Armée), Porte Dauphine (northeast, on av. Foch), or Porte d'Auteuil (southeast, on av. de la Porte d'Auteuil). Take the RER to Avenue Foch or Avenue Henri Martin. In the park are numerous cafes and restaurants. A miniature train runs to the Jardin d'Acclimatation from Porte Maillot—a fun touch for kids. You won't be able to do the whole of the Bois in one day, but to see a maximum of sites, do as Parisians do, and grab a self-service Vélib' bike for the day (1.70€, then free for 30 minutes; see p 168). There's a handy bike station near the park's entrance at Porte Maillot: no. 16003 at 2 bis boulevard André-Maurois.

⑥ Parc de Bagatelle. In the shadow of a bijou château built for Marie-Antoinette, this romantic 18th-century park-within-a-park in the northwest of Bois de Boulogne is a riot of colorful tulips in spring, and the rose garden blooms spectacularly by late May. A sequence of little bridges, grottoes, and water features also make it one of Paris's most popular trysting spots. ☎ 01-40-67-97-00. Métro: Porte d'Auteuil or Jasmin.

Romantic Parc de Bagatelle.

⑦ ★★ kids Jardin d'Acclimatation. Those with small children may want to head straight to this amusement park on the north end of Bois de Boulogne, which boasts colorful rides, a small zoo, and a kid-size train. *See p 29, ⑥.*

⑧ ★ Fondation Louis-Vuitton. Architect Frank Gehry's latest Parisian creation—all futuristic glass and metal sails—is stunningly incongruous when seen emerging through the Bois de Boulogne's tree-lined paths. Inside, expect cutting-edge art exhibitions by a plethora of international names, and contemporary classical music concerts. *See p 43, ⑤.*

⑨ ★★ Jardin de Shakespeare. This has to be one of the most beautiful open-air theaters in the world—a lawn encircled by bright, buzzing flowerbeds and draping trees. Every summer, it becomes the idyllic stage for Shakespeare and classical French children's theater productions. *In the Jardin Pré-Catelan. www.jardin shakespeare.com. Métro: Porte de la Muette.* ●

The Best Dining

Dining Best Bets

Best **for Steak Frites**
★ Le Relais de l'Entrecôte $$ *15 rue Marbeuf, 8th (p 111)*

Best **for High Tea**
★ Angélina $$ *226 rue de Rivoli, 1st (p 106)*

Best **for Kids**
★ Breakfast in America $ *17 rue des Ecoles, 5th (p 107)*

Best **Cheap Meal in 19th-Century Surroundings**
★ Bouillon Chartier $ *7 rue du Faubourg Montmartre, 9th (p 107)*

Best **Cutting-edge Cuisine**
★★★ Le Grand Restaurant $$$ *7 rue d'Aguesseau, 8th (p 111)*

Best **Vegetarian**
★★ Le Potager du Marais $$ *22 rue Rambuteau, 3rd (p 111)*

Best **Seafood**
★ Les Fables de la Fontaine $$$ *131 rue St-Dominique, 7th (p 111)*

Best **for a Michelin-Starred Feast**
★★★ La Dame de Pic $$$$$ *20 rue du Louvre, 1st (p 110)*

Best **Gourmet Asian**
★★★ Shangri-La $$$$$ *10 av. d'Iéna, 16th (p 112)*

Best **for Food Critics**
★★★ Le Grand Véfour $$$$$ *17 rue de Beaujolais, 2nd (p 111)*

Best **Food Truck**
★★ Le Camion qui Fume $ *(mostly) 132 avenue de France, 13th (p 110)*

Best **for Contemporary French Cuisine**
★★ Septime $$$$ *80 rue de Charonne, 11th (p 112)*

Best **Cheap Lunch**
★ Higuma $ *32 bis rue Ste-Anne, 2nd (p 109)*

Best **Romantic Summer Splurge**
★★ Lasserre $$$$$ *17 av. Franklin Roosevelt, 8th (p 110)*

Best **Celebrity-Chef Restaurant**
★★★ Clover $$ *5 rue Perronet, 7th (p 108)*

Best **Trendy Pizzas**
★ East Mamma $ *67 rue Bichat, 10th (p 109)*

Best **Food in a Tourist Spot**
★ Le Fumoir $$ *6 rue de l'Amiral de Coligny, 1st (p 110)*

Brlow: Au Pied de Cochon serves fresh seafood around the clock. Previous page: La Bauhinia brasserie, in the Shangri La Hotel, serves French and Chinese cuisine.

Right Bank (8th & 16th–17th)

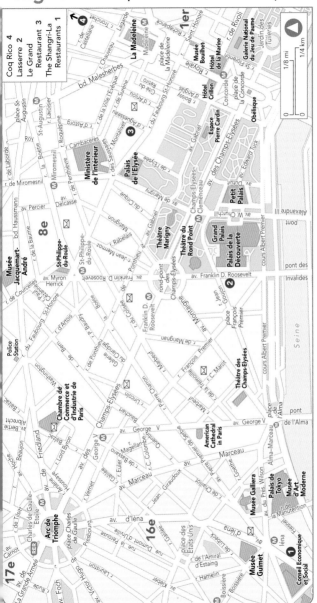

Coq Rico 4
Lasserre 2
Le Grand Restaurant 3
The Shangri-La Restaurants 1

Right Bank (1st–4th & 9th–11th)

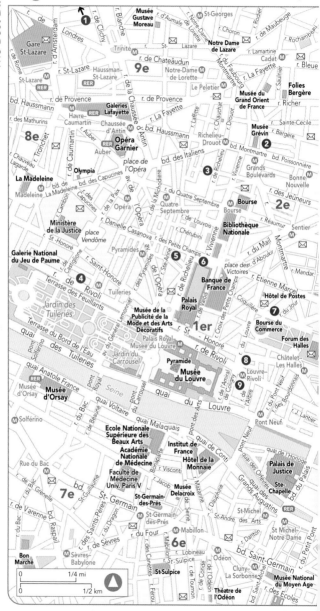

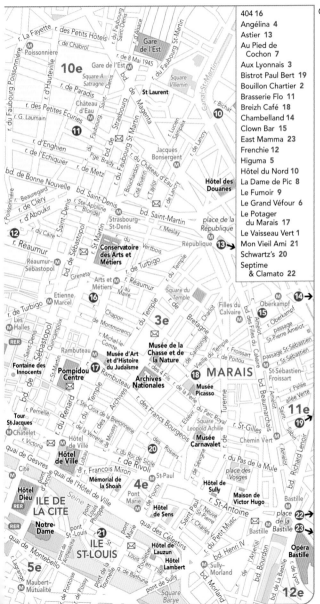

Left Bank (5th–6th)

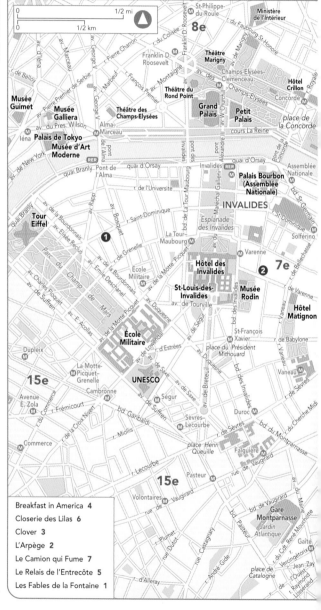

Breakfast in America **4**
Closerie des Lilas **6**
Clover **3**
L'Arpège **2**
Le Camion qui Fume **7**
Le Relais de l'Entrecôte **5**
Les Fables de la Fontaine **1**

La Madeleine

Opéra de
Paris Garnier

Musée Grévin

Ministère
de la Justice

Bourse
des
Valeurs
2e

1er

Banque
de France

Hôtel
de Postes

Comédie
Française

Palais
Royal

Bourse du
Commerce

Palais Royal–
Musée du Louvre

Forum des
Halles

Pompidou
Centre

Musée
du Louvre

Musée
d'Orsay

Hôtel
de Ville

Musée
d'Orsay

Hôtel
de Ville

Ecole Nationale
Supérieure des
Beaux Arts

Palais de
Justice

❸ Académie
Nationale
de Médecine

ILE DE LA
CITÉ

Hôtel
Dieu

Musée
Delacroix

Notre-
Dame

St-Sulpice

LATIN QUARTER

Bon
Marché

St-Sulpice
6e

La
Sorbonne

Palais du
Luxembourg

Lycée
Louis
Le Grand

❹

Alliance
Française

Jardin du
Luxembourg

Panthéon

5e

❺

❻ Port-Royal

MONTPARNASSE

Cimetière du
Montparnasse

14e

❼

13e

Les Gobelins

The Best Dining

Restaurants A to Z

★ **404** MARAIS *NORTH AFRICAN* Step through this restaurant's 16th-century doorway and you're in another world—a supercool Berber world of poufs, North African carpets, and mouthwatering Moroccan dishes. Feeling hungry? The harira soup starter (chickpeas, lamb, and lentils) is almost a meal on its own. Follow it with the 404 Couscous (with lamb skewers and hot merguez sausages) and you'll be reaching for your belt buckle. But do save room for dessert: The pastries and Berber pancakes with honey are delectable. *69 rue des Gravilliers, 3rd.* ☎ *01-42-74-57-81. Entrees 17€–26€. MC, V. Lunch & dinner daily, brunch Sat & Sun. Métro: Arts et Métiers. Map p 102.*

★ **Angélina** TUILERIES *TEA SHOP* This traditional salon de thé serves its high-society patrons tea, pastries, and sandwiches on silver platters. If you have a sweet tooth, try the Mont Blanc, a gooey meringue, cream, and chestnut cake. The hot chocolate is some of the best in Paris too. *226 rue de Rivoli, 1st.* ☎ *01-42-60-82-00. www.angelina-paris.fr. Tea 6€–15€, entrees 14€–22€. AE, MC, V. Breakfast, lunch & tea daily. Métro: Tuileries or Concorde. Map p 102.*

An assortment of appetizers at 404.

★★ **Astier** OBERKAMPF *FRENCH* This red-and-white-checkered dining institution reworks vintage staples, such as smoked herring and potato salad, wild-boar terrine, and braised Charolais beef, with modern flair. The staff is friendly, the wine list long, and the managers also own the next-door Italian restaurant and fine-food épicerie, so if Astier is all booked up, you won't go hungry. *44 rue Jean-Pierre Timbaud, 11th.* ☎ *01-43-57-16-35. www.restaurant-astier.com. 4-course prix-fixe 45€, lunchtime entrees 15€. Lunch & dinner daily. MC, V. Métro: Oberkampf. Map p 102.*

★ **Au Pied de Cochon.** LES HALLES *FRENCH* Where else in Paris can you get such a good meal at 3am? Specialties include onion soup, grilled pigs' feet with béarnaise sauce, and *andouillettes* (sausages). On the street outside, the restaurant sells some of the freshest oysters in town. *6 rue Coquillière, 1st.* ☎ *01-40-13-77-00. www.pied decochon.com. Entrees 17€–48€. Breakfast 6.10€ AE, DC, MC, V. Daily 24 hr. Métro: Les Halles or Louvre Rivoli. Map p 102.*

★ **Aux Lyonnais** GRANDS BOULEVARDS *LYONNAIS* Famed chef Alain Ducasse, the best in Paris at Lyonnais cuisine, creates such dishes as parsleyed calf's liver, pike dumplings, skate meunière, and peppery coq au vin in a restaurant designed to look like a 19th-century bistro. *32 rue St-Marc, 2nd.* ☎ *01-42-96-65-04. www.alain-ducasse.com. Reservations required. Prix-fixe menu 34€ (lunch), 35€ (dinner), 3-course average 45€. AE, DC, MC, V. Lunch & dinner Tues–Fri, dinner Sat. Métro: Grands Boulevards. Map p 102.*

Diners under the vaulted arcades of the Marais district.

★★★ kids Bistrot Paul Bert

FAIDHERBE FRENCH This locals' haunt has old tile floors and a real zinc bar—just as a Parisian bistro should. The food is just as authentic, and also delicious: crispy duck confit with garlicky potatoes, homemade pâtés, and possibly the best île flottante (whisked egg whites in a vanilla sauce) in town. *11 rue Paul Bert, 12th.* ☎ *01-43-72-24-01. Entrees 19€–24€. 3-course menu 38€. MC, V. Lunch & dinner Tues–Sat. Métro: Faidherbe-Chaligny. Map p 102.*

★ kids Bouillon Chartier LES

HALLES *TRADITIONAL FRENCH* This unpretentious, affordable fin-de-siècle restaurant has soaring ceilings, fabulous brasswork, and straightforward cooking—try the beef bourguignon (in red-wine sauce), the pavé (thick steak), or the fish. To avoid the lines, arrive early or late (it's open until midnight). *7 rue du Faubourg Montmartre, 9th.* ☎ *01-47-70-86-29. www.bouillon-chartier.com. Entrees 9€–14€. MC, V. Lunch & dinner daily. Métro: Grands Boulevards. Map p 102.*

★★ Brasserie Flo NORTHEAST

PARIS *TRADITIONAL FRENCH* This well-known restaurant is a bit

hard to find, down a discreet cobbled passage, but you'll be glad you tracked it down when you try the onion soup, sole meunière, or guinea hen with lentils. *7 cour des Petites-Ecuries, 10th.* ☎ *01-47-70-13-59. www.brasserieflo-paris.com. Reservations recommended. Entrees 20€–40€, prix-fixe lunch & dinner 29€–36€. AE, DC, MC, V. Lunch & dinner daily. Métro: Château d'Eau or Strasbourg-St-Denis. Map p 102.*

★ kids Breakfast in America

LATIN QUARTER *AMERICAN* Homesick Americans make a bee-line to this diner, which could have been transported here straight from the streets of Chicago. The menu features such favorites as pecan pie, freshly squeezed OJ, burgers with grilled onions and fries, and brownies. *17 rue des Ecoles, 5th.* ☎ *01-43-54-50-28. www.breakfast-in-america.com. Entrees 7€–17€. MC, V. Breakfast, lunch & dinner daily. Métro: Cardinal Lemoine. Map p 104.*

★ kids Breizh Café MARAIS

CREPERIE You could be in Brittany at this upbeat modern creperie, which uses top-notch, mostly organic produce in its unusual and delicious fillings: Think potato and smoked herring, or 70% cocoa solids in the chocolate dessert crêpes. You can wash it all down with one of 15 artisanal ciders. *109 rue Vieille-du-Temple, 3rd.* ☎ *01-42-72-13-77. www.breizhcafe.com. Crêpes 6€–15€. MC, V. Lunch & dinner Wed–Sun. Métro: Filles du Calvaire. Map p 102.*

★ kids Chambelland

OBERKAMPF *ORGANIC GLUTEN-FREE* Every single product in this fabulous bakery and cafe is gluten-free. But don't be fooled: So utterly delicious are the items (think door-stop sandwiches made with bread baked in the cellar, and sweet chestnut muffins) that most of the clientele don't have gluten allergies. Come for breakfast, lunch, or an early-evening snack (closing is at 8pm); and on a sunny day sit outside and watch the locals stroll to and fro across the tranquil square. *14 rue Ternaux, 11th.* ☎ *01-43-55-07-30. http://chambelland.com. Sandwiches 6€. MC, V. Breakfast & lunch Tues–Sun. Métro: Parmentier or Oberkampf. Map p 102.*

★ **Closerie des Lilas** MONTPARNASSE *TRADITIONAL FRENCH* This restaurant and brasserie was a favorite of Gertrude Stein and Picasso (not to mention Lenin and Trotsky—a revolution marches on its stomach, apparently). Have a champagne julep before stuffing yourself with veal ribs with cider or filet of beef in peppercorn sauce. *171 bd. du Montparnasse, 6th.* ☎ *01-40-51-34-50. www.closerie deslilas.fr. Reservations far in advance for the restaurant, not needed for the brasserie. Restaurant entrees 28€–60€, prix-fixe 52€ (lunch); brasserie entrees 23€–33€. AE, DC, V. Lunch & dinner daily. Métro: Port Royal or Vavin. Map p 104.*

★★★ **Clover** SAINT GERMAIN DES PRES *MODERN FRENCH* Only 20 lucky people can eat in this long, narrow dining room per

Putting the finishing touches on some gluten-free pastries at Chambelland.

seating, so make sure you book in advance. Your forward-planning will be rewarded with some of the most innovative, spontaneous cooking in the city—perhaps scallops served on a Paris paving stone, or duck and foie-gras pastries with shavings of truffles. There's an appetizing wine list as well. *5 rue Perronet, 7th.* ☎ *01-75-50-00-05. www.clover-paris.com. Prix-fixe lunch 28€, 4-course menu 42€. MC, V. Lunch & dinner Tues–Sat. Métro: Saint Germain des Prés. Map p 104.*

★★★ **Clown Bar** BASTILLE/MARAIS *MODERN FRENCH* This charming restaurant is the lair of food-savvy locals who squeeze into its jam-packed dining room to sample chef Sota Atsumi's innovative takes on French classics, such as panko-fried snails and hearty duck pie. If the menu doesn't convince you, the setting should: Adorned in clown-themed Belle Epoque tiles, it's one of the prettiest dining rooms in town. Rumor has it that Toulouse Lautrec used to prop himself up at the zinc bar. *114 rue Amelot, 3rd.* ☎ *01-43-55-87-35. www.clown-bar-paris.fr. Entrees 16€–23€. MC, V. Lunch & dinner Wed–Sun. Métro: Filles du Calvaire or Oberkampf. Map p 102.*

★ **Coq Rico** MONTMARTRE *ROTISSERIE* Bohemian-bourgeois foodies climb up Montmartre's Butte for a table at this "bistro of beautiful birds." And rightly so: The pedigreed roast chicken is succulent every time and comes with lip-smacking gravy and crunch-perfect *frites*. Add to that the humongous *mille-feuilles au chocolat* (layers of pastry and chocolate cream), and the barnyard-chic decor, and you're in rotisserie heaven. *98 rue Lepic, 18th.* ☎ *01-42-59-82-89. Entrees 22€–40€, whole chickens for 2 to 4 people 86€–98€. MC, V. Lunch & dinner daily. Métro: Blanche. Map p 101.*

★ **kids East Mamma** BASTILLE ITALIAN/PIZZA Since opening in 2015, East Mamma has taken the city by storm. The reason? The tastiest, freshest pizzas, pastas, and cocktails in town, served in a beautiful rustico-1970s dining room with an open kitchen. To avoid the evening lines, arrive before 6:50pm or after 9pm. There's another location at 107 bd Richard Lenoir, 11th. *133 rue du Faubourg St-Antoine, 11th.* ☎ 01-43-41-32-15. www.bigmamma. fr. Pizzas from 11€. MC, V. Lunch & dinner daily. Métro: Ledru Rollin. Map p 102.

★ **Frenchie** SENTIER *MODERN FRENCH* In the gentrifying Sentier garment district, this teeny restaurant is one of the buzziest eateries in town. Book at least 1 month in advance for the 7pm sitting (3 months for 9:30pm). Get in, and you'll rejoice over dishes like red tuna with preserved lemon, and chicken in gooseberry and mustard sauce. If it's full, turn up anyway (at 6:30pm): you can leave your name with the staff, then wait in their wine bar. If there's a no-show they'll call you; if not, you can still fill up on great finger food. *5 rue du Nil, 2nd.* ☎ 01-40-39-96-19. www.frenchie-restaurant.com. Entrees

The elegant dining room at La Dame de Pic.

37€, 5-course tasting menu 68€. MC, V. Lunch & dinner Mon–Fri. Métro: Sentier or Bonne Nouvelle. Map p 102.

Higuma OPERA JAPANESE Delicious-smelling steam fills the air at this popular, no-frills Japanese canteen, where you can get a giant bowl of soup, rice, or noodles piled high with meat, seafood, or vegetables for around 9€. If there's no room, walk 5 minutes to sister restaurant Higumas at 163 rue St-Honoré (1st) or 27 bd des Italiens (2nd). *32 bis rue Ste-Anne, 1st.* ☎ 01-47-03-38-59. www.higuma.fr. Prix-fixe menu from 11€, entrees 7€. MC, V. Lunch & dinner daily. Métro: Pyramides. Map p 102.

★ **Hôtel du Nord** CANAL SAINT MARTIN *FRENCH* With 1930s-inspired decor and oodles of history (it gave its name to Marcel Carné's 1938 classic movie, *Hôtel du Nord*), this low-key canal-side eatery is perfect for an inexpensive meal with atmosphere. My favorites are the beef Carpaccio with *frites*, and, for dessert, the crème-brûlée. Simple, but satisfying! *102 quai de Jemmapes, 10th.* ☎ 01-40-40-78-78. www.hoteldunord.org. Entrees 16€–22€, prix-fixe lunch 15€. MC, V. Lunch & dinner daily. Métro: République or Jacques Bonsergent. Map p 102.

Higuma features an open kitchen, tasty soups, and low prices.

People-watch in the trendy 9th arrondissement from the terrace at Le Vaisseau Vert.

★★★ La Dame de Pic LOUVRE
CONTEMPORARY FRENCH Run by Michelin-starred chef Anne-Sophie Pic, this restaurant exudes savoir-faire. Choose your menu using your sense of smell: The waiters offer perfumed cards that correspond to ingredients used in the dishes. Then tuck into veal with bacon and saffron, or pigeon with rhubarb, and such desserts as strawberry and mint baba—all as photogenic as they are delicious. *20 rue du Louvre, 1st.* ☎ *01-42-60-40-40. www.ladamedepic.fr. Reservations recommended. Entrees 35€–70€, prix-fixe lunch 49€, prix-fixe dinner 80€–125€. MC, V. Lunch & dinner Mon–Sat. Métro: Louvre-Rivoli. Map p 102.*

★★ L'Arpège INVALIDES *FRENCH*
Supplies for this exclusive eatery come from chef Alain Passard's own farms in the Sarthe, Eure, and Mont-Saint-Michel regions, where horses replace polluting machinery, and pesticides (when necessary) are vegetable-based. Expect such Michelin-starred dishes as roasted Brittany turbot with smoked potatoes and blue lobster in honey. *84 rue de Varenne, 7th.* ☎ *01-47-05-09-06. www.alain-passard.com. Entrees 60€–140€. AE, MC, V. Mon–Fri noon–2:30pm & 7:30–10:30pm. Métro: Varenne. Map p 104.*

★★ Lasserre CHAMPS ELYSEES
HAUTE FRENCH Eating here, with gold cutlery and fine porcelain, waiters plying to your every whim, and Michelin-starred food on your plate, is a treat available to only a lucky few. If you can afford it, do it, especially in summer, when the restaurant roof opens to let in the warm breeze. Lunch is less than half the price of dinner, for the same food. *17 av. Franklin Roosevelt, 8th.* ☎ *01-43-59-02-13. www.restaurant-lasserre.com. Reservations recommended. Prix-fixe lunch 90€, prix-fixe dinner 195€, entrees 60€–110€. MC, V. Lunch & dinner Thurs–Fri, dinner Tues–Sat. Métro: Champs Elysée Clémenceau. Map p 101.*

★★ Le Camion qui Fume
BIBLIOTHEQUE *FOOD TRUCK BURGERS* "The Smoking Truck" pioneered the food truck trend in Paris, and it's still one of the best. Try the Bleu burger (with *Fourme d'Ambert* blue cheese, caramelized onions, and port sauce); the homemade onion rings and slaw are excellent too. Perhaps that's why there's always a queue? Check the website for the exact location, but you can usually catch it outside the MK2 cinema in the 13th. You can buy their burger recipe book too. *132 ave de France, 13th.* ☎ *01-84-16-33-75. Entrees 9€. MC, V. Lunch & dinner Tues–Sun. Métro: Bibliothèque François Mitterand or Quai de la Gare. Map p 104.*

★ Le Fumoir LOUVRE *BISTRO*
This handy spot near the Louvre and Arts Décoratifs museums has a faithful following from Paris's literary and media crowds. Sink into a Chesterfield armchair and order a refreshing cocktail, or fill up on Franco-Scandinavian dishes like herrings with cucumber cream or rump steak with bone marrow. *6 rue de l'amiral de Coligny, 1st.* ☎ *01-42-92-00-24. www.lefumoir.com. Entrees*

average 20€; lunch from 23€; prix-fixe dinner from 35€. AE, MC, V. Lunch & dinner daily. Métro: Louvre-Rivoli. Map p 102.

★★★ Le Grand Restaurant

CHAMPS ELYSEES *CONTEMPO-RARY HAUTE CUISINE* This sleek restaurant not only looks good (all steely greys and geometric diamond-shapes, including a futuristic glass ceiling), it's also the city's most exciting place for a meal-splurge. Genius chef Jean-François Piège delights with such dreamy dishes as air-blown potato with caviar, a spaghetti tower with belly pork and truffles, and venison served on sugared chestnuts. *7 rue Aguesseau, 8th.* 01-53-05-00-00. www.jeanfrancoispiege.com. *Reservations required. Prix-fixe lunch 80€, prix-fixe dinner 180€–220€. AE, DC, MC, V. Lunch & dinner Mon–Fri. Métro: Madeleine or Franklin D. Roosevelt. Map p 101.*

★★★ Le Grand Véfour TUILE-

RIES *TRADITIONAL FRENCH* This romantic, historic, expensive place is where the Revolution was rumored to have been plotted. It's also where super-talented chef Guy Martin serves specialties such as lamb cooked with sweet wine, Breton lobster, and cabbage sorbet in dark-chocolate sauce. The upstairs dining room sports sketches drawn by artists such as

You can get modern French comfort food at Septime, or tapas next door at Clamato.

Chagall. *17 rue de Beaujolais, 1st.* 01-42-96-56-27. www.grand-vefour.com. *Reservations required. Entrees 84€–128€, prix-fixe lunch 115€, prix-fixe dinner 240€. AE, DC, MC, V. Lunch & dinner Mon–Thurs, lunch Fri. Closed Aug. Métro: Louvre-Palais Royal or Pyramides. Map p 102.*

★★ Le Potager du Marais

MARAIS *VEGETARIAN* Vegetarians and vegans flock to this organic offering, arguably the best of its kind in Paris. The welcome is warm, and many items are gluten-free. *24 rue Rambuteau, 3rd.* 01-57-40-98-57. www.lepotagerdumarais.fr. *Entrees 13€–21€. MC, V. Lunch & dinner daily. Métro: Rambuteau. Map p 102.*

🚸 Le Relais de l'Entrecôte

MONTPARNASSE *FRENCH* When you're hankering after a decent *steak-frites* (steak and fries), this is the place to come. The only real choice on the menu is for dessert (think chocolate profiteroles or lemon sorbet); for the rest it's the cut of day, skinny fries, and the restaurant's secret sauce. Wine starts at a reasonable 18€/bottle. Other branches can be found at 20 rue Saint-Benoît, 6th, and 14 rue Marbeuf, 8th. *101 bd du Montparnasse, 6th.* 01-46-33-82-82. www.relaisentrecote.fr. *Entrees 27€. AE, DC, MC, V. Lunch & dinner daily. Métro: Vavin. Map p 104.*

★ Les Fables de la Fontaine

EIFFEL TOWER *SEAFOOD* One of the city's best seafood restaurants draws crowds with its fresh fried shrimp, baked sea bass with a rich, creamy sauce, big bowls of mussels, and fine oysters. The restaurant is small, so tables fill up quickly. Book the second sitting if you want to linger. *131 rue St-Dominique, 7th.* 01-44-18-37-55. www.lesfables delafontaine.net. *Entrees 21€–28€, lunch menus from 25€, 6-course prix-fixe 70€. MC, V. Lunch & dinner daily. Métro: Ecole Militaire. Map p 104.*

★ **Le Vaisseau Vert** PLACE DE CLICHY *MODERN FRENCH* Off the beaten tourist path in the trendy 9th arrondissement, this cozy neo-bistro is the place to pretend you're a local. Sink into the marshmallow-cushioned banquettes, tell the waiters about your food allergies or dislikes, then open your mind to the chef's fusion creations (nothing is marked on the menu—only the price and the wine), which according to the market's offerings and the chef's mood, may include butternut and rose velouté and shrimp with avocado and wasabi cream. Desserts aren't copious, but the rest is so inventive it can be forgiven. *10 rue Parme, 9th.* ☎ *01-43-21-95-68. www.le-vaisseau-vert.fr. Prix-fixe lunch from 28€. Prix-fixe 8-course tasting menu dinner 69€ MC, V. Lunch & dinner Mon–Fri. Métro: Place de Clichy. Map p 102.*

★★ **Mon Vieil Ami** ÎLE ST-LOUIS *CONTEMPORARY FRENCH* This slice of gastronomy is where chef Antoine Westermann prepares traditional French cuisine with a modern twist. Vegetables take pride of place alongside perfect meat and fish, creating such wonderful *plats* as slow-braised roebuck with celery, quince, and chestnuts; and seafood casserole topped with tomatoes and tender baby squid. *65 rue St-Louis-en-l'Île, 4th.* ☎ *01-40-46-01-35. www.mon-vieil-ami.com. Reservations required. Prix-fixe menu*

lunch 16€, dinner 48€, entrees 25€. AE, MC, V. Lunch & dinner Wed–Sun. Métro: Pont Marie. Map p 102.

★ **kids Schwartz's** MARAIS *JEWISH* This New York–style Jewish deli bustles throughout the day with hungry folk looking to fill up on smoked herring, pastrami, chunky bagels, burgers, and hot dogs. The cheesecake is a treat. *16 rue des Ecouffes, 4th.* ☎ *01-48-87-31-29. www.schwartzsdeli.fr. Entrees 9.50€–24€. AE, DC, MC, V. Lunch & dinner daily. Métro: St-Paul. Map p 102.*

★★ **Septime & Clamato** NORTHEAST PARIS *CONTEMPORARY FRENCH* This rustic-chic eatery draws fans from across the city for flawless dishes such as succulent pork with caramelized rutabaga and smoked duck with ricotta. The lunch menu is a steal at 28€, and the next-door seafood tapas bar, Clamato, makes you feel as though you've been transported to the seaside. *80 rue de Charonne, 11th.* ☎ *01-43-67-38-29. www.septime-charonne.fr. Entrees 25€, prix-fixe lunch 28€, dinner 65€. MC, V. Lunch & dinner Tues–Fri, dinner Mon. (Clamato Wed–Sun dinner, Sat–Sun lunch). Métro: Charonne. Map p 102.*

★★★ **Shangri-La Restaurants** CHAILLOT *FRENCH & ASIAN* The palatial **Hôtel Shangri-La** (p 146) gives you three fabulous high-end eating opportunities: **Shang Palace,** the city's first-ever gourmet Cantonese restaurant; **L'Abeille,** a marvelous gastronomic French restaurant overlooking the interior garden; and **La Bauhinia** brasserie, which serves lip-smacking Chinese and French dishes. *10 av. Iéna, 16th.* ☎ *01-53-67-19-98. www.shangri-la.com. Entrees 60€–90€, prix-fixe lunch from 80€. AE, DC, MC, V. Lunch & dinner daily. Métro: Iéna. Map p 101.* ●

L'Abeille, at the Shangri-La Hotel, overlooks the garden.

Nightlife Best Bets

Best Bohemian Bar
★ Chez Prune, 36 rue Beaurepaire, 10th (p 122)

Best Chic Cocktails
★★★ Le Coq, 12 rue du Château d'Eau, 10th (p 123)

Best Place to Steal a Kiss
★★ La Palette, 43 rue de Seine, 6th (p 122)

Best Wine Bar
★★ Le Baron Rouge, 1 rue Théophile-Roussel, 12th (p 124)

Best for Paris-Brewed Beer
★★ Paname Brewing Company, 41 bis Quai de la Loire (p 123)

Best for Ping-Pong Fans
★★ Gossima, 4 rue Victor Gelez, 11th (p 122)

Best for Fans of Papa
★★★ Harry's Bar, 5 rue Daunou, 2nd (p 122)

Best for Dinner & a Boogie
★★ Wanderlust, 32 quai d'Austerlitz, 13th (p 120)

Best Outdoor Partying
★★ Rosa Bonheur, 2 allée de la Cascade, Parc des Buttes Chaumont, 19th (p 123)

Best Hip Club
★★ Le Cartel Club, 8 rue Arsène Houssaye, 8th (p 120)

Best Speakeasy
★★ Candelaria, 52 rue Saintonge, 3rd (p 122)

Best Waterfront Location
★★ Batofar, 11 quai François Mauriac, 13th (p 120)

Best Cutting-Edge Club
★★ Le Social Club, 142 rue de Montmartre, 2nd (p 120)

Best for the Latest Electro Sounds
★★ Rex Club, 5 bd. Poissonnière, 2nd (p 120)

Best Gay Bars
Open Café & Café Cox, 15 & 17 rue des Archives, 4th (p 121)

Best Lesbian Bar
3W Kafé, 8 rue des Ecouffes, 4th (p 121)

Best Boudoir
★★★ Le Bar de L'Hôtel, 13 rue des Beaux-Arts, 6th (p 123)

Below: Batofar is a barge turned hip dance club. Previous page: Locals flock to Le Baron Rouge for its excellent selection of wines.

Right Bank (8th & 16th–17th)

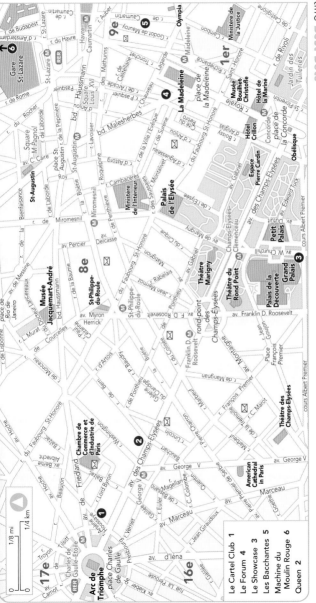

Le Cartel Club 1
Le Forum 4
Le Showcase 3
Les Bacchantes 5
Machine du
Moulin Rouge 6
Queen 2

Right Bank (1st–4th & 9th–11th)

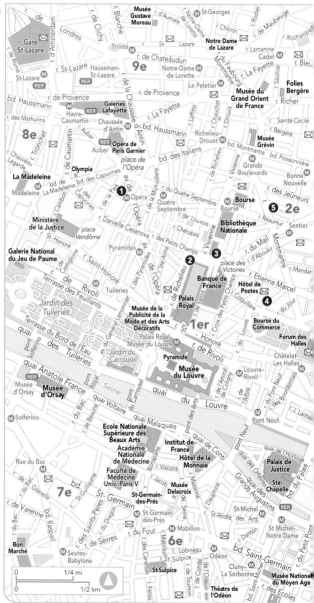

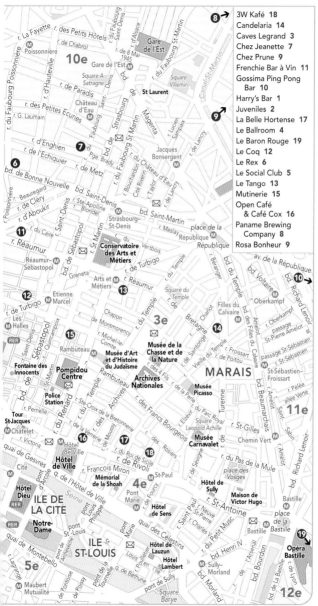

Left Bank (5th–6th)

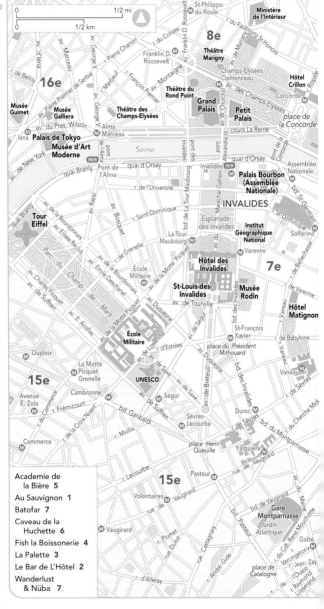

Academie de
la Bière **5**

Au Sauvignon **1**

Batofar **7**

Caveau de la
Huchette **6**

Fish la Boissonerie **4**

La Palette **3**

Le Bar de L'Hôtel **2**

Wanderlust
& Nüba **7**

Nightlife A to Z

Dance Clubs

★★ Batofar BIBLIOTHEQUE At this hip club, on a converted barge on the Seine, the rotating DJs attract hundreds of 20- and 30-somethings. In the summer, the quayside turns into an extension of the boat, with food, a bar, and deck chairs. *11 quai François Mauriac, 13th.* ☎ *09-71-25-50-61. www.bato far.org. Cover free–15€. Métro: Quai de la Gare. Map p 118.*

Caveau de la Huchette LATIN QUARTER This rocking club has an emphasis on good times and loud funk, jazz, and classic swing; the crowd tends to be in their 30s and older. *5 rue de la Huchette, 5th.* ☎ *01-43-26-65-05. www.caveau delahuchette.fr. Cover 10€–15€. Métro: St-Michel. Map p 118.*

★★ Le Cartel Club CHAMPS ELYSEES This uber-trendy, Mexican-themed club drips in shabby-chic style and serves 30 tequilas at the bar. Music-wise, hip hop and deep house draw a stream of fashionistas, so book a table if you want to get in; the bouncers are notoriously difficult. *4 rue Arsène Houssaye, 8th.* ☎ *06-43-74-53-39. www.cartelclubparis.com. Cover free. Métro/RER: Charles de Gaulle-Etoile. Map p 115.*

Le Showcase CHAMPS ELYSEES Underneath pont Alexandre III, inside an old boat hangar, this happening club packs in the young and energetic for nightly shows by French and international rock, pop, and electro bands. There are DJ nights with renowned names, too. *Pont Alexandre III, 8th.* ☎ *01-45-61-25-43/resa@ showcase.fr. www.showcase.fr. Cover up to 20€. Métro: Champs-Elysées Clémenceau. Map p 115.*

★★ Le Social Club BOURSE This funky club is where the serious French electronic music and techno lovers go. Internationally acclaimed producers and DJs splice the night, and live bands occasionally pump things up. *142 rue de Montmartre, 2nd.* ☎ *01-40-28-05-55. www.paris socialclub.com. Cover free–20€. Métro: Bourse or Grands Boulevards. Map p 116.*

★★ Machine du Moulin Rouge MONTMARTRE Set in the night-club adjoining Paris's most famous cabaret, this is the latest hot spot for electronic music lovers. Expect DJ sets by famous names, a big dance floor, and youthful fauna soaking up the vibes. *90 bd. de Clichy, 18th.* ☎ *01-53-41-88-89. www.lamachine dumoulinrouge.com. Cover free–30€. Métro: Blanche. Map p 115.*

Queen CHAMPS ELYSEES This cheesy, very-late-night, gay-friendly club attracts a mixed crowd of corporate workers kicking back, ladies out for a night of dancing, and tourists in the know. International DJs regularly play, and it's one of the only places to provide clubbing every night of the week. *102 av. des Champs-Elysées, 8th.* ☎ *01-53-89-08-90. www.queen.fr. Cover free–20€. Métro: George-V. Map p 115.*

★★ Rex Club GRANDS BOULE-VARDS This place is known for its cutting-edge electronic music, with top DJs playing weekly and frequent free nights. Check local listings to see who's at the helm. *5 bd. Poisson-nière, 2nd.* ☎ *01-42-36-10-96. www. rexclub.com. Cover up to 20€. Métro: Bonne Nouvelle. Map p 116.*

★★ Wanderlust & Nüba AUS-TERLITZ The riverside Cité de la Mode et du Design (fashion and design school) now has two hip night venues: Quay-level Wander-lust is where stylish crowds gyrate

Nightlife Basics

Over the last 5 years, Paris's night-scene has exploded, from exclusive clubs headed by international DJs, to intimate speakeasies and inventive mixology cocktail bars. Many of the city's bars and cafes chip in, too, by staying open until 1 or 2am. If you plan to hit a trendy nightclub, you should know that most are open 11pm to 6am, and that Parisian bouncers—*physionomistes* (literally "face-checkers")—are extremely picky. Dress up, smile, and hope they let you in; or ensure entry the expensive way by reserving a table with bottle service, where you pay around 150€ for a bottle of champagne or a spirit.

The legal drinking age in France is 18. Expect to pay around 5€ for a glass of wine or 4€ for beer in a bar or café, and 13€ to 20€ for a cocktail. Drinks in nightclubs usually start at 10€.

to French touch electro, while top-deck Nüba offers panoramic views and a chill DJ beach hut. Make a night of it and dine at Wanderlust before you party. *32 & 36 quai d'Austerlitz, 13th.* ☎ *01-70-74-41-74 (Wanderlust restaurant; no phone in club) or* ☎ *01-76-77-34-85 (Nüba). www.wanderlustparis.com or www. lenuba.com. No cover. Métro/RER: Gare d'Austerlitz. Map p 118.*

Gay & Lesbian Bars & Clubs

3W Kafé MARAIS This fun lesbian bar offers a jam-packed program, from clubbing and karaoke, to lesbian movie screenings and burlesque cabaret nights. Men are welcome too, if they arrive with a woman. *8 rue des Ecouffes, 4th.* ☎ *01-48-87-39-26. www.facebook.com/3w. kafe. Métro: St. Paul. Map p 116.*

Le Tango (aka La Boîte à Frissons) REPUBLIQUE Open on weekends, this wacky, hetero-friendly gay and lesbian dance hall plays cheesy Madonna songs and accordion music alike. Couples practice dancing the foxtrot and tango early on, and then a DJ takes over and plays everything except techno. *13 rue au Maire, 2nd.*

☎ *01-42-72-17-78. www.boite-a-frissons.fr. Cover varies. Métro: Arts et Métiers. Map p 116.*

Mutinerie MARAIS More than just a party spot, this shabby LGBT bar acts as a local cafe, library, concert venue, and even a yoga center. DJs spin everything from ragga and pop to cool electro and rock. *176-178 rue St. Martin, 3rd.* ☎ *01-42-72-70-59. No cover. Métro: Rambuteau or Etienne Marcel; RER Châtelet-les-Halles. Map p 116.*

Open Café & Café Cox MARAIS This pair of gay men's bars includes two independent businesses, but there's so much traffic between them that they're often thought of as a single place. You'll find the most mixed gay crowd in Paris here. *15 & 17 rue des Archives, 4th. Open Café:* ☎ *01-42-72-26-18. www.opencafe.fr. Café Cox:* ☎ *01-42-72-08-00. www.cox.fr. Métro: Hôtel-de-Ville. Map p 116.*

Pubs & Bars

★ **Académie de la Bière** LATIN QUARTER This rustic-looking "academy of beer" can get downright raucous. Most of the beers on

Hemingway fans and expats flock to Harry's Bar, birthplace of the Sidecar.

tap come from Belgium. Soak it up with delicious *moules-frites*. *88 bd. de Port-Royal, 5th.* ☎ *01-43-54-66-65. www.academie-biere.com. RER: Port Royal. Map p 118.*

★★ Candelaria MARAIS What this tiny taqueria lacks in space it makes up for in trendiness—especially at night, when a young, hip crowd makes a beeline for the speakeasy-style cocktail bar hidden behind the tacos counter. Try—if you dare—the spicy *Guêpe Verte* (Green Wasp), made from Ocho Blanco tequila infused with hot pepper, coriander, cucumber, and lime. *52 rue de Saintonge, 3rd.* ☎ *01-42-74-41-28. www.candelariaparis.com. Métro: Filles du Calvaire. Map p 116.*

Chez Jeanette STRASBOURG-SAINT-DENIS The decor in this bar has changed little since the 1940s. Nowadays crowds of trendy 30-somethings lap up the cheap wine, while the occasional old regular sweeps in, Jack Russell in tow, oblivious to the change of clientele. *47 rue du Faubourg St-Denis, 10th.* ☎ *01-47-70-30-89. Métro: Strasbourg-St-Denis or Château Eau. Map p 116.*

★ Chez Prune CANAL SAINT-MARTIN This casual spot serves excellent, well-priced food, including some vegetarian dishes (from 13€), plus coffee, beer, and wine to local arty types and cool do-littlers

taking in the canal-side view. *36 rue Beaurepaire, 10th.* ☎ *01-42-41-30-47. Métro: République. Map p 116.*

★★ Gossima Ping Pong Bar NORTHEAST PARIS Set in a converted garage, this quirky, vintage-style bar is the only place in Paris you can drink cocktails and play ping pong at the same time. With two floors of tables, a thrashing sound system, and an all-round jovial atmosphere, it's a top spot for a night out with friends. *4 rue Victor Gelez, 11th.* ☎ *01-48-07-43-35. www.facebook.com/GossimaPing PongBar. Métro: Père Lachaise or Rue Saint-Maur. Map p 116.*

★★★ Harry's Bar OPERA This place is sacred to Hemingway disciples as the place where he and the rest of the ambulance corps drank themselves silly during the Spanish Civil War. The White Lady and the Sidecar were both invented here. A pianist plays in the cellar; the area upstairs is somewhat less sophisticated. Filled with expats, this place is more fun than you might think. *5 rue Daunou, 2nd.* ☎ *01-42-61-71-14. www.harrysbar.fr. Métro: Opéra or Pyramides. Map p 116.*

★★ La Palette ST-GERMAIN-DES-PRES This is a favorite rendezvous for students from the nearby fine-arts school. It's also rather romantic (especially the fresco-painted back room). A drink here means following in the steps

The decor of Chez Jeanette, in the 10th arrondissement, is vintage 1940s.

Don't miss the frescoes in the back room of La Palette.

of Ernest Hemingway and Jim Morrison. A handy base for exploring Saint-Germain's art galleries. *43 rue de Seine, 6th.* ☎ *01-43-26-68-15. Métro: Odéon. Map p 118.*

★★ **Le Ballroom** PALAIS-ROYAL/ LES HALLES After a juicy steak in the upstairs Beef Club, descend the "secret" staircase for a soirée in one of the city's best underground cocktail bars. It feels as though you've stepped into a speakeasy, with dark lighting and vintage decor (not to mention the Mafia-like bouncers). Expect well-mixed drinks. *58 rue Jean-Jacques Rousseau, 1st.* ☎ *09-52-52-89-34. www. eccbeefclub.com. Métro: Louvre-Rivoli or Les Halles. Map p 116.*

★★★ **Le Bar de L'Hôtel** ST-GERMAIN-DES-PRES This wee hotel bar is appropriately theatrical (a Victorian color scheme, baroque touches) when you consider that its regulars tend to be in the film industry—or want to be. This was the hotel where Oscar Wilde died, impoverished and alone; it's a lovely historic place for a drink and a ponder. *13 rue des Beaux-Arts, 6th.* ☎ *01-44-41-99-00. www.l-hotel. com. Métro: St-Germain-des-Prés. Map p 118.*

★★★ **Le Coq** REPUBLIQUE Darkly lit, with 70s-style touches, this trendsetting mixology cocktail

bar has made a name for itself by reviving old-fashioned French spirits like *Chartreuse* and daring to mix "pure" French products like cognac with "lower-grade" alcohols like cider. When you fancy a nibble, croque monsieurs and cheese platters are at hand to soak everything up. *12 rue du Château d'Eau, 10th.* ☎ *01-42-40-85-68. Métro: Jacques Bonsergent or République. Map p 116.*

★ **Le Forum** MADELEINE This smart, business-crowd favorite is like a London private club—all oak paneling, single malts, and brass. On the drinks menu (aside from the *digestifs*) are delicious cocktails, such as the French Cup (champagne, elderflower liqueur, lime juice, and violet syrup). *4 bd. Malesherbes, 8th.* ☎ *01-42-65-37-86. www.bar-le-forum.com. Métro: Madeleine. Map p 115.*

★★ **Paname Brewing Company** CANAL SAINT-MARTIN Set in a converted 19th-century warehouse, this hip waterside joint serves five beers that it brews on-site. Choices range from the refreshing, amber-hued *Barge du Canal* to the *Bête Noire* (aka Black Beast), a delicious dark ale with a licorice/caramel finish. *41 bis Quai de la Loire, 19th.* ☎ *01-40-36-43-55. Métro: Laumière or Ourcq. Map p 116.*

★★ **Rosa Bonheur** NORTHEAST Smack bang in the un-touristy Parc des Buttes Chaumont (a beautiful urban park set in former quarries), this is where those in-the-know come for after-hour drinking and partying. It's magical looking out across the moonlit park, drink in hand, with nothing but the rustling of trees (and like-minded Parisians) for company. *2 alléé de la Cascade, 19th; after dark enter at 7 rue Botzaris, opposite no. 74.* ☎ *01-42-00-00-45. www.rosabonheur.fr. Métro: Botzaris or Jourdain. Map p 116.*

Wine Bars

★ **Au Sauvignon** ST-GERMAIN-DES-PRES This tiny bar has tables overflowing onto the terrace, where a cheerful crowd downs wines ranging from cheap Beaujolais to the pricey Grand Crus. *80 rue des St-Pères, 7th. ☎ 01-45-48-49-02. Métro: Sèvres-Babylone. Map p 118.*

★ **Caves Legrand** BOURSE Nestled in the chocolate-box Passage Vivienne (a covered passage), this old-world wine shop doubles as a bar, a delicatessen, and a bookshop. Excellent seasonal menus for food and wine pairings complete the offering. *1 rue de la Banque, 2nd. ☎ 01-42-60-07-12. www.caves-legrand.com. Métro: Bourse. Map p 116.*

★★ **Fish la Boissonerie** SAINT-GERMAIN International, after-work crowds pile into this playful wine bar–cum–restaurant, for a glass of something tasty and an excellent fish-focused menu. Sidle up to the bar, or opt for a sit-down dinner—either way, you're in for a treat. *69 rue de Seine, 6th. ☎ 01-43-54-34-69. Métro: Saint Germain des Prés. Map p 118.*

★★ **Frenchie Bar à Vin** SENTIER Off the beaten tourist track north of Les Halles, this adorable wine bar belongs to Frenchie, the acclaimed restaurant over the road (see p 109). Fans come for French wine for every budget and delicious small tasting menus. Get here early if you

Le Ballroom is a speakeasy-style cocktail lounge underneath the Beef Club.

The historic Bar de L'Hôtel.

don't want to queue; no reservations. *6 rue du Nil, 2nd. ☎ 01-40-39-96-10. www.frenchie-restaurant. com. Métro: Sentier or Réamur Sebastopol. Map p 116.*

★ **Juveniles** BOURSE This sleek place with a trendy crowd prides itself on its enormous wine cellar with labels from around the world. *47 rue des Richelieu, 1st. ☎ 01-42-97-46-49. Métro: Palais Royal. Map p 116.*

La Belle Hortense MARAIS The fact that this quirky bar has a bookshop within its walls makes it a perpetual favorite for bookish wine lovers. *31 vieille du Temple, 4th. ☎ 01-48-04-71-60. www.cafeine.com. Métro: Hôtel-de-Ville. Map p 116.*

★★ **Le Baron Rouge** BASTILLE Be prepared to fight for elbow room at this popular locals' haunt (opposite the Aligre market), where excellent wine is sold by the glass and drunk on wine barrels posing as tables. Grab a plate of charcuterie or oysters (when in season). *1 rue Théophile-Roussel, 12th. ☎ 01-42-72-76-85. Métro: St-Paul. Map p 116.*

★★ **Les Bacchantes** MADELEINE This place, just down the road from Printemps department store, is a top spot for a post-shopping tipple. Around 50 wines grace the board and exposed beams add character. *21 rue Caumartin, 9th. ☎ 01-42-65-25-35. www.lesbacchantes.fr. Métro: Opéra or Madeleine. Map p 115.* ●

Arts & Entertainment **Best Bets**

Best **Theater for Musicals**
★★★ Théâtre du Châtelet, *1 place du Châtelet, 1st (p 134)*

Best **Place to Walk in the Phantom's Footsteps**
★★★ Opéra Garnier, *Place de l'Opéra, 9th (p 133)*

Best **Place to Hear Classical Music**
★★★ Philharmonie de Paris, *221 avenue Jean-Jaurès, 19th (p 133)*

Best **Theater**
★ Comédie Française, *Place Colette, 1st (p 134)*

Best **Drag Show**
★ Cabaret Michou, *80 rue des Martyrs, 18th (p 129)*

Best **Place to Hear Modern French Chanson**
★ Les Trois Baudets, *64 bd. de Clichy, 18th (p 131)*

Best **Place to See Dance**
★ Théâtre National de Chaillot, *1 place du Trocadéro, 16th (p 133)*

Best **Chic Cabaret**
★★ Lido, *116 bis av. des Champs-Elysées, 8th (p 129)*

Best **Place for 20-Somethings**
★★ La Flèche d'Or, *102 bis rue de Bagnolet, 20th (p 130)*

Best **Place to See a Movie**
★ La Pagode, *57bis rue de Babylone, 7th (p 134)*

Best **Overall Jazz Club**
★★★ Duc des Lombards, *42 rue des Lombards, 1st (p 130)*

Best **Nouvelle Orleans Jazz**
★★★ Le Sunset/Le Sunside, *60 rue des Lombards, 1st (p 131)*

Best **Live Music with Your Meal**
★★ La Bellevilloise, *19–21 rue Boyer, 20th (p 130)*

Best **Indie Rock Concerts**
★ La Boule Noire, *120 bd. de Rochechouart, 18th (p 130)*

Below: The Opéra Bastille was inaugurated in 1989 for the Revolution's bicentennial. Previous page: The ornate ceiling of the Opéra Garnier.

Right Bank (8th & 18th)

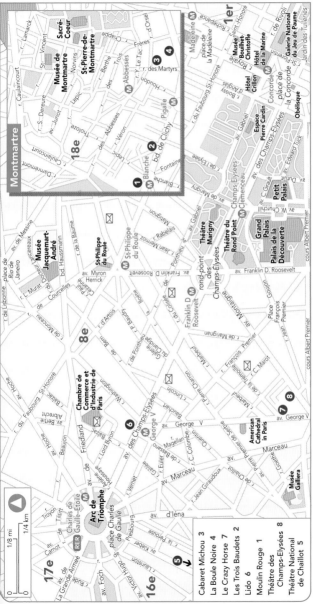

Montmartre

Cabaret Michou 3
La Boule Noire 4
Le Crazy Horse 7
Les Trois Baudets 2
Lido 6
Moulin Rouge 1
Théâtre des
Champs-Elysées 8
Théâtre National
de Chaillot 5

Right Bank & Left Bank

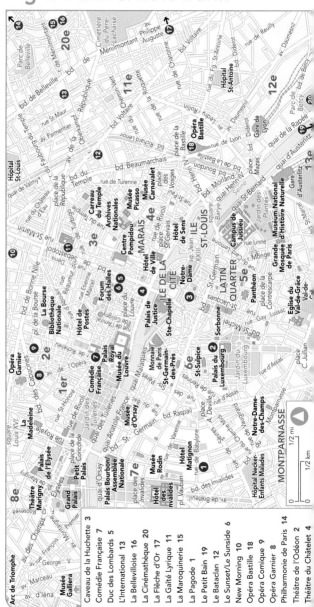

Arts & Entertainment A to Z

Cabarets

★ **Cabaret Michou** PIGALLE
This eccentric place is run by a veteran impresario whose 20 cross-dressing belles lip-sync to Whitney Houston and Mireille Mathieu while wearing bizarre costumes. If you don't have dinner, you must stand at the bar and pay a compulsory 40€ for your first drink. *80 rue des Martyrs, 18th.* ☎ *01-46-06-16-04. www.michou.com. Cover including dinner (not drinks) & show 110€–140€. Métro: Pigalle. Map p 127.*

★ **Le Crazy Horse** CHAMPS ELYSEES   This sophisticated joint's nude revue thrives on genuinely good choreography and the beauty of the women, who dance dressed in little more than light. Not surprisingly, it's popular with businessmen, but women too will be surprised at how mesmerizing the show is. *12 av. George-V, 8th.* ☎ *01-47-23-32-32. www.lecrazyhorseparis.com. Reservations recommended. Cover including 2 drinks per person 125€, show only 105€. Dining options available. Métro: George-V or Alma-Marceau. Map p 127.*

★★ **Lido** CHAMPS ELYSEES   This glossy club puts on multimillion-euro performances in a dramatic reworking of the classic Parisian cabaret show, with special effects, including aerial and aquatic ballets—even an occasional ice rink. *116 bis av. des Champs-Elysées, 8th.* ☎ *01-40-76-56-10. www.lido.fr. Show w/half bottle champagne per person from 115€, dinner & show 165€–400€. Métro: George-V. Map p 127.*

★ **Moulin Rouge** MONTMARTRE Toulouse-Lautrec immortalized this windmill-topped building and its scantily clad cancan dancers (this is where the risqué dance was invented). Today, it's true to its original theme and very cheesy, but the dancing is perfectly synchronized, and the girls are all beautiful. *Place Blanche, 18th.* ☎ *01-53-09-82-82. www.moulinrouge.fr. Show only from 87€, show & half bottle champagne from 210€, dinner & show 190€–420€. Métro: Blanche. Map p 127.*

Jazz, Rock & More
★ **Caveau de la Huchette** LATIN QUARTER   This celebrated

The windmill atop the Moulin Rouge is a landmark in Montmartre.

La Bellevilloise is an entertainment emporium housing multiple venues.

jazz and swing cave draws a young crowd, mostly university students, who dance to the music of well-known jazz combos. Robespierre hung out here in his time, so you can tell everyone you're here for the history. *5 rue de la Huchette, 5th.* ☎ *01-43-26-65-05. www.cave audelahuchette.fr. Cover 13€–15€. Métro: St-Michel. RER: St-Michel-Notre-Dame. Map p 128.*

★★★ Duc des Lombards

CHATELET This thriving jazz club has seen all the greats of Paris's jazz era pass through its doors. Today, it features performances nightly that range in style from free jazz to hard bop. Tables can be reserved, and meals (prepared with mostly fair-trade produce) are served. *42 rue des Lombards, 1st.* ☎ *01-42-33-22-88. www.ducdeslombards.com. Cover varies. Métro: Châtelet. Map p 128.*

★★ La Bellevilloise

MENILM-ONTANT This multidisciplinary venue (set inside France's first cooperative building) has several bars, two restaurants, a nightclub, an exhibition space, and a concert hall where some of Paris's most exciting bands have been launched. It's a place to relax, soak up the atmosphere, and spend the whole evening. *19–21 rue Boyer, 20th.* ☎ *01-46-36-07-07. www.labellevillo ise.com. Cover varies. Metro: Gambetta, or Ménilmontant. Map p 128.*

★ La Boule Noire

PIGALLE The Black Ball is one of those intimate, divey Parisian haunts that attract such biggies as the Dandy Warhols, Metallica, Cat Power, Franz Ferdinand, and Jamie Cullum. Despite the star-studded lineup, the cover tends to hover around the 22€ mark, making this one of the cheapest venues around. *120 bd. Rochech-ouart, 75018.* ☎ *01-49-25-81-75. www.laboule-noire.fr. Cover varies. Metro: Anvers or Pigalle. Map p 128.*

★★ La Flèche d'Or

PERE LACHAISE This funky rock, indie, and electro venue not only has highly credible acts (from both France and abroad), and it has the advantage of being set in a unique building—a former train station with a room that hangs over the tracks. A popular choice for trendy music buffs. *102 bis rue de Bagnolet, 20th.* ☎ *01-44-64-01-02. www.flech edor.fr. Cover varies. Métro: Alexan-dre-Dumas. Map p 128.*

★★ La Gaité Lyrique

HAUT MARAIS For those into digital art and off-beat culture, this former opera house (where Offenbach cre-ated the operetta genre) is a show-case for emerging digital art forms. After visiting the art installations, you can frequently attend an elec-tronic pop/rock concert in the Grand Salle, where the walls are made of giant speakers. *3 bis rue Papin, 3rd.*

☎ 01-53-01-51-51. www.gaite-lyrique.net. Cover varies. Métro: Réamur-Sébastopol. Map p 128.

Le Bataclan REPUBLIQUE This 1864 music hall was at the center of the tragic November 2015 terrorist attacks in Paris. At press time, future plans for the venue were unclear, but it's long been a flagship of Paris's music scene. Check the website for updates. 50 bd. Voltaire, 11th. ☎ 01-43-14-00-30. www.le-bataclan.com. Cover varies. Métro: Oberkampf. Map p 128.

★ Le Petit Bain BIBLIOTHEQUE This wooden and chartreuse rectangle, floating on the Seine, is one of the city's best concert venues, with a stream of up-and-coming bands and a handful of well-known French musicians. Dine in the restaurant beforehand or sip a cool *bière* on the upper terrace. Then watch Paris's lights reflect like diamonds on the water. 7 port de la Gare, 13th. ☎ 01-43-49-68-92. www.petitbain. org. Cover varies. Métro: Quai de la Gare. Map p 128.

★ Les Trois Baudets PIGALLE Between 1947 and 1966, this small theater launched more musical

careers than anywhere else (Gainsbourg, Brel, and Henri Salvador all started here). Nowadays it's Paris's main francophone music theater, with a jam-packed program of rock, electro, folk, *chanson*, and slam poetry. 64 bd. de Clichy, 18th. ☎ 01-42-62-33-33. www.lestroisbaudets.com. Cover varies. Metro: Pigalle. Map p 127.

★★★ Le Sunset/Le Sunside CHÂTELET This staple of the Parisian jazz circuit is two bars in one, with separate jazz shows going on simultaneously. The look is minimalist, and artists are both European and U.S.-based. Le Sunside favors classic jazz, and Le Sunset goes for electric jazz and world music. Take your pick. 60 rue des Lombards, 1st. ☎ 01-40-26-46-60. www.sunset-sunside.com. Cover varies. Métro: Châtelet. Map p 128.

L'International OBERKAMPF Arty types flock to this grungy bar for its winning formula of cheap beer and free live music. A stream of on-the-up bands play here, making it a great joint in which to spot the talent of the future and get familiar with Paris's electro-rock

Best Free Shows in Paris

As you stroll along the river, keep your eyes peeled for free entertainment by street performers. In the summer, the area at the southeastern tip of the Île de la Cité, behind Notre-Dame, becomes a stage of sorts when performance artists, musicians, and jugglers put on a show against the backdrop of the cathedral. Notre-Dame itself also often hosts free classical music concerts—as do other churches, from quaint neighborhood chapels to icons like Saint-Germain-des-Prés. The cultural website L'Officiel du Spectacles lists free recitals (in French; www.offi.fr). Or for something hip, cross the Périphérique and go to Glazart (7-15 ave Porte de la Villette, 19th; ☎ 01-40-36-55-65; www.glazart.com). Set in a former bus station, this funky venue turns its front lot into a fake beach each summer, and offers free techno, indie, pop, and rock concerts.

Buying Tickets

The easiest way to get tickets nowadays is online, in advance, from the venue's website. If you're staying in a first-class hotel, your concierge can probably arrange your tickets, too. A service fee may be added, but you won't waste precious sightseeing hours securing hard-to-get tickets.

Cheaper tickets, with discounts of up to 50%, can be found at the **Kiosque Théâtre,** 15 place de la Madeleine, 8th (no phone; www.kiosquetheatre.com; Métro: Madeleine). It offers leftover tickets at about half-price on performance day. Tickets are sold Tuesday to Saturday from 12:30 to 8pm and Sunday from 2 to 8pm. Students with ID can often get last-minute tickets by inquiring at the box office an hour before curtain time.

If you haven't left for Paris yet and are having trouble getting advance tickets for cabaret performances, check with **Keith Prowse** (www.keithprowse.com). The company will mail tickets to you or leave tickets at the box office for pickup prior to the performance. There's a markup of about 25% over box-office prices on each ticket, which includes handling charges. Keith Prowse sells to customers all over the world, including the U.S., Canada, the U.K., Australia, and New Zealand. Another good place to try is any branch of the **FNAC** media store (or www.fnac.com). It handles tickets for most museums, concerts, and shows across France. The Champs Elysées branch is open until midnight (p 88).

---

scene. *5–7 rue Moret, 11th.* ☎ *01-49-29-76-45. www.linternational.fr. No cover. Métro: Menilmontant. Map p 128.*

Maroquinerie BELLEVILLE Up-and-coming rock acts take center stage at this hip concert venue, which doubles as a restaurant, bar, and literary cafe. You can easily spend the whole night here. *23 rue Boyer, 20th.* ☎ *01-40-33-35-05. www.lamaroquinerie.fr. Cover varies. Métro: Ménilmontant or Gambetta. Map p 128.*

★ **New Morning** EASTERN PARIS Jazz fanatics pack this respected club to drink, talk, and dance, not to mention check each other out—this is one of the city's "it" places to see and be seen. Such celebs as

Spike Lee and Prince have been spotted here. The club is popular with African and European musicians. *7–9 rue des Petites-Ecuries, 10th.* ☎ *01-45-23-51-41. www.new morning.com. Cover varies. Métro: Château d'Eau. Map p 128.*

Opera, Dance & Classical
★★★ **Opéra Bastille** BAS-TILLE This huge, contemporary building hosts outstanding opera performances, such as Mozart's *Marriage of Figaro* and Tchaikovsky's *Queen of Spades,* in its three concert halls. Symphony and dance performances are held here occasionally as well. *2 place de la Bastille, 4th.* ☎ *08-92-89-90-90. www.operadeparis.fr. Tickets 10€–210€. Métro: Bastille. Map p 128.*

★★ Opéra Comique BOURSE
Come to this charming venue, built in the 1880s, for light opera on a smaller scale than at the city's major opera houses. It's a lovely place to see *Carmen*, *Don Giovanni*, or *Tosca*. **Note:** Closed for renovations until end of 2016. *5 rue Favart, 2nd.* ☎ *08-25-01-01-23. www.opera-comique.com. Tickets 15€–100€. Métro: Richelieu-Drouot. Map p 128.*

Theater Tip

Many theaters are closed over the summer, so check beforehand to avoid disappointment. Also, where possible make advance reservations: Parisians are enthusiastic theatergoers, and tickets can go like hotcakes.

★★★ Opéra Garnier OPERA
The Phantom did his fictional haunting here. Now the opera house is home to the city's ballet scene, although it still hosts opera from time to time. Charles Garnier's 1875 building is a rococo wonder with a ceiling painted by Chagall. There are even beehives on the roof, which produce the Opéra honey for sale in the shop. *Place de l'Opéra, 9th.* ☎ *08-92-89-90-90. www.operadeparis.fr. Tickets* 10€–210€. *Métro: Opéra, RER: Auber. Map p 128.*

★★★ Philharmonie de Paris
VILLETTE   This multimillion-euro structure and its gargantuan annex (the former Cité de la Musique) house a state-of-the-art concert hall, libraries, and a museum on musical instruments across the ages. It has an eclectic program, ranging from Baroque quartets to symphonic orchestras, opera recitals, and jazz ensembles—all big names. *221 avenue Jean-Jaurès, 19th.* ☎ *01-44-84-44-84. www.philharmoniedeparis.fr. Tickets 10€–196€. Métro: Porte de Pantin. Map p 128.*

Théâtre des Champs-Elysées
CHAMPS ELYSEES   National and international orchestras (such as the Vienna Philharmonic) fill this Art Deco theater with sound, to the delight of its well-dressed audiences. *15 av. Montaigne, 8th.* ☎ *01-49-52-50-50. www.theatrechampselysees.fr. Tickets 10€–115€. Métro: Alma–Marceau. Map p 127.*

★ Théâtre National de Chaillot
TROCADERO   In the sumptuous, Art Deco Palais de Chaillot, this contemporary dance theater offers a consistently excellent, avant-garde program of contemporary dance

Indie bands are the staple fare at La Flèche d'Or, in the 20th arrondissement.

An art instillation at La Gaîté Lyrique.

and theater. It also provides some of the city's most breathtaking Eiffel Tower views from its bar and restaurant, where you can eat before the show. *1 place du Trocadéro, 16th.* ☎ *01-53-65-31-00. www.theatre-chaillot.fr. Tickets 35€–39€. Métro: Trocadéro. Map p 127.*

Theater & Musicals

★ **Comédie Française** PALAIS ROYAL Those with even a modest understanding of French will enjoy a sparkling production at this national theater, where the main goal is to keep the classics alive while promoting contemporary authors. *Place Colette, 1st.* ☎ *01-44-58-15-15. www.comedie-francaise.fr. Tickets 10€–70€. Métro: Palais Royal–Musée du Louvre. Map p 128.*

★ **Théâtre de l'Odéon** ODEON More than just a theater, the Odéon hosts debates on literature, philosophy, and European politics. On stage, quality plays are produced in different European languages, including (occasionally) English. *Place de l'Odéon, 6th.* ☎ *01-44-85-40-40. www.*

theatre-odeon.fr. Tickets 14€–40€. Métro: Odéon. Map p 128.

★★★ **Théâtre du Châtelet** CHÂTELET This Belle Epoque masterpiece is the only place in Paris to perform Broadway standard musicals in English with full orchestras and parts sung by some of the world's best artists. Previous triumphs have included *Sweeney Todd* and *The Sound of Music.* The program is completed with top-notch classical concerts, opera, and dance. *1 place du Châtelet, 1st.* ☎ *01-40-28-28-40. www.chatelet-theatre.com. Tickets 20€–110€. Métro/RER: Châtelet. Map p 128.*

Film

★ **La Cinémathèque** BERCY In a quirky, cruise-ship inspired building designed by Frank Gehry, you can retrace the history of cinema in the museum (home to the *Metropolis* robot) and then take in a movie. The center is known for holding fabulous retrospectives on master filmmakers. *51 rue de Bercy, 12th.* ☎ *01-71-19-33-33. www.cinematheque.fr. Tickets museum 5€, museum & movie 8€. Métro: Bercy. Map p 128.*

★ **La Pagode** INVALIDES In a 19th-century pagoda, this photogenic movie theater's main screening room is adorned in silk and ornate sculpted woodwork. It's a sumptuous, old-world spot for both art-house and "grand-public" movies (mostly in VO or original language—including English), and there's a tiny Japanese garden with seating. *57 bis rue de Babylone, 7th.* ☎ *01-45-55-48-48. www.etoile-cinemas.com. Tickets 9.80€ Métro: St-François-Xavier. Map p 128.* ●

9 The Best **Lodging**

Lodging **Best Bets**

Best **Budget Sleep**
★ Le Vert Galant $ 43 rue Croule-barbe, 13th (p 148)

Best **for Swimming**
★★ Molitor by Mgallery $$$ 3 rue Nungesser et Coli, 16th (p 149)

Best **Boutique Hotel**
★ L'Hôtel $$$$ 13 rue des Beaux-Arts, 6th (p 148)

Best **Kid-Friendly Hotel**
★★ Hôtel Lion d'Or $$ 5 rue de la Sourdière, 1st (p 145)

Coolest Hostel
★ Generator Hostel $ 11 place du Colonel Fabien, 10th (p 142)

Best **Luxury Hotel**
★★★ Hôtel Shangri-Là $$$$$ 10 av. d'Iéna, 16th (p 146)

Best **21st-Century Luxury**
★★★ Les Bains Paris $$$$$ 7 rue du Bourg-l'Abbé, 3rd (p 148)

Best **Hip Hotel**
★★ Mama Shelter $$ 107 rue de Bagnolet, 20th (p 148)

Best **Eco-Friendly Hotel**
★★★ Solar Hôtel $ 22 rue Boulard, 14th (p 150)

Best **Family-Run Hôtel**
★★★ Hôtel Louison $$$ 105 rue de Vaugirard, 6th (p 145)

Best **"Only in Paris" Hideaway**
★★★ Pension les Marronniers $$ 78 rue d'Assas, 6th (p 149)

Best **Place to Detox**
★ Hôtel Gabriel $$$ 25 rue du Grand Prieuré, 11th (p 145)

Best **for Cocktail Lovers**
★★ Grand Pigalle Hotel $$$ 29 rue Victor Massé, 9th (p 142)

Best **Value B&B**
52 Clichy $$ 52 rue de Clichy, 9th (p 149)

Lodging Tip

From world-class palaces to tiny B&Bs, Paris has it all—except huge rooms (unless you fork out for a suite). Many hotels are in historic buildings that cannot be changed structurally, so rooms are generally "cozy." Price-wise, always look for Internet discounts on the hotels' own websites; hit the right dates and you can sometimes get up to 50% off. Discount travel sites, such as www.booking.com, www.expedia.com, and www.venere.com, also offer deals on select hotels. Prices vary with the season. August (low season) is usually cheapest; the rest of the year fluctuates, peaking during trade fairs and fashion week (check dates at www.fashionweekdates.com). When choosing your hotel, here's a brief guide to the arrondissements (districts): Postcodes are from 75001 to 75020. Areas 1 (75001) to 8 (75008) are very central; 9 to 11 and 17 to 20 are the city's up-and-coming, trendy areas; and 12 to 16 are largely residential but have plenty of atmosphere. Arrondissement 13 contains the city's main Chinese neighborhood.

Previous page: Spectacular views from the Shangri La Hotel.

Right Bank (8th & 16th–18th)

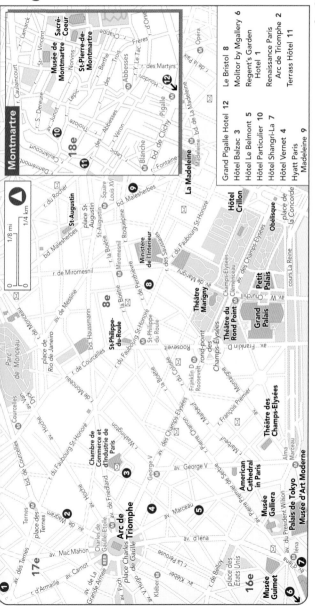

Grand Pigalle Hotel **12**
Hôtel Balzac **3**
Hôtel Le Belmont **5**
Hôtel Particulier **10**
Hôtel Shangri-La **7**
Hôtel Vernet **4**
Hyatt Paris
Madeleine **9**

Le Bristol **8**
Molitor by Mgallery **6**
Regent's Garden
Hotel **1**
Renaissance Paris
Arc de Triomphe **2**
Terrass Hôtel **11**

Right Bank (1st–4th & 9th–11th)

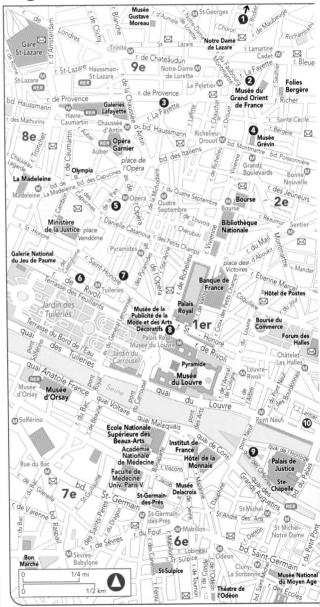

r. de Amsterdam
Londres
r. de Clichy
r. Blanche
Musée Gustave Moreau
r. d'Aumale
r. de Notre-Dame de Lorette
St-Georges
Choron
r. Rodier
r. de Maubeuge
Rochambeau
❶

Gare St-Lazare
r. de Rome
r. St-Lazare
r. d'Amsterdam
Trinité
Lazare
r. de Chateâudun
Notre Dame de Lazare
Lamartine
La Fayette
Cadet
Saulnier
r. Bleue

St-Lazare RER
r. de Provence
Haussman-St-Lazare RER
9e
Notre-Dame de Lorette
Le Peletier
du Faubourg Montmartre
Musée du Grand Orient de France
❷
Folies Bergère
Richer

bd. Haussmann
r. des Mathurins
r. de Provence
Galeries Lafayette
Havre-Caumartin RER
Chaussée d'Antin
La Fayette
Laffitte
Le Peletier
Chauchat
Richelieu-Drouot
Sainte-Cecile
Bergère
Musée Grévin
❹

8e
r. Tronchet
r. de Caumartin
Auber
bd. Haussmann
Auber RER
Opéra Garnier
Auber
bd. des Italiens
Richelieu
Vivienne
bd. Montmartre
bd. Poissonnière
Bonne Nouvelle

Chauveau Lagarde
Olympia
place de l'Opéra
Grands Boulevards
r. des Jeûneurs
2e

La Madeleine
Madeleine
La Madeleine
bd. de la Madeleine
bd. des Capucines
av. de l'Opéra
Opéra
r. de la Michodière
du Quatre Septembre
Bourse
Bourse
r. Réaumur
Sentier

Ministère de la Justice
place Vendôme
r. des Capucines
❺
Quatre Septembre
de Louvois
r. Chérubini
Bibliothèque Nationale
r. du Mail

Galerie National du Jeu de Paume
r. de Castiglione
r. Saint-Honoré
r. Danielle Casanova
r. des Petits Champs
Vivienne
place des Victoires
r. d'Aboukir
Mandar

❻
r. de Rivoli
Tuileries
❼
r. des Pyramides
Ste-Anne
r. de Richelieu
Banque de France
Etienne Marcel
r. Coquillère
Hôtel de Postes
r. du Jour

Jardin des Tuileries
Terrasse des Feuillants
Terrasse du Bord de l'Eau
quai des Tuileries
av. du Général Lemonnier
Musée de la Publicité de la Mode et des Arts Décoratifs
❽
Palais Royal
Palais Royal-Musée du Louvre
1er
r. de Rivoli
r. Croix des Petits Champs
r. de Valois
r. du Louvre
Bourse du Commerce
Forum des Halles
Châtelet-Les Halles

quai Anatole France
pont Solférino
Seine
pont Royal
Jardin du Carrousel
Pyramide
Musée du Louvre
r. de l'Amiral de Coligny
Louvre-Rivoli
r. de l'Arbre
Pont Neuf
r. des Bourdonnais
r. J. Lantier
❿

Musée d'Orsay
Musée d'Orsay
quai Voltaire
pont du Carrousel
quai du
Louvre
pont des Arts
Pont Neuf

Solférino
r. du Bac
r. de Beaune
Ecole Nationale Supérieure des Beaux-Arts
Académie Nationale de Médecine
Institut de France
Hôtel de la Monnaie
quai de Conti
quai des Grands Augustins
quai de l'Horloge
Palais de Justice
❾
Ste-Chapelle

Rue du Bac
r. de Bac
r. de Grenelle
7e
r. St-Guillaume
bd. St-Germain
r. Bonaparte
r. Visconti
r. Jacob
Faculté de Médecine Univ. Paris V
St-Germain-des-Prés
Musée Delacroix
r. Mazarine
r. Dauphine
St-André des Arts
St-Michel RER
St-Michel-Notre Dame
r. du Petit Pont

r. de Varenne
bd. Raspail
r. des Saints-Pères
r. du Dragon
St-Germain-des-Prés
r. de Seine
Mabillon
Odéon
bd. Saint-Germain
Danton

Bon Marché
Sèvres-Babylone
r. de Sèvres
r. du Four
6e
r. du Mabillon
r. des Canettes
St-Sulpice
r. Lobineau
St-Sulpice
r. de Tournon
Odéon
Cluny-La Sorbonne
r. des Ecoles
Musée National du Moyen Age

0 ___ 1/4 mi
0 ___ 1/2 km
⬆
r. de Condé
r. de l'Odéon
Théâtre de l'Odéon
bd. Saint-Michel
r. Férou

Generator Hostel 16
Hôtel Amour 1
Hôtel Banke 3
Hôtel Britannique 10
Hôtel Chopin 4
Hôtel du Bourg Tibourg 12

Hôtel du Louvre 8
Hôtel Duo 13
Hôtel Eugène en Ville 2
Hôtel Gabriel 17
Hôtel Henri IV 9
Hôtel Lion d'Or 7
Hôtel Meurice 6
Hôtel Saint-Louis en l'Isle 11
Hôtel Westminster 5
Les Bains Paris 14
Mama Shelter 18
Providence 15
St-Christopher's Inn 16

Left Bank (5th–7th, 13th)

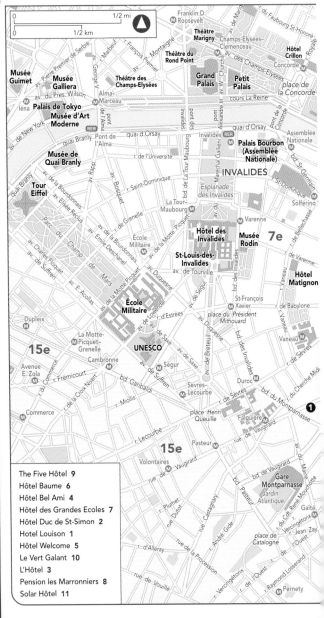

The Five Hôtel **9**
Hôtel Baume **6**
Hôtel Bel Ami **4**
Hôtel des Grandes Ecoles **7**
Hôtel Duc de St-Simon **2**
Hotel Louison **1**
Hôtel Welcome **5**
Le Vert Galant **10**
L'Hôtel **3**
Pension les Marronniers **8**
Solar Hôtel **11**

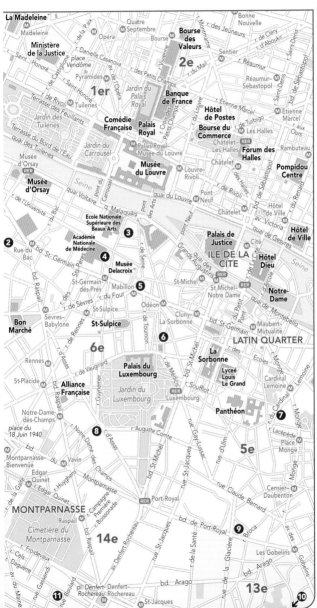

La Madeleine
Madeleine M
Ministère
de la Justice
r. St-Honoré
r. de Castiglione place
Vendôme
Quatre
Septembre M
Opéra M
Bourse M
r. Danielle Casanova
Pyramides M
r. St-Honoré
Tuileries M
r. de Rivoli
Terrasse des Feuillants
Jardin des
Tuileries
Terrasse du Bord de l'Eau
quai des Tuileries
Musée
d'Orsay
RER
Musée
d'Orsay
r. de l'Université
bd. St-Germain
r. du
Bac
Rue du
Bac M
Académie
Nationale
de Médecine
Musée
Delacroix
St-Germain-
des-Prés M
r. de Sèvres
Bon
Marché
Sèvres-
Babylone M
St-Placide M
Rennes M
Notre-Dame-
des-Champs M
place du
18 Juin 1940
Montparnasse-
Bienvenüe M
Edgar
Quinet M
MONTPARNASSE
Cimetière du
Montparnasse
r. Froidevaux
r. Cels
r. Daguerre
bd. Raspail
Denfert-
Rochereau M
Denfert-
Rochereau
St-Jacques M

2e
Bourse
des
Valeurs
Bonne
Nouvelle M
r. des Jeuneurs
r. de Cléry
r. d'Aboukir
Sentier M
r. Réaumur
Réaumur
r. du Mail
Réaumur-
Sébastopol M
1er
Banque
de France
Hôtel
de Postes
r. Etienne Marcel
Etienne
Marcel M
Comédie
Française
Palais
Royal
Bourse du
Commerce
de Turbigo
Les Halles M
Palais Royal-
Musée du Louvre M
Châtelet-
Les Halles RER
Forum des
Halles
Rambuteau M
Musée
du Louvre
Châtelet M
des Halles
Pompidou
Centre
quai du Louvre
Pont
Neuf
Louvre-
Rivoli M
r. de Rivoli
Hôtel
de Ville M
Hôtel
de Ville
Châtelet M
av. Victoria
quai de Gesvres
Hôtel
de Ville
Ecole Nationale
Supérieure des
Beaux Arts
Palais de
Justice
ILE DE LA
CITÉ
Cité M
Hôtel
Dieu
Seine
quai de la Tournelle
Notre-
Dame
St-Michel
Notre Dame RER
quai de Montebello
Musée
d'Orsay
St-Michel M
Maubert-
Mutualité M
Cluny-
La Sorbonne M
bd. St-Germain
LATIN QUARTER
Odéon M
r. des Ecoles
La
Sorbonne
r. Monge
6e
Palais du
Luxembourg
r. de Médicis
La
Sorbonne
Lycée
Louis
Le Grand
Cardinal
Lemoine M
Soufflot
Luxembourg RER
Panthéon
r. du Cardinal Lemoine
Alliance
Française
Jardin du
Luxembourg
r. Auguste Comte
r. Lacépède
Place
Monge M
5e
rue Gay-Lussac
rue d'Ulm
Censier-
Daubenton M
rue Claude-Bernard
Port-Royal RER
bd. de Port-Royal
r. de la Santé
r. Broca
Les Gobelins M
bd. Arago
13e
St-Sulpice
St-Sulpice M
Mabillon M
r. du Four
r. de Seine
r. de Tournon
Rue du
Bac
14e
Raspail M
Vavin M
r. Edgar Quinet
bd. du Montparnasse
bd. Raspail

❶ ❷ ❸ ❹ ❺ ❻ ❼ ❽ ❾ ❿ ⓫

Hotels A to Z

The Five Hôtel LATIN QUARTER
The fun rooms here are small but impressive, with Chinese lacquer, velvet fabrics, fiber-optic lighting that makes you feel as though you're sleeping under a starry sky, and your own room fragrance. In all, it's a fine design hotel and convenient base for exploring the Left Bank. *3 rue Flatters, 5th.* ☎ *01-43-31-74-21. www.thefive hotel.com. 24 units. Double 133€– 284 €. MC, V. Métro: Les Gobelins. RER: Port Royal. Map p 140.*

★ **Generator Hostel** COLONEL FABIEN   Set in a revamped office block, this funky, next-generation hostel offers vintage-chic dorms and private rooms with their own rooftop-view terraces. The other draws are the cafe (overlooking a garden; it's a great spot for breakfast), and the rooftop bar, which serves snacks, plays music, and offers uninterrupted views over the city. You're a 15-minute walk from the Gare du Nord Eurostar terminal, too. *9-11 place du Colonel Fabien, 10th.* ☎ *01-70-98-84-00. www.generatorhostels.com. 198 units. Shared rooms from 29€,*

private rooms from 55€. MC, V. Métro: Colonel Fabien. Map p 138.

★★ **Grand Pigalle Hotel**
PIGALLE   This new hipster hang-out calls itself a B&B, but don't be fooled: the second "B" refers to "beverages" served in its neo–Art Deco bar—a low-lit little treasure offering craft cocktails and over 200 wines. Rooms are artfully vintage with bold wallpaper and granny-chic headboards. Corner rooms look up at Montmartre (ask when you book). You couldn't ask for a better spot for exploring both trendy SoPi (South Pigalle) and Montmartre's cobbled streets. *29 rue Victor Massé, 9th.* ☎ *01-85-73-12-00. www.grandpigalle.com. 37 units Double 185€–241€. MC, V. Métro: Pigalle. Map p 137.*

★ **Hôtel Amour** PIGALLE
Rooms in this boutique hotel are individually decorated by progressive artists such as Sophie Calle, M&M, and Pierre Le Tan. The result in some is risqué (photos of bare bottoms), but if you mind, what are you doing in Pigalle? The brasserie-bar with a hidden garden is a hit

The funky, individually decorated rooms at the Hôtel Amour feature original works of art.

with Paris's trendy crowd. *8 rue Navarin, 9th.* ☎ *01-48-78-31-80. www.hotelamourparis.fr. 20 units. Double 135€–310€. AE, MC, V. Métro: Pigalle or St Georges. Map p 138.*

★★ **Hôtel Balzac** CHAMPS-ELYSEES This Belle Epoque mansion with a pretty courtyard is luxuriously designed with ostentatious 19th-century touches and king-size beds. Its elegant restaurant is a hit with locals, who come for its relatively low prices (45€ a head) and intimate atmosphere. *6 rue Balzac, 8th.* ☎ *01-44-35-18-00. www.hotelbalzac.com. 70 units. Double 400€–900€. AE, DC, MC, V. Métro: George-V. Map p 137.*

★ **Hôtel Banke** OPERA This smart hotel has a breathtaking neo–Belle Epoque lobby, left over from a time when the building was a bank (hence the name). Rooms are stylish in browns and reds, and beds have ultra-comfy mattresses. The restaurant offers a menu with a Spanish twist. *20 rue Lafayette, 9th.* ☎ *01-55-33-22-22. www.derbyhotels.com. 94 units. Double 280€–540€. AE, MC, V. Métro: Le Peletier. Map p 138.*

★★★ **Hôtel Baume** ODEON Set on a tranquil street near the neo-classical Théâtre de l'Odéon (and a 5-minute walk from the Luxembourg gardens), this chic neo-'30s-style hotel offers exquisite rooms (all pinks, blues, or terracottas) that follow themes such as jewelry, fashion, design, and film. Some have private terraces, and some suites are so big you feel as though you're in an apartment. There's a quaint little walled breakfast terrace to boot. *7 rue Casimir Delavigne, 6th.* ☎ *01-53-10-28-50. www.baume-hotel-paris.com. 35 units. Double 252€–370€. AE, MC, V. Métro: Odéon. Map p 140.*

The Hôtel Banke is lodged in—you guessed it—a former bank building.

★ **Hôtel Bel-Ami** LATIN QUARTER Recently restored, this sleek, arts-conscious hotel has a minimalist look with a clean design aesthetic. Earth-tone guest rooms have a Zen-like air. Check the website for deals. *7–11 rue St-Benoit, 6th.* ☎ *01-49-27-09-33. www.hotel-bel-ami.com. 115 units. Double 280€–470€. AE, DC, MC, V. Métro: St-Germain-des-Prés. Map p 140.*

★ **Hôtel Britannique** HOTEL DE VILLE Tastefully modern and plush, this place has cultivated a kind of English graciousness. Guest rooms are small but nicely appointed and soundproof. The location is so central, you can walk almost anywhere. *20 av. Victoria, 1st.* ☎ *01-42-33-74-59. www.hotel-britannique.com. 39 units. Double 152€–359€. AE, DC, MC, V. Métro: Châtelet. Map p 138.*

★ **Hôtel Chopin** GRANDS BOULEVARDS This intimate hotel is hidden inside a curious 19th-century covered passage. The Victorian lobby has elegant woodwork, rooms are comfortably furnished, and the staff is friendly. *10 bd. Montmartre, 9th.* ☎ *01-47-70-58-10. www.hotelchopin-paris-opera.com.*

36 units. Double 87€–147€. Métro: Grands Boulevards. Map p 138.

★★ Hôtel des Grandes Ecoles

LATIN QUARTER This country house—with its old-fashioned floral wallpaper, chintz, and lace—is a welcome break from the city hub-bub. The bucolic feel continues in the flower-filled garden, where noisy traffic dissolves into the twit-tering of birds—the perfect place for a lazy breakfast. Rooms are spotlessly clean and the welcome is friendly. *75 rue Cardinal Lemoine, 5th.* ☎ *01-43-26-79-23. www.hotel-grandes-ecoles.com. 51 units. Double 135€–165€. MC, V. Métro: Cardinal Lemoine. Map p 140.*

★ Hôtel du Bourg Tibourg

MARAIS Hotels with far less style can cost twice as much as this well-located place. Rooms are small but comfortable, with romantic modern decor and lush fabrics in everything from leopard print to stripes. *19 rue du Bourg-Tibourg, 4th.* ☎ *01-42-78-47-39. www.hoteldubourgtibourg. com. 30 units. Double 290€–380€. AE, MC, V. Métro: Hôtel-de-Ville. Map p 138.*

★ Hôtel Duc de St-Simon

INVALIDES A sweet courtyard offers your first glimpse into this

The Hôtel des Grandes Ecoles features a peaceful garden.

hopelessly romantic hotel that has seduced the likes of Lauren Bacall. Rooms are filled with antiques, objets d'art, and lush fabrics. Some have terraces overlooking a garden. *14 rue de St-Simon, 7th.* ☎ *01-44-39-20-20. www.hotelducdesaint simon.com. 34 units. Double 295€–365€. AE, MC, V. Métro: Rue du Bac. Map p 140.*

★★ Hôtel du Louvre LOUVRE

This former home of painter Camille Pissarro is now a sort of Belle Epoque luxury hotel, resplen-dent with marble, bronze, and gilt galore. Guest rooms are replete with antiques and heavy fabrics. *Place André Malraux, 1st.* ☎ *01-44-58-38-38. www.hoteldulouvre.com. 177 units. Double 365€–490€. AE, DC, MC, V. Métro: Palais Royal or Louvre Rivoli. Map p 138.*

★★ Hôtel Duo MARAIS One of

the city's trendiest hotels, with a location right in the heart of the Marais. Decor has an old- meets new-world charm thanks to sleek rooms all dressed up in cool browns, creams, and bold-print wallpaper. It's also one of the only hotels in the area to have its own sauna. *11 rue du Temple, 4th.* ☎ *01-42-72-72-22. www.duo-paris. com. 45 units. Double 210€–430€. AE, DC, MC, V. Métro: Hôtel-de-Ville. Map p 138.*

★ Hôtel Eugène en Ville

GRANDS BOULEVARDS Steely grays and cornflower blues, mixed with dandy-esque touches such as drawings of dogs in top hats, lend an industrial-baroque feel to this spanking new hotel. Rooms are smallish but tasteful, with black and white accents. Should you wish to eat in, the hotel has a handy can-teen, serving rather good wine and charcuterie/cheese platters. *6 rue Bouffaut, 9th.* ☎ *01-40-22-04-34. www.eugeneenville.fr. 66 units. Dou-*

Camille Pissaro once lived in the palatial building that houses the Hôtel du Louvre

ble 170€–245€. MC, V. Métro:
Le Peletier or Grands Boulevards.
Map p 138.

★ **Hôtel Gabriel** REPUBLIQUE
Relaxing massages, healthy food,
and Zen decor are what you get at
Paris's first-ever detox hotel. Come
here to wind down and escape the
city life outside. *25 rue du Grand
Prieuré, 11th.* ☎ *01-47-00-13-38.
www.hotelgabrielparis.com. 40 units.
Double 149€–405€. MC, V. Métro:
République. Map p 138.*

★★★ **Hôtel Henri IV** THE
ISLANDS This is possibly Paris's
best budget hotel, at the heart of
the Île de la Cité, near Notre-Dame
and pont Neuf. Rooms are very
basic but clean, and the top-floor
rooms have balconies. Only 11
rooms have en suite bathrooms
with toilets. The sandy square just
in front is a perfect spot for a game
of *boules*. Book way in advance.
25 place Dauphine, 1st. ☎ *01-43-
54-44-53. www.henri-paris-hotel.com.
15 units. Double 80€–90€. MC, V.
Métro: Pont Neuf. Map p 138.*

★★ **Hôtel Le Belmont** CHAMPS
ELYSEES Luxurious, beautiful, and
kitted out with a spa, this gem of a
hotel throws you back to the Napoleon III era, with opulent furnishings
and deep wood paneling. Rooms
are theatrical (quite literally when it

comes to the stage-curtain headboards) and the black marble in the
bathrooms sparkles like onyx. For
an extra treat, book a body mas-
sage in the Carita spa (130€) or
check out the Turkish bath and
gym. *30 rue de Bassano, 16th.*
☎ *01-53-57-75-00. www.belmont-
paris-hotel.com. 74 units. Double
210€–375€. MC, V. Métro: Kléber or
Georges V. Map p 137.*

★★ **kids Hôtel Lion d'Or**
TUILERIES The "Golden Lion" has
bright, simple rooms, plus fully furnished apartments that sleep up to
five people. It's well located, too,
right near the Louvre. *5 rue de la
Sourdière, 1st.* ☎ *01-42-60-79-04.
www.hotel-louvre-paris.com. 27 units.
Double 148€–265€, apt 230€–300€.
MC, V. Métro: Tuileries. Map p 138.*

★★★ **kids Hôtel Louison**
MONTPARNASSE/SAINT-GERMAIN
Rooms in this family-run hotel are
lushly decorated in thick, patterned
fabrics and parquet floors. The
hearty breakfasts are served in a
bistro-style room that feels like a
Left Bank institution. Families are
welcome here, but the atmosphere
is nonetheless romantic, too. *105
rue Vaugirard, 6th.* ☎ *01-53-63-25-
50. www.louison-hotel.com. 42 units.
Double 188€–385€. AE, MC, V.
Métro: Montparnasse or St-Placide.
Map p 140.*

Guests' health and well-being come first at the Hôtel Gabriel.

★★ **Hôtel Meurice** CONCORDE
Salvador Dalí once made this hotel
his headquarters. It's gorgeous,
with perfectly preserved mosaic
floors, hand-carved moldings, and
an Art Nouveau glass roof. Rooms
are sumptuous and individually
decorated, some with fluffy clouds
and blue skies painted on the ceilings. *228 rue de Rivoli, 1st.*
☎ *01-44-58-10-10. www.meurice-
hotel.com. 160 units. Double 750€–
1,065€. AE, DC, MC, V. Métro:
Tuileries or Concorde. Map p 138.*

★★★ **Hôtel Particulier** MONT-
MARTRE You'll be hard-pressed
to find somewhere more romantic
or stylish than this hidden gem, nestled down a leafy passage by a rock
called Rocher de la Sorcière (Witch's
Rock). Avant-garde artists have
given each room a special touch.
The hotel's a favorite local haunt
too, thanks to its excellent brunches
and cocktails. *23 av. Junot, 18th.*
☎ *01-53-41-81-40. www.hotel-partic
ulier-montmartre.com. 5 units. Double
360€–590€. MC, V. Métro: Lamarck-
Caulincourt. Map p 137.*

★ **Hôtel Saint-Louis en l'Isle**
ÎLE ST-LOUIS A charming family
atmosphere reigns at this antiques-
filled hotel in a 17th-century town
house. Rooms are small but well

decorated, there are lots of lovely
touches, and the location is excellent. Great value for the price. *75
rue St-Louis-en-l'Île, 4th.* ☎ *01-46-
34-04-80. www.hotelsaintlouis.com.
19 units. Double 165€–255€. MC, V.
Métro: Pont Marie or St-Michel-
Notre-Dame. Map p 138.*

★★★ **Hôtel Shangri-La** CHAIL-
LOT Set inside the 19th-century
palace Napoleon built for his great-
nephew Prince Roland Bonaparte,
this hotel drips with fine furniture,
chandeliers, and antiques. But
there's a modern edge, too, in the
classy rooms, lounge, and two
superlative eateries: **L'Abeille** for
haute French cuisine (p 112) and **La
Bauhinia** brasserie, which mixes
Asian and French flavors. The spa
has one of the city's loveliest pools.
10 av. d'Iéna, 16th. ☎ *01-53-67-19-
98. www.shangri-la.com. 81 units.
Double 740€–1,200€. AE, DC, MC, V.
Métro: Iéna. Map p 137.*

★★ **Hôtel Vernet** ETOILE In
Paris's Golden Triangle (a luxe shopping district), this oasis of charm
attracts guests drawn by the nearby
designer shops on avenues Georges
V and Montaigne. Contemporary
styling throughout contrasts nicely
with the Haussmann-era building—
especially its restaurant, which

sports a stunning Belle Époque glass cupola (with ironwork by Eiffel himself). *25 rue Vernet, 8th.* ☎ *01-44-31-98-00. www.hotelvernet-paris.fr. 50 units. Double 270€–420€. AE, MC, V. Métro: Kléber or George V. Map p 137.*

★★ Hôtel Welcome SAINT-GERMAIN-DES-PRES Nestled among the art galleries and cafes of Saint-Germain, this quaint hotel oozes atmosphere, with wooden beams, old furniture, classic red-and-cream drapes, and street views from most bedrooms. A real steal for such a good Left Bank location. *66 rue de Seine, 6th.* ☎ *01-46-34-24-80. www.hotelwelcomeparis.com. 29 units. Double 137€–240€. MC, V. Métro: St-Germain-des-Prés or Odéon. Map p 140.*

★★★ Hôtel Westminster OPERA This gorgeous hotel is favored by shoppers who prowl Place Vendôme, Rue du Faubourg Saint-Honoré, and the department stores around Opéra Garnier for chic attire. Decor is resolutely stylish: classic marbles, deep woods, and plush fabrics. The Michelin-starred restaurant is known for its fine contemporary French cuisine. *13 rue de la Paix, 2nd.* ☎ *01-42-61-57-46. www.warwickwestminsteropera. com. 102 units. Double 230€–680€.*

AE, MC, V. Métro: Opéra. RER: Auber. Map p 138.

Hyatt Paris Madeleine MADE-LEINE This palace hotel is a citadel of luxurious 21st-century living. High ceilings and neo–Art Deco touches make the hotel airy and dramatic. The sleek fittings add to the luxury, as do the rich fabrics and precious wooden furniture. *24 bd. Malesherbes, 8th.* ☎ *01-55-27-15-34. www.paris.madeleine.hyatt. com/hyatt/hotels. 86 units. Double 430€–750€. AE, DC, MC, V. Métro: St-Augustin. Map p 137.*

★★★ kids Le Bristol CHAMPS-ELYSEES Paris's most discreet palace hotel is a favorite with celebrities, politicians, and royalty. Guest rooms are lavish, large, and luxurious. The swimming pool has views over the whole city. In the summer, the three-Michelin-starred restaurant, Epicure, opens onto Paris's biggest palace garden (1,500 sq. m/16,000 sq. ft.), and its one-starred 114 Faubourg brasserie is well worth crossing Paris for. If you can't afford a room, observe the glitterati over a cocktail in the bar. You might even meet Fa-raon and Kléopatre, the resident cats—they're a hit with kids. *112 rue du Faubourg St-Honoré, 8th.* ☎ *01-53-43-43-00. www.hotel-bristol.com. 170*

Opt for a romantic dinner on the terrace of your suite at the Hôtel Meurice.

One of the stylish rooms at L'Hôtel.

units. Double 800€–2,200€. AE, DC, MC, V. Métro: Franklin-D.-Roosevelt. Map p 137.

★★★ Les Bains Paris MARAIS

What started as a 19th-century bathhouse (where Proust once bathed), became a famous night-club in 1978—a place where film stars, artists, and supermodels threw wild parties that generally ended in the baths. Today it's the city's edgiest hotel and still draws A-listers. Room-wise, expect under-stated opulence in distressed walls and vintage furniture. The blood-red restaurant serves food until midnight, and the basement har-bors a nightclub and the revamped baths. *7 rue du Bourg-l'Abbé, 3rd.* ☎ *01-42-77-07-07. www.lesbains-paris.com. 39 units. Double 380€–750€. MC, V. Métro: Etienne Marcel or Arts et Métiers. Map p 138.*

★ Le Vert Galant GOBELINS

Set around a serene garden and attached to an excellent Corsican restaurant, it isn't hard to see why this is one of the city's best budget hotels. Some rooms even have kitchenettes so you can save money by cooking. Sidle up to a table in the garden after a long day's sight-seeing. It's a wonderful spot for winding down, drink in hand. *43 rue Croulebarbe, 13th.* ☎ *01-44-08-83-50. http://vertgalant.hotel-restaurant-paris.com. 17 units. Double 90€–150€. MC, V. Métro: Gobelins. Map p 140.*

★ L'Hôtel SAINT-GERMAIN-DES-PRES

The hotel where Oscar Wilde died is now one of the Left Bank's most distinctive boutique hotels. Each guest room is different, some with fireplaces, some with fabric-covered walls. There's a swimming pool in the cellar, and the restaurant is one of the best in town. *13 rue des Beaux-Arts, 6th.* ☎ *01-44-41-99-00. www.l-hotel.com. 20 units. Double 255€–680€. AE, DC, MC, V. Métro: St-Germain-des-Prés. Map p 140.*

★★ Mama Shelter PERE-LACHAISE

Rooms in this starkly modern design hotel, set in a con-verted car park, are full of fun touches, such as lights made of superhero Halloween masks and 24" wall-mounted iMacs with TV, radio, and web access. Downstairs, a bar, pizza parlor, and restaurant draw a crowd of international trend-ies. It's still the place to see and be seen. *107 rue de Bagnolet, 20th.* ☎ *01-43-48-48-48. www.mamashel ter.com. 170 units. Double 90€–400€. MC, V. Métro: Alexandre Dumas or Porte de Bagnolet. Map p 138.*

★★ Molitor by Mgallery BOIS DE BOULOGNE

Once an Art Deco swimming pool, inaugurated in 1929 by Johnny Weissmuller (the Olympic gold medal winner who went on to play Tarzan), this stunning, art-themed hotel—from its rooftop bar down to its basement Clarins spa—feels like a secret. It's an excellent spot for sports fans: The Roland Garros tennis grounds are across the road, and it's near both the Parc des Princes stadium and the Auteuil racetrack in the Bois de Boulogne (see p 97). The cool, retro-inspired rooms are understatedly chic; the two pools are a godsend in summer. *3 rue Nungesser et Coli, 16th.* ☎ *01-56-07-08-50. www.mgallery.com. 124 units. Double 270€–460€. AE, MC, V. Métro: Michel-Ange Molitor. Map p 137.*

★★★ Pension les Marronniers LUXEMBOURG

This is one of the city's very last pensions de famille (boarding houses)—perfect for nostalgic travelers looking for a slice of bygone Paris. It has been in the owner's family since the 1930s and offers great views over the Luxembourg Gardens. Rooms are cluttered—just as they should be. Some share washing facilities. Half-board is available. *78 rue d'Assas, 6th.* ☎ *01-43-26-37-71. www.pension-marronniers.com. 7 units. Double 94€–120€. No credit cards. Weekly and monthly rentals. Métro: Notre-Dame des Champs or Vavin. Map p 140.*

★★★ Providence RÉPUBLIQUE

In the heart of Paris's shabby-chic "hipsterland" (spreading from the Canal St-Martin to the Marais), this atmospheric retro-design hotel woos with dark flowery wallpaper, claw-foot bathtubs, metro tiles, and chintzy light shades. The kitschy bar/restaurant serves lip-smacking bistro fare, and in-room perks include iMacs, free VOD (video on demand), and bars with icemakers. *90 rue René Boulanger, 10th.* ☎ *01-46-34-34-04. www.hotelprovidenceparis.com. 22 units. Double 190€–270€. MC, V. Métro: République or Jacques Bonsergent. Map p 138.*

Bed & Breakfasts in Paris

For a special, intimate Parisian experience, consider booking a B&B. Here are some reliable places to try: **Alcôve & Agapes** (☎ 01-44-85-06-05; www.bed-and-breakfast-in-paris.com), with more than 100 regularly inspected addresses throughout central Paris; **Hôtes Qualité Paris** (www.hotesqualiteparis.fr), which has a long, trustworthy selection verified by City Hall; and **Alastair Sawday's** (www.sawdays.co.uk), which lists many special B&Bs and apartments to rent. To live like a local in trendy SoPi (south Pigalle, below Montmartre), try **52 Clichy,** 52 rue de Clichy, 9th (☎ 01-44-53-93-65; www.52clichy.com; from 105€), a fabulous B&B for two, with a separate flat that sleeps up to four people. Breakfast is copious; the balcony views over Paris's steely rooftops picturesque; and the welcome, by expat owner Rosemary, perfect. She can even give you a makeover (prices on request), as she's an image consultant by trade.

The young and stylish flock to Mama Shelter, in the 20th arrondissement.

★★★ kids Regent's Garden Hotel CHAMPS-ELYSEES

A good, guilt-free night's sleep is guaranteed in this environmentally friendly hotel, whose efforts to reduce carbon emissions have earned it the difficult-to-obtain European Ecolabel. Rooms are elegant, in bold stripes and patterns; there's a relaxing spa and a flower-filled courtyard—perfect for breakfast alfresco. *6 rue Pierre Demours, 8th.* ☎ *01-45-74-07-30. www.hotel-regents-paris.com. 40 units. Double 179€–300€. AE, MC, V. Métro: Ternes or Charles de Gaulle–Etoile. Map p 137.*

★★ Renaissance Paris Arc de Triomphe CHAMPS-ELYSEES

Order a Paris Sky View Room and watch the Eiffel Tower twinkle from your balcony in this trendy five-star hotel. It has elegantly modern architecture, and if you fancy non-French cuisine, the Macassar restaurant serves scrumptious Indonesian-inspired dishes like ikan dabu dabu (roasted marinated swordfish with basmati rice and sauce vierge). *39 av. de Wagram, 17th. 01-55-37-55-37. www.marriott.com. 118 units. Double from 236€–560€. MC, V. Métro: Ternes. Map p 137.*

★★★ Solar Hôtel DENFERT-ROCHEREAU

Paris's first low-budget, environmentally friendly hotel has a fabulous concept: Modern rooms without frills but with A/C, TV, and phones; a pretty garden where you can eat the free organic breakfast and hire bikes; static prices year-round; and a genuine low-carbon charter. *22 rue Boulard, 14th.* ☎ *01-43-21-08-20. www.solarhotel.fr. 34 units. Double 89€. MC, V. Métro/RER: Denfert-Rochereau. Map p 140.*

St-Christopher's Inn STALIN-GRAD

This English youth hostel chain, set inside an old boat hangar, has funky decor and unbeatable prices. Private rooms and dormers are marine-themed. Dorms are single-sex and mixed, so check when you book. *159 rue de Crimée, 19th.* ☎ *01-40-34-34-40. www.st-christophers.co.uk. 350 beds. Dorm from 27€, double 48€–60€. MC, V. Métro: Crimée. Map p 138.*

★ Terrass Hôtel MONTMARTRE

This hotel is a find, with a marble-floored lobby, blond-oak paneling, and contemporary art. Guest rooms have high ceilings and sophisticated, retro-inspired decor. The rooftop bar/restaurant is coveted by Parisians for its uninterrupted views, which include the Eiffel Tower. *12 rue Joseph de Maistre, 18th.* ☎ *01-46-06-72-85. www.terrass-hotel.com. 100 units. Double 247€–450€. MC, V. Métro: Place de Clichy or Blanche. Map p 137.* ●

152

Decadent Versailles

The Best Day Trips & Excursions

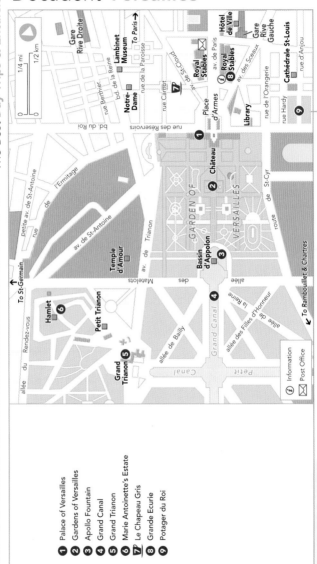

1 Palace of Versailles
2 Gardens of Versailles
3 Apollo Fountain
4 Grand Canal
5 Grand Trianon
6 Marie Antoinette's Estate
7 Le Chapeau Gris
8 Grande Ecurie
9 Potager du Roi

Previous page: The Fountain of Apollo at Versailles.

Yes, it's touristy, and yes, it will be crowded in the summer, but come anyway. Versailles must be seen to be believed, and it is well worth the 35-minute journey. It took 40,000 workers 50 years to convert Louis XIII's hunting lodge into this extravagant palace. The major work was started in 1678 by Jules Hardouin Mansart under Louis XIV, and before it was finished, entire forests had been moved to make way for its extensive gardens. It was here in the 18th century that French royalty lived a life of such excess in a time of widespread poverty that it spurred a revolution.

❶ ★★★ Palace of Versailles. One of the first things you'll notice when you arrive is that this vast palace of 2,300 rooms is dwarfed by the grounds, which stretch for miles. Inside the palace, it's all over-the-top, all the time. The king and his family lived in the Petits Appartements much of the time. One room, the Cabinet of the Meridian, was where Marie Antoinette finally gave birth to an heir in 1781, after 11 years of marriage. The King's Grand Appartement contains the Hercules Salon, where the ceiling is painted with the *Apotheosis of Hercules*. The elaborate Mercury Salon is where the body of Louis XIV lay in state after his death. But the apartments pale in comparison to the 71m-long (233-ft.) Hall of Mirrors designed by Mansart. The Hall of Mirrors was designed to reflect sunlight back into the garden and remind people that the "Sun King" lived here. On June 28, 1919, the treaty ending World War I was signed in this hall. Elsewhere in the palace there's an impressive Clock Room, designed in 1753 by architect Jacques-Ange Gabriel, with a gilded-bronze astronomical clock that is supposed to keep perfect time until 9999. ⏱ *2 hr.*

❷ ★★★ Gardens of Versailles. These vast, varied, vainglorious gardens were created by the landscape architect André Le Nôtre, who used lakes, canals, geometric flower beds, long avenues, fountains, and statuary to devise a French Eden. Thousands of men moved tons of soil, trees, and rock for the plan. The result—beautifully maintained for hundreds of years—is simply breathtaking. ⏱ *2 hr.*

❸ Apollo Fountain. Created in 1670 by Jean-Baptiste Tuby after a drawing by Charles Le Brun, Versaille's most famous fountain depicts Apollo's chariot.

The Sun King's Hall of Mirrors reflects natural light back into the garden at Versailles.

The Pomp of Versailles Gardens

Each weekend between the end of March and November, the palace's fountains spurt to the rhythms of Baroque music during the 60- to 90-minute **Grandes Eaux Musicales,** a wonderful exhibition that takes you back to the time of the Sun King. Every Tuesday between April and October (except June), classical music fills Le Nôtre's landscaped patchworks from 10:30am to 6pm during **Les Jardins Musicaux.**

④ Grand Canal. On St. Louis Day (Aug 25), the sun sets in perfect alignment with this 1.6km (1-mile) canal, surrounded by lush forests

⑤ ★★ Grand Trianon. The elegant Grand Trianon was designed in 1687 by Jules Hardouin Mansart. It was later the home of Napoleon and his family. Then, in 1963, President Charles de Gaulle had it turned into a guesthouse for French presidents. The northern wing, the Trianon-sous-Bois, is still used today for presidential functions. ◷ *30 min.*

Travel Tip

Both the Grand Trianon and Marie Antoinette's estate can be reached by the "Petit Train" from the Parterre Nord (☎ 01-39-54-22-00; www.train-versailles.com; 7.50€ adults, 5.80€ ages 11–18, free for under 11s). The round trip is

narrated by a guide and takes 50 minutes, but you can hop on and hop off at each site.

⑥ Marie Antoinette's Estate. Louis XVI's young wife is famed for her desire to flee the pomp of the Versailles court. Her retreat was this estate—made up of the Queen's Gardens, the **Hameau de la Reine** (a lovely thatch-roofed hamlet of fanciful faux farmhouses), and the **Petit Trianon** (a perfectly scaled gem of a building that architecture buffs flip for; it was also a meeting place for Louis XV and Madame de Pompadour). ◷ *30 min.*

⑦ Le Chapeau Gris. Outside the palace grounds, stop for a bite of French country cuisine in Versailles's oldest restaurant, whose building dates back to the construction of

The gardens of Versailles nearly outdo the palace itself.

the château. The prix-fixe menus, at 24€ and 31€, are excellent values. *7 rue Hoche.* ☎ *01-39-50-10-81. www. auchapeaugris.com. Closed Tues– Wed. $$.*

❽ Grande Ecurie. The famous Versailles horses are kept in high style here and trained in a variety of equine performance arts. You can watch the horse trainers at work on Saturday, Sunday, and some weekdays, or take in a performance on weekend afternoons or evenings (and some Thursdays). For times, check the website or call in advance. ◷ *1 hr. 15 min. Near the palace entrance on av. Rockefeller.* ☎ *01-48-39-18-03. www.bartabas.fr. Admission 12€, performances 25€.*

❾ Potager du Roi. This enclosure, made up of 5,000 fruit trees tapered into extravagant shapes, is where the Sun King's fruit and vegetable plot stood. The garden (built between 1678 and 1683) is now separate from the château and well worth visiting. You can even buy the fruit and veggies grown here in the boutique. ◷ *30 min. Access via Rue du Maréchal Joffr (left main entrance).* ☎ *01-39-24-62-62. www.potager- du-roi.fr. Admission 4.50€ (7€ weekends), free for children 12 & under. Apr–Oct Tues–Sun 10am–6pm; Jan– Mar Tues & Thurs 10am–6pm; Nov– Dec Tues & Thurs 10am–6pm, Sat 10am–1pm. Closed May 1 & during Christmas school holidays.*

Versailles: Practical Matters

Versailles (☎ 01-30-83-78-00; www.chateauversailles.fr) is open Tuesday to Sunday from 9am to 5:30pm (Apr–Oct until 6:30pm). The gardens are open daily year-round from 8am to 6pm (Apr–Oct until 8:30pm). Admission to the château is 13€ to 15€. Admission to the Grand Trianon and Marie Antoinette's estate is 6€ to 10€. Admission to the gardens is free (except during the Grandes Eaux, when it's 8€). However, the best and easiest way to visit Versailles is to buy a *Passeport Versailles* (18€–25€; free for children 17 and under and visitors 25 and under from the E.U., except during the Grandes Eaux and Jardins Musicaux events—see box facing page), which allows quick access to all the sites. The 2-day passport is a good value if you plan to stay overnight. Buy tickets online or at an FNAC (p 132). If you already have your ticket when you arrive, head straight to door A. To buy your ticket, head to the information/ ticket point in the south wing. For tickets to the Grand Trianon and Marie Antoinette's estate, head straight to that entrance in the gardens.

There are two stations in Versailles—Rive Gauche (the nearest one to the château) and Rive Droite. To get to the former, take RER C from central Paris to Versailles–Rive Gauche; or take a normal train from Gare St-Lazare to Versailles–Rive Droite and then walk 10 minutes. By car, take the A-13 from Paris to the Versailles-Château exit. Pay parking is available on the Place d'Armes. The trip to Versailles takes about 30 to 40 minutes by car or train.

Disneyland Paris

1. Main Street, USA
2. Frontierland
3. Adventureland
4. Fantasyland
5. Auberge de Cendrillon
6. Discoveryland
7. Disney Village
8. Walt Disney Studios Park

Pirates of the Caribbean

Adventureland

Adventure Isle

Peter Pan's Flight

Indiana Jones et le Temple du Péril

3

La Cabane des Robinson

Le Passage d'Aladdin

Disneyland Railroad Frontierland Depot

Critter Corral

2

Frontierland

Legends of the Wild West

The Chaparral Stage

River Rogue Koolboats

Shootin' Gallery

Pocahontas Indian Village

Big Thunder Mountain

Riverboat Landing

Phantom Manor

8

WALT DISNEY STUDIOS

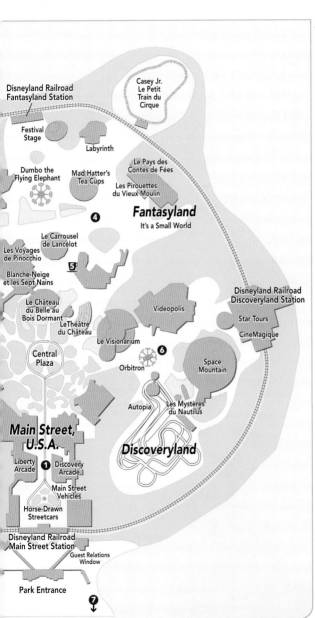

Disneyland Railroad
Fantasyland Station

Casey Jr.
Le Petit
Train du
Cirque

Festival
Stage

Labyrinth

Le Pays des
Contes de Fées

Dumbo the
Flying Elephant

Mad Hatter's
Tea Cups

Les Pirouettes
du Vieux Moulin

❹

Fantasyland

It's a Small World

Le Carrousel
de Lancelot

Les Voyages
de Pinocchio

❺

Blanche-Neige
et les Sept Nains

Le Château
du Belle au
Bois Dormant

Vidéopolis

Disneyland Railroad
Discoveryland Station

Star Tours

CinéMagique

Le Théâtre
du Château

Le Visionarium

❻

Central
Plaza

Orbitron

Space
Mountain

Autopia

Les Mystères
du Nautilus

Main Street,
U.S.A.

Discoveryland

Liberty
Arcade

❶ Discovery
Arcade

Main Street
Vehicles

Horse-Drawn
Streetcars

Disneyland Railroad
Main Street Station

Guest Relations
Window

Park Entrance

❼

Disneyland Paris is a blessing for travelers with kids who have wearied of the museums and churches and just want to go on the rides for a day, pleasepleaseplease*please!* Overall, there's little difference between this amusement park and those in Florida and California, except here the cheeseburgers come with *pommes frîtes* instead of fries. There are two main parks: Disneyland Park, with its five lands, and Walt Disney Studios Park, split into lots.

❶ Main Street, USA. Immediately after entering the park, you'll find yourself in an idealized American town, complete with horse-drawn carriages and street-corner barbershop quartets. This is also a good spot to catch a parade. Throughout the day (and sometimes in the evening), all the Disney characters pass by on colorful floats, dancing and waving, putting everyone in a party mood.

❷ Frontierland. In this "pretend America," it's a conveniently short hop to the West, particularly if you board one of the steam-powered trains that takes you through a Grand Canyon diorama to get to it (you can catch the train at Main Street). Pocahontas's Indian village is a fine spot to get young kids away from the crowds. If it gets too hot, you and the kids can ride the nearby paddle-wheel steamship.

Sleeping Beauty's Castle.

❸ Adventureland. The trains will take you on to Adventureland, where swashbuckling pirates battle near the Swiss Family Robinson's treehouse. If that's too tame, head for the Indiana Jones and the Temple of Peril ride, which travels backward at breakneck speed, or get wet fighting the ghostly Pirates of the Caribbean.

❹ Fantasyland. Young children will be charmed by Sleeping Beauty's Castle (*Le Château de la Belle au Bois Dormant*) and its idealized interpretation of a French château, complete with the obligatory fire-breathing dragon in its dungeon. From here, a visit with Dumbo the Flying Elephant may be necessary, and perhaps a whirl on the giant teacup ride.

❺ Auberge de Cendrillon. If you're looking for a nice sit-down lunch, try this restaurant for traditional French dining in Cinderella's country inn. (Reservations are recommended.) Otherwise, take your pick from any of the dozens of dining options scattered throughout the park—just don't expect high standards or healthy options. *Fantasyland.* ☎ 01-60-30-40-50. $$$–$$.

❻ Discoveryland. Explore the visions of the future displayed here, with designs drawn from the works of Jules Verne and H. G. Wells, as well as from more modern fictional creations, like the *Star Wars* universe. This is the park's most popular area,

Disneyland Paris: Practical Matters

Drive 32km (20 miles) along the A4 east from Paris to exit 14, take the Disneyland® Paris Express shuttle (from one of four stops in central Paris), or take the RER A to the Marne-la-Vallée–Chessy stop (about 40 min.). The park is at Marne-la-Vallée, Paris (☎ 08-25-30-05-00 at 0.15€/min; www.disneylandparis.com). Parking is 15€ per day. Admission for 1 day (one park) is 63€ adults, 57€ ages 3–11, and free for children 2 and under; a 1-day hopper (both parks) is 74€ adults and 67€ ages 3–11. Disneyland Park is open September to mid-June Monday through Friday 10am to 8pm and Saturday through Sunday 10am to 9pm, and mid-June to August daily 10am to 11pm. Walt Disney Studios Park is open winter daily 10am to 6pm, and summer daily 10am to 7pm. (These are guidelines, and opening hours and prices may change.) The resort was designed as a total vacation destination, so within the enormous compound there are not only the two parks but also six hotels, campgrounds, the Village Disney entertainment center, a 27-hole golf course, and dozens of restaurants and shops.

with its own version of Space Mountain (which emulates Jules Verne's version of what a trip from Earth to the moon would be like) and a Jedi Training Academy where kids learn to wield lightsabers.

❼ Disney Village. This haven for adults features endless entertainment options—dance clubs, snack bars, restaurants, shops, and bars. There's also a massive 3-D IMAX cinema, where you can see all the latest blockbusters.

❽ Walt Disney Studios Park. Split into four lots (Toon Studio, Backlot, Front Lot, and Production Courtyard), the second park emphasizes film production and special effects. Feel the flames as you play an extra in the *Armageddon* disaster movie, plunge 13 floors down an elevator shaft in the Twilight Tower of Terror, or shrink down to the size of Remy the rat and try to escape from Gusteau's kitchen in the 4-D ride, Ratatouille: The Adventure.

Grown-ups can find plenty of entertainment in Disney Village.

The Cathedral at Chartres

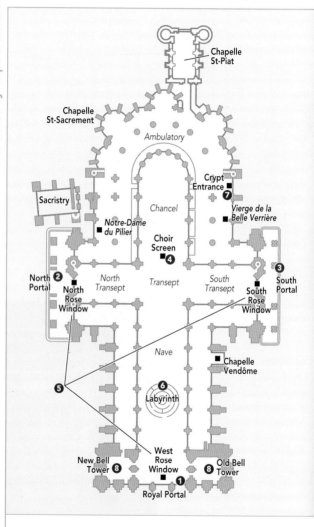

Chapelle St-Piat

Chapelle St-Sacrement

Ambulatory

Sacristy

Chancel

Crypt Entrance ■ **7**

Vierge de la Belle Verrière ■

Notre-Dame du Pilier ■

Choir Screen ■ **4**

North Portal **2**

North Transept

Transept

South Transept

South Portal **3**

North Rose Window

South Rose Window

Nave

Chapelle Vendôme ■

5

6 Labyrinth

West Rose Window ■

New Bell Tower **8**

Old Bell Tower **8**

1 Royal Portal

1 Royal Portal		**5** Rose Windows	
2 North Portal		**6** Floor Labyrinth	
3 South Portal		**7** Crypts	
4 Choir Screen		**8** Towers	

An hour from Paris, standing at the gateway to the Loire Valley, Chartres represents the highest architectural and theological aspirations of the Middle Ages in France. The cathedral was much the same in medieval times as it is now, which should give you a sense of how impressive it must have been in 1260, when it was completed. At night between April and October, a mind-blowingly beautiful light show is projected onto its facade.

The cathedral's facade.

❶ Royal Portal. The sculpted bodies around it are elongated and garbed in long, flowing robes, but their faces are almost disturbingly lifelike—frowning, winking, and smiling. Christ is shown at the Second Coming—his descent to Earth on the right, his ascent back to Heaven on the left.

❷ & ❸ North and South Portals. Both portals are carved with biblical images, including the expulsion of Adam and Eve from the Garden of Eden.

❹ Choir Screen. This celebrated screen dates to the 16th century. It has 40 niches holding statues of biblical figures. Don't be so dazzled by all the stained glass (see next stop) that you overlook its intricate carvings.

❺ ★★★ Rose Windows. No cathedral in the world can match Chartres for its 12th-century glass (saved from damage during World War I and World War II by parishioners who removed it piece by piece and stored it safely). It gave the world a new color—Chartres blue—and it is absolutely exceptional. All the windows are glorious, but the three rose windows may be the best.

❻ Floor Labyrinth. Many Gothic cathedrals once had labyrinths like the one on the floor of the nave, but virtually all were destroyed over

A Special Place to Stay near Chartres

With its moat, forest walks, and 60 hectares (148 acres) of gardens, the Renaissance ★★ **Château d'Esclimont** is a fairy-tale place to stay and dine. It's between Chârtres and Paris at St Symphorien Le Château (☎ 02-37-31-15-15; www.grandesetapes.com; double rooms from 200€; lunch from 29€, dinner from 49€). The gourmet restaurant (think French classics like beef tournedos and lobster) overlooks the gardens. Rooms are stately, with marble bathrooms and thick drapes, and children are welcomed with teddy bears and games.

Chartres: Practical Matters

From Paris's Gare Montparnasse, trains run directly to Chartres (1 hr.). By car, take A-10/A-11 southwest from the Périphérique and follow signs to Le Mans and Chartres (about 1½ hr.). The cathedral (Cloître Notre-Dame; ☎ 02-37-21-59-08; www.cathedrale-chartres.org) is open daily 8:30am to 7:30pm (until 10pm Tues, Fri, & Sun in July). Audio-guides are available for 6.20€. Guided tours of the cathedral are available in English twice a day (Easter–Oct) by lecturer Malcolm Miller at noon and 2:45pm Monday through Saturday (at noon only Nov–Easter, and only if there are more than eight participants). Admission is 10€. For tour information, inquire in the gift shop or contact Miller at ☎ 02-37-28-15-58 or millerchartres@aol.com.

Any trip to the cathedral should include a visit to the medieval cobbled streets of **Chartres's Vieux Quartier (Old Quarter),** which stretches from the cathedral down to the Eure River. On **Rue Chantault,** the 800-year-old houses have wonderfully colorful facades. Right next to the cathedral, the **Musée des Beaux Arts de Chartres,** at 29 Cloître Notre-Dame (☎ 02-37-90-45-80; admission 3.40€) has an excellent collection covering the 16th through the 20th centuries. You'll find a vibrant food market Saturdays and Wednesday mornings in the market hall at Place Billard, near the cathedral. There's also a flower market Tuesdays, Thursdays, and Saturdays at Place du Cygne. For lunch, try **Le Saint-Hilaire,** 11 rue Pont St-Hilaire (☎ 02-37-30-97-57; www.restaurant-saint-hilaire.fr), a traditional French restaurant.

time, so this one, which dates from around 1200, is very rare. It is thought that such labyrinths represented the passage of the soul to heaven. Its 261.5m (858-ft.) path was either walked in prayer as a symbolic pilgrimage to Jerusalem or as a path of repentance, in which case the sinner would cover the distance on his or her knees.

❼ Crypts. Those who would like to visit the cathedral's underbelly can usually only do so as part of a guided tour in French (2.70€). Tag along even if your French is nonexistent to see the wondrous crypt, medieval frescoes, and contemporary stained glass.

❽ Towers. The evolution of Gothic architecture was influenced by the cathedral's 12th-century towers, which can be climbed for sweeping views across the Beauce countryside. Architect Viollet-le-Duc considered the 105m (344-ft.) spire of the Old Bell Tower (also called the Tour du Midi) to be flawless. The flamboyant Gothic New Bell Tower is one of the tallest in France. Huff and puff your way to the top and admire the village of Chartres's tiled rooftops. *Cloître Notre-Dame.* ☎ *02-37-31-22-07. www.cathedrale-chartres.monuments-nationaux.fr. Admission 7.50€. Mon–Sat 9:30am–12:30pm & 2pm–5pm (May–Sept until 6pm), Sun 2pm–5pm (May–Sept until 6pm).* ●

Before You Go

Visitor Information

The **Office de Tourisme et des Congrès** (25 rue des Pyramides, 1st; ☎ 01-49-52-42-63; www. parisinfo.com; daily 9am–7pm, from 10am Nov–Apr) is the city's main tourist information office, providing information on hotels, restaurants, excursions, shopping, transport and events. Other offices dotted around the city (closed during major holidays) include: **Anvers** (72 bd Rochechouart, 9th; daily 10am–6pm); **Gare du Nord** (18 rue de Dunkerque, 10th; Mon–Sat 8am–7pm; **Gare de Lyon** (20 bd Diderot, 12th; Mon–Sat 8am–6pm); and **Porte de Versailles** (1 place de la Porte de Versailles, 15th; daily during trade fairs 11am–7pm).

The international website for tourism in France is www.rendezvousen france.com. For comprehensive information about traveling to Paris and Île de France, including hotels, sightseeing, and notices of special events check out www.parisinfo.com and www.visitparisregion.com.

The Best Times to Go

Paris is less crowded in **August,** when the locals traditionally take their annual holiday. This is also a time for some of Paris's best outdoor festivals. However, some shops, restaurants, and galleries close for 2 weeks at the beginning of the month (usually until Aug 15). You may want to avoid **late September/early October,** when both the annual auto and Paris Fashion Week shows attract thousands of enthusiasts. Spring in Paris is still a good time to come, but so too is December, when many hotels have

Previous page: Traveling Paris by Métro is an easy and convenient way to get around.

special offers on the run up to Christmas—although you might not get any sunshine.

Weather

Generally speaking, summers are warm and pleasant, with only a few oppressively hot days. Although more and more hotels are adding air-conditioning to the rooms, many cheaper accommodations still get hot and stuffy. Rain is common throughout the year, especially in winter.

Useful Websites

- **www.mappy.fr**, **www.viami chelin.com**, and **www.google. com/maps**: Online maps and journey planner.

- **www.pagesjaunes.fr**: Online phone directory for businesses and services.

- **www.culture.fr**: Extensive listings of upcoming cultural events.

- **www.parissi.com**: Guide to the Parisian music scene, with an emphasis on nightclubs.

- **www.paris.fr**: The City Hall's guide to Paris, with museum and exhibition listings.

Cellphones (Mobile Phones)

If you own a mobile phone (GSM, Triband or quad-band), you should be able to make and receive calls to and from France, and other countries worldwide. Check with your service provider before you leave. Charges can be high, however, because you are usually charged for calls you both make and receive, but a good way around this is getting your phone unlocked before you leave. This will allow you to buy a local SIM card from a French provider. The main ones are **Orange** (www.orange.fr), **Bouygues Telecom** (www.bouygues telecom.fr), and **SFR** (www.sfr.fr).

Car Rentals

There's very little need to rent a car in Paris, but if you do need four wheels, one of the best and cheapest ways to get them is with the self-service **Autolib'** electric-car system. Like its older cousin, the self-service Vélib' bike system (see p 168), you unplug a car, drive away, and then return it to any Autolib' station in the city. To register go to a subscription kiosk, subscribe online (www.autolib.eu), or visit the information office (5 rue Edouard VII, 9th). You'll need your driving license (only International and European driving licenses are accepted), a valid passport and a credit card (Visa, MasterCard).

Once you have your badge, pass it over the sensor at the rental station, unplug the car, and drive away. To return it, select an Autolib' station from the onboard GPS. Park the car and use your badge to activate the recharging unit. Then uncoil the cable and plug the car in. A 1-day subscription is free, but you'll pay 9€ per 30 minutes; a week's rental costs 10€, then 7€ per 30 minutes; a month is 25€ then 6.50€ per 30 minutes.

Or, if you'd rather do things the traditional way, book a car online before you leave your home country. Try **Hertz** (www.hertz.com), **Avis** (www.avis.com), or **Budget** (www.budget.com). If you're in the U.S., you should also consider **AutoEurope** (www.autoeurope.com), which sends you a prepaid voucher, thus locking in the exchange rate.

Getting **There**

By Plane

Paris has two international airports—**Orly** and **Charles de Gaulle (CDG)** (☎ 00-33-1-70-36-39-50 from abroad or ☎ 39-50 in France; www.aeroportsdeparis.fr). RER B operates between the two airports, with two stops for CDG: the first for T1 and T3, the second for T2. A free train, the CDGVAL, connects the terminals and provides service to the train stations. Orly's stop is Anthony; from there, a monorail takes you to the airport. (See "From Orly," below.)

From Charles de Gaulle: RER trains leave every 15 minutes (5am to approximately 12:30am) from the station near Terminal 3, serving several of the major downtown Métro/RER stations including Gare du Nord (for Eurostar and Thalys) and Châtelet-les-Halles, the central hub (trip time: 35 min.). Air France also

operates two shuttle-bus services into Paris: one departing for Place d'Etoile and Porte Maillot (17€), and the other for Gare Montparnasse and Gare de Lyon (17.50€). See the website (www.lescarsairfrance.com) for times. Another option is the **Roissybus** (☎ 32-46; www.ratp.fr), which links the airport to Opéra (RER A Auber/metro Opéra). It costs 11€.

A taxi to the city costs about 60€; the fare is higher at night (8pm–7am). The trip takes 40 to 50 minutes by bus or taxi. Uber's flat rate starts at 50€ for basic service to and from the city center.

From Orly: There are no direct trains to central Paris, but the airport is served by a **monorail** (Orlyval) that takes you to the RER station Anthony, where you can catch line B into the city (trip time about 30 min.). Air France buses (en.lescarsairfrance.com) leave from Orly Ouest and Orly Sud for three stops in Paris: the Gare de Montparnasse train/metro station, Invalides metro, and Place de l'Etoile. A taxi from the airport into Paris costs about 45€ (more at night). It takes 25 minutes to an hour to get to Paris by bus or taxi, depending on traffic. The Uber's rates start at 40€ for a basic car.

Beauvais Airport (☎ 08-92-68-20-66, 0.34€/min; www.aeroportbeauvais.com) is served by low-cost airlines such as Ryanair and Wizz and lies around 80km (50 miles) from Paris. Buses to Porte Maillot leave roughly 20 minutes after flights have landed. To return to the airport, catch the bus at least 3 hours before your flight; the journey takes about 1 hour and 15 minutes. Tickets cost 17€.

By Car

The main highways into Paris are the A-1 from the north (Great Britain and Benelux); A-13 from Rouen, Normandy, and northwest France; A-10 from Bordeaux, the Pyrenees, southwest France, and Spain; A-6 from Lyon, the French Alps, the Riviera, and Italy; and A-4 and A-5 from eastern France.

By Train

North Americans can buy a **Eurailpass** or individual tickets from most travel agencies, or at any office of

Rail Europe (☎ 800/622-8600 in the U.S., 800/361-RAIL in Canada; www.raileurope.com). For details on the rail passes available in the U.K., call the **National Rail,** (☎ 03457-48-49-50; www.nationalrail.co.uk). From the U.K., you can travel to Paris under the English Channel via the Eurostar (trip time about 2½ hr.). Buy tickets directly from **Eurostar** (www.eurostar.com).

By Bus

Bus travel to Paris is available from London and several other cities on the Continent. The arrival and departure point for Europe's largest bus operator, **Eurolines France** (www.eurolines.fr; ☎ 08-92-89-90-91, 0.34€/min. from France), is a 15- to 25-minute Métro ride from central Paris, at the terminus of Métro line 3 (Galleini). Because Eurolines doesn't have sales agents outside Europe, most non-European travelers wait until they reach England or the Continent to buy their tickets. Any European travel agent can arrange this for you, or you can book online at www.eurolines.co.uk (☎ 08717-8181-77 from the U.K.). Before you travel between London and Paris by bus, check the Eurostar website for offers, as train tickets sometimes dip to as little as 66€ return—about 30€ more than a bus ticket, but you may find spending the extra cash worthwhile for the upgrade in comfort and speed.

Getting **Around**

Paris Orientation

Paris is encircled by the *périphérique*, a busy ring-road linking the city center to its suburbs and France's highway system (*autoroutes*). Everything within the *périphérique* is classified as the city center. The River Seine runs

east-west through it, splitting the city into the Right Bank (north of the Seine), and the Left Bank (south). Together, the Right and Left Banks are divided into 20 sectors called *arrondissements* with postcodes beginning with 75 (designating central Paris) and numbered from 1 to 20 (75001 to 75020; or abbreviated to 1st to 20th). The numbers spiral out clockwise, like the shell of a snail, starting at 1 (around the Louvre) and finishing at 20 (around Père Lachaise). In terms of atmosphere, arrondissements 1 to 8 cover most tourist sights, from the Louvre and Notre-Dame to the Eiffel Tower and the Champs-Elysées. Literary Paris, with its cafes and the Sorbonne University, is concentrated around the 5th and 6th. The 9th to 11th and 17th to 20th are the city's trendiest areas (including the Canal St-Martin, Montmartre, and the Père Lachaise cemetery), although some parts may look shabby. Avoid La Chapelle and Barbès-Rochechouart (18th) at night. The 12th to 16th are largely residential areas but still have plenty of bars and restaurants. The 13th is where you'll find the city's main Chinese quarter. The 16th is very chic, with grand buildings and prices to match.

Getting Around by Public Transportation

The **Métro** network is vast, reliable, and cheap, and within Paris you can transfer between the subway and the **RER** (Réseau Express Régional) regional trains at no extra cost. The Métro runs from roughly 5:30am to 12:30am Sunday to Thursday (until about 1:30am Fri–Sat and the night before public holidays; 2am on line 2). Detailed information is at www.ratp.fr.

The Métro is reasonably safe at any hour, but use your common sense and be on your guard for pickpockets; on-board beggars are also frequent. Châtelet-les-Halles RER is best avoided at night, as troublemakers tend to loiter there. For ticket advice, see below.

Buses are slower than the Métro but reliable and offer sightseeing opportunities. Most buses run from 6:30am to 9pm, after which a nighttime service (Noctilien) covers key areas until about 5:30am. Some services are limited on Sunday and public holidays. At certain stops, signs list the destinations and numbers of the buses serving that point. Bus and Métro fares are the same, and you can use the same tickets on both, but you'll need a separate ticket for each (you can't transfer from one to the other on the same ticket).

Trams are the latest addition to the network. There are three lines in central Paris (T2, T3a, and T3b), which run around the outskirts of the city, roughly following the *périphérique* (ring-road). Tram fare is the same as on the Métro and on buses, but you will need a separate ticket.

Buying Tickets

Single journey tickets, or packs of 10 tickets (un carnet, pronounced car-*nay*) can be bought from a machine in the subway station (with cash or a credit card). Individual tickets cost 1.80€ and a pack of 10 is 14.10€ (prices as of press time; they may be higher once you get there). If you plan to ride the Métro a lot, the Paris Visite pass (sold at all RATP machines and ticket booths in the Métro) may be worthwhile. You get unlimited rides for 1, 2, 3, or 5 days for access to zones 1 to 3, which includes central Paris and its nearby suburbs, or zones 1 to 5, which includes Disneyland (zone 5), Versailles (zone 4), and the Charles de Gaulle (zone 5) and Orly (zone 4) airports. It is valid only from the first time you use it, so you can buy it in advance (www.ratp.fr). Remember to fill in your name (and your children's names) as well as the series number on the card and the date of its first use. Prices range from 11.15€ to 61.55€, depending on the zone covered and the number of days.

By Taxi

The revolutionary Uber taxi service is available in Paris (minus Uber-Pop), and the smartphone app works exactly the same way as at home (www.uber.com). Or you can hail a taxi when its sign reads LIBRE or if it sports a full green or white light. The flag drops at 6.86€, and you pay 1€ to 1.50€ per kilometer (more at night). Cabs are scarce during rush hour and when the Métro closes. Don't use an unlicensed cab under any circumstances; you could find yourself the victim of robbery, or worse. Or if you'd like to hire a taxi with a chauffeur for a single journey or even the whole day, try **Paris Moving,** a friendly, reliable service run by husband-and-wife duo Fabrice and Gwladys Grüngrass (22 bd. des Filles du Calvaire, 75011; www. parismoving.com; ☎ 06-60-45-21-50 or 06-24-27-10-59; contact@parismoving.com). Other options are **Les Taxis Bleus** (☎ 36-09; www.taxisbleus.com) or **Taxi G7** (☎ 36-07; www.taxisg7.fr; call ☎ 36-49 if you want an eco-friendly taxi.

By Car

Driving in Paris is not recommended. Parking is difficult, traffic is dense, and networks of one-way streets make navigation, even with the best of maps, a problem.

By Foot

The best way to take in the city is to walk. The center is very pedestrian-friendly, and you're bound to make a few unexpected discoveries along the way.

By Bike

Paris does have cycle paths, even if you have to compete with heavy traffic, and it's a fine way to sightsee.

The best deal for short journeys is the **Vélib',** Paris's excellent self-service bike scheme, available 24/7. A subscription is 1.70€ for 1 day and 8€ for 1 week. You can take a bike from any stand (there are more than 20,000 across the city), use it, replace it, and take a new one (you can even buy a ticket online at http://en.velib.paris.fr). If a rack is full, check the map on the service point for the nearest stand. Tickets can be bought with your credit card at any service point. You'll have to authorize a 150€ deposit, which will be taken from your card only if the bike is not returned, and type in a PIN of your choice. The machine will give you a card with a code that you can use to unlock the bikes. To use the machines, travelers must have credit cards with chips, which not all cards have (especially in the U.S.). To get around it, buy your subscription online beforehand.

The first 30 minutes are free. Every additional 30 minutes costs 1€ extra (e.g., if you keep the bike for 6 hours, you'll pay an extra 12€.

Fast **Facts**

APARTMENT RENTALS   In Paris, **Alcôve & Agapes** (☎ 07-64-08-42-77; www.bed-and-breakfast-in-paris. com) promotes upmarket B&B accommodations. **Good Morning Paris** (☎ 01-47-07-28-29; www. goodmorningparis.fr) also has more than 100 rooms in the city, plus apartments for two to four people (from 121€); or try the excellent **Hôtes Qualité Paris** (www. hotesqualiteparis.fr), with apartments approved by the City of Paris for rental.

The U.K.-based **Alastair Sawdays** (www.sawdays.co.uk) also offers an excellent collection of charming B&Bs and tourist apartments in Paris. **New York Habitat** (☎ 212/255-8018; www.nyhabitat. com) rents furnished apartments and vacation accommodations in Paris and the south of France. **Airbnb** (www.airbnb.com)—an Internet community—is also a good source for private vacation rentals, offering direct contact with residents across Paris.

ATMS/CASHPOINTS The easiest and best way to get cash abroad is through an ATM—the **Cirrus** and **PLUS** networks span the globe. Most banks charge a fee for international withdrawals—check with your bank before you leave home.

BABYSITTERS Most expensive and some moderately priced hotels offer babysitting services, usually subcontracted to local agencies and requiring at least 24 hours' notice. Also try the American Church's basement bulletin board, where English-speaking (often American) students post notices to offer babysitting services. The church is at 65 quai d'Orsay, 7th (☎ 01-45-62-05-00; www.acparis. org; Métro: Invalides).

BANKS & CURRENCY EXCHANGE Most banks are open Monday to Friday from 9am to 5pm and on Saturday mornings. Most no longer keep cash on-site, offering only cash machines. If you have money to change, look for a Travelex counter (www.travelex.fr); there's a handy one at 8 place de l'Opéra, 2nd, and at the city's main train stations. Traveler's checks are generally no longer accepted anywhere in France. A better option (if you really don't want to withdraw cash with your usual card) is to buy a pre-paid, reloadable MasterCard Cash Passport (www.cashpassport. com), which works like a usual credit card with a pin and a chip.

BUSINESS HOURS Shops tend to be open from 9:30am to 7pm, but opening hours can be a little erratic. Some traditional shops open at 8am and close at 8 or 9pm, but the lunch break can last up to 3 hours, starting at 1pm. Most museums close 1 day a week (Mon or Tues) and on some national holidays.

CONSULATES & EMBASSIES U.S. Embassy, 2 av. Gabriel, 8th (☎ 01-43-12-22-22; www.france. usembassy.gov); **Canadian Embassy,** 35 av. Montaigne, 8th (☎ 01-44-43-29-00; www.canada international.gc.ca); **U.K. Embassy,** 35 rue Faubourg St-Honoré, 8th (☎ 01-44-51-31-00; www.gov.uk/ government/world/france); **U.K. Consulate,** 16 bis rue d'Anjou, 8th (☎ 01-44-51-31-02); **Irish Embassy,** 12 av. Foch, 16th (☎ 01-44-17-67-00; www.embassyofireland.fr); **Australian Embassy,** 4 rue Jean-Ray, 15th (☎ 01-40-59-33-00; www. france.embassy.gov.au); **New Zealand Embassy,** 7ter rue Lêonard-de-Vinci, 16th (☎ 01-45-01-43-43; www.nzembassy.com/france).

CREDIT CARDS Credit cards are a safe way to carry money. They also provide a convenient record of all your expenses, and they generally offer good exchange rates. You can also withdraw cash advances from your credit cards at banks or ATMs (cashpoints), provided you know your PIN. Keep in mind that when you use your credit card abroad, most banks charge a fee.

CUSTOMS Customs restrictions for visitors entering France differ for citizens of the European Union and for citizens of non-E.U. countries.

For U.S. Citizens For specifics on what you can bring back from your trip to France, download the free pamphlet *Know Before You Go* online at www.cbp.gov, or contact U.S. Customs Border Protection (CBP) (☎ 877/CBP-5511, or 202/325-8000 from abroad).

For Canadian Citizens For a clear summary of Canadian rules, call for the booklet *I Declare*, issued by the Canada Customs and Revenue Agency (☎ 800/461-9999 in Canada, or 204/983-3500 from outside Canada; www.cbsa-asfc.gc.ca).

For U.K. Citizens For more information, contact **HM Revenue & Customs** at ☎ 0300/200-3700, or consult the website www.hmrc.gov. uk or www.gov.uk/browse/business/imports-exports.

For Australian Citizens A helpful brochure available from Australian consulates or customs offices is *Know Before You Go*. For more information, call the **Australian Customs Service** at ☎ 1300/363-263 (61/2 9313-3010 from outside Australia), or go to www.customs. gov.au.

For New Zealand Citizens Request the free pamphlet *New Zealand Customs Guide for Travelers*, Notice no. 4, from New Zealand Customs Service, The Customhouse, 17–21 Whitmore St., Box 2218, Wellington (☎ 0800/428-786; or 64/9 927-8036 from overseas; www.customs.govt.nz).

DENTISTS See "Emergencies," below.

DOCTORS See "Emergencies," below.

DRUGSTORES After regular hours, ask at your hotel where the nearest 24-hour pharmacy is. You'll also find the address posted on the doors or windows of other drugstores in the neighborhood. One all-night drugstore is **Pharmacie du Drugstore des Champs Elysées,** 133 av. des Champs-Elysées, 8th (☎ 01-47-20-39-25; www.pharmacie-drugstore-champselysees.com).

ELECTRICITY France uses the 220-volt system (two round prongs), so you will need an adapter for all electronic equipment (cellphone, computer, etc.).

EMERGENCIES For the **police,** call ☎ 17. To report a **fire,** call ☎ 18. For an **ambulance,** call the fire department at ☎ 18, or the S.A.M.U. ambulance company at ☎ 15. From anywhere in Europe, including France, the **general emergency number** is ☎ 112. If you need non-urgent medical attention, practitioners in most fields can be found at the Centre Médical Europe, 44 rue d'Amsterdam, 9th (☎ 01-42-81-93-33; www.centre-medical-europe. com). For **emergency dental service,** call S.O.S. Urgences Stomatologie et Dentaire, ☎ 01-43-36-36-00. **Hospitals with English-speaking staff** are Hôpital Américain, 63 bd. Victor Hugo, Neuilly-sur-Seine (92) (☎ 01-46-41-25-25; www.american-hospital.org), and Hôpital Franco Britannique, 3 rue Barbes, Levallois Perret (92) (☎ 01-47-59-59-59; www.ihfb.org).

U.K. nationals will need a European Health Insurance Card (EHIC) to receive free or reduced-cost health benefits during a visit to a European Economic Area (EEA) country (European Union countries plus Iceland, Liechtenstein, and Norway) or Switzerland.

The quickest way to apply for one in the U.K. is online (www.nhs. uk/ehic), by calling ☎ 0300/3301-350 (44-191-218-1999 from abroad), or by getting a form from the post office. You still pay upfront for treatment and related expenses; the doctor will give you a form to reclaim most of the money (about 70% of doctor's fees and 35%–65% of medicines/prescription charges), which you should send off while still in France (see the EHIC website for details, or see www.dh.gov.uk/travellers). Non-E.U. nationals—with the exception of Canadians, who have the same rights as E.U. citizens to medical treatment in France—need comprehensive travel insurance that covers medical treatment overseas. Even then, you pay bills upfront and apply for a refund.

EVENT LISTINGS *L'Officiel des Spectacle* (consultable online; www.offi.fr) provides listings of everything that's going on in the city. Another handy website is http://spectacles.premiere.fr. *Le Figaro* carries a special listings supplement every Wednesday. Or try the online magazine **Gogo Paris** (www.gogoparis.com) and the expat info website, **Anglo Info** (www.paris.angloinfo.com/whatson).

FAMILY TRAVEL The official website of the French Tourist Board, Atout France (http://int.rendez-vousenfrance.com/en) has sections on family travel. The website www.france4families.com is a very useful resource, with lots of general information about France from a family perspective, plus guides to all regions, including Paris. If your trip to Paris is part of a wider tour of France, another good site is www.totstotravel.co.uk, which details family-friendly properties to rent outside Paris and gives valuable info about traveling in France with children, including tips on what to pack.

LGBT TRAVELERS The center of gay and lesbian life is in the Marais. Paris's largest gay bookstore is **Les Mots à la Bouche,** 6 rue Ste-Croix-de-la-Bretonnerie, 4th (☎ 01-42-78-88-30; www.motsbouche.com). To find listings and events focused on Paris, try www.qweek.fr. The city's tourist office website (www.parisinfo.com) lists gay clubs, hotels, and associations in the "Practical Paris" section.

HOLIDAYS Public holidays include New Year's Day (Jan 1), Easter Monday (Mar or Apr), Labor Day (May 1), Victory Day 1945 (May 8), Ascension Day (40 days after Easter), Whit Monday (11 days after Ascension Day), National Day/Bastille Day (July 14), Assumption Day (Aug 15), All Saints' Day (Nov 1), Armistice Day 1918 (Nov 11), and Christmas Day (Dec 25).

INSURANCE Nowadays most upper-end credit cards provide some travel insurance. North Americans with homeowner's or renter's insurance are probably covered for lost luggage. If not, inquire with **Travel Assistance International** (☎ 800/821-2828; www.travelassistanceinternational.com) or **Travelex** (☎ 800/228-9792; www.travelexinsurance.com). These insurers can also provide trip-cancellation, medical, and emergency evacuation coverage abroad.

INTERNET ACCESS Most hotels offer Internet access (sometimes at a price); alternatively, many cafes offer Wi-Fi. There are also more than 260 free Wi-Fi spots dotted around the city (check www.paris.fr for details). To surf the Net and for printing services, try **Milk,** open 24/7, at 31 bd Sebastopol, 1st (☎ 01-42-33-68-17; www.milklub.com).

LIQUOR LAWS Supermarkets, grocery stores, and cafes sell alcoholic beverages. The legal drinking age is 18. Hours of cafes vary; some even stay open 24 hours. It's illegal to drive while drunk. If convicted, motorists face a stiff fine and a possible prison term.

LOST PROPERTY If your luggage is lost, immediately file a lost-luggage claim at the airport, detailing the luggage contents. For most airlines, you must report delayed, damaged, or lost baggage within 4 hours of arrival. If you lose any belongings in Paris, try the **Service des Objets Trouvés** (Lost-Property Bureau), 36 rue des Morillons, 15th (☎ 08-21-00-25-25), which collects everything that is found in the city. You might be lucky.

MAIL/POST OFFICES Most post offices (La Poste) in Paris are open Monday through Friday from 8am to 7pm and Saturday from 8am to noon. However, the **main post office,** at 52 rue du Louvre (☎ 36-31; www.laposte.fr), is open 24 hours a day for stamps, phone calls, and sending faxes and telegrams. Stamps can usually be purchased from your hotel reception desk and at cafes with red TABAC signs.

MONEY The currency of France is the euro, which can be used in most other E.U. countries. The exchange rate varies, but at press time, 1 euro was equal to US$1.11. The best way to get cash in Paris is at ATMs or cashpoints (see above). Credit cards are accepted at almost all shops, restaurants, and hotels (although not always American Express or Diner's Club), but you should always have some cash on hand for incidentals and sightseeing admissions. Most taxis accept credit cards. Check with the driver as soon as you get in, or request a card-payment taxi when you reserve.

NEWSPAPERS & MAGAZINES English-language newspapers are available from most kiosks, including the American *International Herald Tribune* and *USA Today* and the British *Times, Guardian,* and *Independent.* The leading French-language domestic papers are *Le Monde, Le Figaro,* and *Libération.*

PASSPORTS If your passport is lost or stolen, contact your country's embassy or consulate immediately. (See "Consulates & Embassies," above.) Before you travel, you should copy the critical pages and keep them in a separate place.

POLICE Call ☎ **17** for emergencies. The principal *Préfecture* (police station) is at 9 bd. du Palais, 4th (☎ 01-53-71-53-71; www.prefecturedepolice.interieur.gouv.fr/English; Métro: Cité).

SAFETY The center of Paris is relatively safe. Look out for pickpockets—especially child pickpockets. Their method is to get very close to a target, ask for a handout, and deftly help themselves to your money or passport. Other methods to watch are card tricks (especially at the base of Montmartre); and if someone picks up a ring in front of you, walk on by. Robbery at gun- or knifepoint is rare, but not unknown. For more information, consult the U.S. State Department's website at www.travel.state.gov; in the U.K., consult the Foreign Office's website, www.fco.gov.uk; and in Australia, consult the government travel advisory service at www.smartraveller.gov.au.

SENIOR TRAVELERS As in most cities, people over the age of 60 qualify for reduced admission to theaters, museums, and other attractions as well as discounted fares on public transportation.

SMOKING Smoking is now illegal in public places (including restaurants, bars, theaters, and public transportation) but is tolerated outside and on cafe terraces. Some hotels still provide smokers' bedrooms (so ask when making reservations); otherwise, they may fine you for smoking in a nonsmoking room.

TAXES Value Added Tax, or VAT (TVA in French) is 20%, but non-E.U. visitors can get a refund when they spend 175.01€ or more in any store that participates in the VAT refund program. The shops will give you a form—a "bordereau de vente"—which you and the shop keeper should sign. You will also choose how you want to be reimbursed (card, bank transfer or cash). The form has a bar code that you scan in a 'Pablo' terminal (or for cash head to the "detaxe" counter).

TELEPHONES Public phones are few and far between. If you can find one, it should accept credit cards To make a **direct international call,** first dial 00, then dial the country code, the area code (minus the first zero), and the local number. The country code for the **U.S. and Canada** is 1; **Great Britain,** 44; **Ireland,** 353; **Australia,** 61; and **New Zealand,** 64. The country code for France is 33. Paris numbers usually begin with 01 (06 or 07 for mobiles).

TICKETS There are many theater ticket agencies in Paris, but buying tickets directly from the box office or at a discount agency can be up to 50% cheaper. Try **Kiosque Théâtre,** 15 place de la Madeleine, 8th; in front of Gare de Montparnasse, 14th; or Place des Ternes, 17th (www.kiosquetheatre.com). Tickets for many shows, sports events, and tours can also be purchased in advance in your home country through your travel agent; try **Keith Prowse** (www.keithprowse. com) for advance tickets to cabaret events and guided visits but expect to pay a commission.

TIPPING In cafes and restaurants, waiter service is included, although you can round the bill up or leave some small change, if you like. The same goes for taxi drivers. In more expensive hotels, a tip of 1€ to 2€ for having luggage carried by a hotel porter is appreciated.

TOILETS If you use a toilet at a cafe or brasserie, it's customary to make some small purchase. In the street, the domed self-cleaning lavatories are an option if you have small change. Some Métro stations have public toilets, but the degree of cleanliness varies. Be prepared—though the infamous "Turkish loo" (a porcelain hole in the floor) is largely a thing of the past, even cafe toilets can leave a lot to be desired.

TOURIST OFFICES For tourist information, try **Office du Tourisme,** 25 rue des Pyramides, 1st (www. parisinfo.com).

TOURS The two largest tour companies are **Globus/Cosmos** (www.globus andcosmos.com) and **Trafalgar** (www. trafalgartours.com). Many major airlines offer air/land package deals that include tours of Paris; ask the airlines or your travel agent for details.

TRAVELERS WITH DISABILITIES
Nearly all modern hotels in France (and those with 3 or more stars) now have rooms designed for people with disabilities, but many older hotels do not, so check when booking. Hotels sensitive to the issue may also have the "Tourisme & Handicaps" label, a sign that they are well-equipped. Most high-speed trains within France have wheelchair access, and guide dogs ride free. Paris's Métro and RER system does have some elevator access, but it is very difficult to use if you're in a wheelchair. There are, however, 60 wheelchair-accessible bus lines. **Paris Info** (www. parisinfo.com) has resources for travelers with disabilities, including a list of accessible hotels and attractions including museums, public swimming pools, and cinemas.

British travelers should contact **Tourism for All** (☎ 0845-124-9971 in the U.K. only; www.tourismforall. org.uk) to access a wide range of travel information and resources for elderly people and those with disabilities.

Paris: A Brief History

2000 B.C. The Parisii tribe founds the settlement of Lutétia alongside the Seine.

52 B.C. Julius Caesar conquers Lutétia during the Gallic wars.

300 A.D. Lutétia is renamed Paris. Roman power begins to weaken in France.

1422 England invades Paris during the Hundred Years' War.

1429 Joan of Arc tries to regain Paris for the French; she is later burned at the stake by the English in Rouen.

1572 The wars of religion reach their climax with the St. Bartholomew's Day massacre of Protestants.

1598 Henri IV endorses the Edict of Nantes, granting tolerance to Protestants.

1643 Louis XIV moves his court to the newly built Versailles.

1789 The French Revolution begins.

1793 Louis XVI and his queen, Marie Antoinette, are publicly guillotined.

1799 A coup d'état installs Napoleon Bonaparte as head of government.

1804 Napoleon declares France an empire and is crowned emperor at Notre-Dame.

1804–15 The Napoleonic wars are fought.

1814 Paris is briefly occupied by a coalition, including Britain and Russia. The Bourbon monarchy is restored.

1848 Revolutions occur across Europe. King Louis-Philippe is deposed by the autocratic Napoleon III.

1870–71 The Franco-Prussian War ends in the siege of Paris. The Third Republic is established, while much of the city is controlled by the revolutionary Paris Commune.

1914–18 World War I rips apart Europe. Millions are killed in the trenches of northeast France.

1940 German troops occupy France during World War II. The French Resistance under General Charles de Gaulle maintains symbolic headquarters in London.

1944 U.S. troops liberate Paris; de Gaulle returns in triumph.

1968 Parisian students and factory workers engage in a general revolt; the government is overhauled in the aftermath.

1994 François Mitterrand and Queen Elizabeth II open the Channel Tunnel.

1995 Jacques Chirac is elected president over François Mitterrand. Paris is crippled by a general strike.

2002 The euro replaces the franc as France's national currency.

2003–04 French opposition to the war in Iraq causes the largest diplomatic rift with America in decades.

2007 Nicolas Sarkozy replaces Jacques Chirac as president of France.

2012 Socialist François Hollande is elected president over Sarkozy.

2013 Gay marriage is legalized.

French Architecture

This section serves as a guide to some of the architectural styles you'll see in Paris. However, it's worth pointing out that very few buildings (especially churches) were built in one particular style. These massive, expensive structures often took centuries to complete, during which time tastes changed and plans were altered.

Romanesque (800–1100)
Romanesque architects concentrated on building large churches with wide aisles. **Saint-Germain-des-Prés** (oldest part, 6th century A.D.) is a good example. The overall building is Romanesque, but by the time builders got to creating the choir, the early Gothic was on—note the pointy arches.

Gothic (1100–1500)
By the 12th century, engineering developments freed church architecture from the thick, heavy walls of Romanesque structures.

Gothic interiors enticed the churchgoers' gaze upward to high ceilings filled with light. The squat, brooding Romanesque exteriors were replaced by graceful buttresses and spires. **Notre-Dame** (1163–1250) is arguably the finest example of Gothic church architecture anywhere in the world.

Renaissance (1500–1630)
In architecture, as in painting, the Renaissance came from Italy and took some time to coalesce. And, as in painting, its rules stressed proportion, order, classical inspiration, and precision, resulting in unified, balanced structures. The 1544 **Hôtel Carnavalet** (23 rue de Sévigné), a Renaissance mansion, exemplifies the style. It now contains the **Musée Carnavalet** (p 63).

Baroque, Rococo, and Neoclassical (1630–1800)
During the reign of Louis XIV (1643–1715). French baroque buildings were grandiose and severely ordered—Versailles is the best model. Opulence was especially pronounced in interior decoration, which increasingly became the excessively detailed and self-indulgent rococo (*rocaille* in French) style. Rococo tastes didn't last long, though, and soon a neoclassical movement was raising such structures as Paris's **Panthéon** (1758), based even more strictly on ancient models than the earlier Renaissance classicism was.

The 19th Century
Architectural styles in 19th-century Paris were eclectic, beginning in a severe classical mode and ending with something of an identity crisis—torn between Industrial Age technology and Art Nouveau's organic vibe. During the reign of Emperor Napoleon III (1852–1870), classicism was reinterpreted in an ornate, dramatic mode. Urban planning was the architectural rage, and Paris became a city of wide boulevards courtesy of **Baron Georges-Eugène Haussmann** (1809–91), commissioned by Napoleon III in 1852 to modernize the city.

Expositions in 1878, 1889, and 1900 were the catalysts for constructing huge glass-and-steel structures that showed off modern techniques. This produced such Parisian monuments as the **Eiffel Tower** and **Gare d'Orsay** (which now houses the Musée d'Orsay). However, the subsequent emergence of the Art Nouveau movement was, in many ways, a rebellion against the late-19th-century industrial zeal. Peaking around the turn of the century, it celebrated curvaceous **Hector Guimard** asymmetrical designs, often based on plants and flowers. It was during this short period that the famous Art Nouveau Métro station entrances were designed; the **Porte Dauphine** (line 2) and **Abbesses** (line 12) entrances are the most intact examples today. But the city's finest Art Nouveau structure is the intricately decorated apartment block at 29 av. de Rapp in the 7th.

The 20th Century
The ravages of war stalled the progress of French architecture for a number of decades, but the latter half of the 20th century saw some of the most audacious architectural projects in French history—and certainly some of the most controversial. It has taken decades for such structures as the **Centre Pompidou** or the **Louvre**'s glass pyramids to become accepted by most Parisians.

The 21st Century
The face of Paris is ever-changing. The new era has already seen the arrival of the **Musée du Quai Branly** (2006), an impressive angular structure designed by Jean Nouvel, whose bright colors and clever use of vegetation are a flagship for 21st-century architecture within the city center. The sleek **Passerelle Simone de Beauvoir** bridge (2006) is another new addition, linking the Bercy district to the François Mitterrand library's towers. The most recent addition to the Louvre museum is a stark, modern structure—nicknamed the *libéllule* (dragonfly), after its undulating roof—in the Cours Visconti. Designed by Mario Bellini and Rudi Ricciotti, it houses the museum's Islamic art collections. In 2014, some futuristic edifices joined the skyline: Frank Gehry's **Fondation Louis Vuitton** (a contemporary art showcase for the Vuitton group), with soaring glass sails, like a glass and concrete ship. On its tail, is Jean Nouvel's **Philharmonie de Paris** concert venue features an avant-garde wooden interior and a facade of Modernist bird mosaics.

Useful Phrases & Menu Terms

It's amazing how often a word or two of halting French will change your host's disposition. At the very least, try to learn basic greetings, and—above all—the life-raft phrase, *Parlez-vous anglais?* ("Do you speak English?")

Useful Words & Phrases

ENGLISH	FRENCH	PRONUNCIATION
Yes/No	**Oui/Non**	wee/noh
Okay	**D'accord**	dah-core
Please	**S'il vous plaît**	seel voo play
Thank you	**Merci**	mair-see
You're welcome	**De rien**	duh ree-ehn
Hello (during daylight)	**Bonjour**	bohn-jhoor
Good evening	**Bonsoir**	bohn-swahr
Good-bye	**Au revoir**	o ruh-vwahr

ENGLISH	FRENCH	PRONUNCIATION
What's your name?	**Comment vous appellez-vous?**	kuh-*mahn* voo za-pell-ay-voo?
My name is	**Je m'appelle**	*jhuh* ma-pell
How are you?	**Comment allez-vous?**	kuh-*mahn* tahl-ay-voo?
So-so	**Comme ci, comme ça**	kum-*see*, kum-*sah*
I'm sorry/Excuse me	**Pardon**	pahr-*dohn*
Do you speak English?	**Parlez-vous anglais?**	par-lay-voo zahn-*glay*?
I don't speak French	**Je ne parle pas français**	jhuh ne parl pah frahn-*say*
I don't understand	**Je ne comprends pas**	jhuh ne kohm-*prahn* pas
Where is . . . ?	**Où est . . . ?**	ooh eh . . . ?
Why?	**Pourquoi?**	poor-*kwah*?
Here/There	**Ici/Là**	ee-*see*/lah
Left/Right	**à Gauche/à Droite**	a goash/a drwaht
Straight ahead	**Tout droit**	too drwah

Food, Menu & Cooking Terms

ENGLISH	FRENCH	PRONUNCIATION
I would like	**Je voudrais**	jhe voo-*dray*
to eat	**manger**	mahn-*jhay*
Please give me	**Donnez-moi, s'il vous plaît**	doe-nay-*mwah*, seel voo play
a bottle of	**une bouteille de**	ewn boo-*tay* duh
a cup of	**une tasse de**	ewn tass duh
a glass of	**un verre de**	uh vair duh
a cocktail	**un apéritif**	uh ah-pay-ree-*teef*
the check/bill	**l'addition/la note**	la-dee-see-*ohn*/la noat
a knife	**un couteau**	uh koo-*toe*
a napkin	**une serviette**	ewn sair-vee-*et*
a spoon	**une cuillère**	ewn kwee-*air*
a fork	**une fourchette**	ewn four-*shet*
a fixed-price menu	**un menu**	uh may-*new*
Is the tip/service included?	**Est-ce que le service est compris?**	ess-ke luh ser-*vees* eh com-*pree*?
Waiter!/Waitress!	**Monsieur!/Mademoiselle!**	mun-*syuh*/mad-mwa-*zel*
Wine list	**Une carte des vins**	ewn cart day *van*
Appetizer	**Une entrée**	ewn en-*tray*
Main course	**Un plat principal**	uh plah pran-see-*pahl*
Tip included	**Service compris**	sehr-*vees* cohm-*pree*
Tasting/Chef's menu	**Menu dégustation**	may-*new* day-gus-ta-see-*on*

Index

See also Accommodations and Restaurant indexes, below.

Photo **Credits**

abadesign: p 7. Alden Gewirtz: p 18; p 46. aldorado / Shutterstock.com: p 66, bottom. Alessandro Colle / Shutterstock.com: p 34. Amy Murrell: p 124, top; p 148. Anastasia Petrova / Shutterstock.com: p 63, bottom. Antonshutterstock / Shutterstock.com: p 17. Botond Horvath / Shutterstock.com: p 163. Christoph Bauer: p 114. Claudia Carlsen: p 94. Cosmin Sava / Shutterstock.com: p 32. Courtesy of 404: p 106. Courtesy of Au Pied de Cochon/ Raoul Dobremel: p 100. Courtesy of Bonpoint: p 76. Courtesy of Chambelland Bakery/ Maud Bernos : p 108. Courtesy of Hotel Amour: p 142. Courtesy of Hotel Banke: p 143. Courtesy of Hotel du Louvre: p 145. Courtesy of Hotel Gabriel: p 146. Courtesy of Hotel Meurice: p 147. Courtesy of La Dame de Pic/ Francois Goize: p 109, top. Courtesy of Le Vaisseau Vert: p 110. Courtesy of Pring: p 85, bottom. Courtesy of Septime/ François Flohic: p 111. Courtesy of Shangri La: p iii, top; p 99; p 112; p iii, second from bottom; p 135. craigfinlay: p 83, top. cyberien 94: p 83, bottom. David Jafra: p 159. Denis Pepin: p 4. Douglas LeMoine: p 88, top. Ekaterina Pokrovsky: p 59. Elisabeth Blanchet: p 39, bottom; p 123. Emily Goodwin: p 49, top. EQRoy / Shutterstock.com: p 70, top. Eric Bréchemier: p 134. esinel: p 23. f11photo / Shutterstock.com: p 14. foto.fritz: p 74, top. Georgios Makkas: p 61, top. Gideon: p iii, second from top; p 113. Henry Marion: p 57. HOTEL DES GRANDES ECOLES <hotel.grandes.ecoles@free.fr>: p 144. Hung Chung Chih / Shutterstock.com: p 37. Jean-Pierre Dalbéra: p 42, top; p 54, top; p 63, top. jorisvo / Shutterstock.com: p 161. Jose Ignacio Soto / Shutterstock.com: p 58, bottom; p 153. Katchooo: p 126. Kemal Taner / Shutterstock.com: p 49, bottom. Kiev. Victor / Shutterstock.com: p 8, bottom; p ii, second from top; p ii, second from bottom; p 19; p 38; p 70, bottom; p 75; p 91; p 95. Kristen Pelou: p 124, bottom. lapas77 / Shutterstock.com: p 58, top. Lee Winder: p 45, bottom. lembi / Shutterstock.com: p 62, bottom. Lena Ivanova / Shutterstock.com: p ii, bottom; p 89. Lilyana Vynogradova / Shutterstock.com: p 3, top. Isantilli: p ii, third from top; p 47. Luis Irisarri: p 86. Lyubov Timofeyeva / Shutterstock.com: p 154. Marina99: p 8, top. Markel Redondo: p 11; p 24; p 39, top; p 62, top; p 66, top; p 69; p 71; p 74, bottom; p 85, top; p 97; p 107; p 109, bottom; p 122, bottom; p 130; p 133; p 150. MarKord / Shutterstock.com: p 13. Marten_House: p 65, right. mary416: p iii, third from top; p 125. meunierd / Shutterstock.com: p 43. nexus 7: p 51. Nikonaft / Shutterstock.com: p 28. Nikonaft / Shutterstock.com: p 3, bottom. ostill / Shutterstock.com: p 53. Paris Tourist Office - Photographer : Daniel Thierry: p 29; p 65, left; p 87, top. photo.ua: p 55. photogolfer / Shutterstock.com: p 54, bottom. pisaphotography / Shutterstock.com: p 42, bottom. Robert Crum: p 22. Rrrainbow / Shutterstock.com: p 45, top; p 50, bottom. Sam Nabi: p 87, bottom. Samot: p 9. saraicat: p 122, top. S-F / Shutterstock.com: p iii, bottom; p 151. spacejulien: p 98. Stefano Ember / Shutterstock.com: p 82. Tallapragada sriram: p 158. Tanya Ustenko: p 50, top. torfo: p 129. Valery Egorov / Shutterstock.com: p 61, bottom. Velishchuk Yevhen / Shutterstock.com: p viii–1; p 67. VLADJ55: p 73. Yury Dmitrienko / Shutterstock.com: p ii, top; p 5.

Notes